European Integration

An Economic Perspective

edited by
Jørgen Drud Hansen

OXFORD
UNIVERSITY PRESS

OXFORD

UNIVERSITY PRESS

Great Clarendon Street, Oxford OX2 6DP

Oxford University Press is a department of the University of Oxford.
It furthers the University's objective of excellence in research, scholarship,
and education by publishing worldwide in

Oxford New York

Athens Auckland Bangkok Bogotá Buenos Aires Cape Town
Chennai Dar es Salaam Delhi Florence Hong Kong Istanbul Karachi
Kolkata Kuala Lumpur Madrid Melbourne Mexico City Mumbai Nairobi
Paris São Paulo Shanghai Singapore Taipei Tokyo Toronto Warsaw

with associated companies in Berlin Ibadan

Oxford is a registered trade mark of Oxford University Press
in the UK and in certain other countries

Published in the United States
by Oxford University Press Inc., New York

British Library Cataloguing in Publication Data

Data available

Library of Congress Cataloging in Publication Data

Data available

ISBN 0-19-870060-1

Typeset in Swift and Argo
by RefineCatch Limited, Bungay, Suffolk
Printed in Great Britain
on acid-free paper by
Bath Press Ltd., Bath, Somerset

Preface

INTEGRATION has been on the European political agenda for more than half a century, but two recent initiatives in particular have significantly changed the European economies. In the mid-1980s, European politicians agreed upon the formation of the Single Market, fulfilling the ambition of creating a Europe with free mobility of goods, persons, services, and capital; and just before the turn of the century, the Economic and Monetary Union was launched and a new common currency, the *euro*, was born. The purpose of this book is to assess how far economic integration has progressed. Has it had a positive impact on the economies of Europe at all? Does Europe still consist of a set of individual economies, or does it make more sense to perceive Europe as one economy?

This book represents a step towards answering these complex questions. The book should be equally valuable to researchers, policy makers, and students of social sciences. Those who want a solid introduction to the issue of European economic integration will find a rich source of factual and theoretical input, as each chapter combines theory and evidence in the analysis of specific areas. Theory is presented in a non-technical way in order to allow all interested readers to follow the arguments of modern economics, while economics students should find it easy to see the parallels to the relevant, formal arguments in their other courses.

Modern economics frequently loses sight of the real world. With this book we try to bridge this gap and present real data and facts together with concepts commonly used in economics. Facts and real world observations are useful inputs for any economist or social scientist, they are the lifeblood of our science. Already simple observations, such as the fact that Portuguese GDP per capita is only 60 per cent of that of Germany, or that unemployment in the EU is around twice that in the USA, trigger and challenge our minds. Why is this so? Our book certainly does not have all the answers, but we believe that we ask some of the right questions.

The book is the result of a two-year collaboration between researchers at the Jean Monnet European Centre of Excellence at the University of Southern Denmark. Although individual authors are assigned to each chapter according to their research interests, the preliminary drafts of each chapter have been thoroughly discussed in the whole group of authors and with members of the Centre. Hence, in the latter sense we accept collective responsibility.

The individual chapters have benefited from comments from and discussions with many colleagues, who cannot all be mentioned here. However, we are especially grateful to Hans Heinrich, Assistant Professor at the University of Southern Denmark, and Morten Hansen, Visiting Professor, EuroFaculty, University of Latvia, for working through the entire manuscript, as well as to Dorrit Andersen-Alstrup for efficient secretarial assistance. Finally, we are indebted to Eva Carlson for translating the manuscript from Danish into English. Her patience and careful assistance have improved the readability of the book tremendously.

On behalf of the authors

Jørgen Drud Hansen

Contents

List of Figures

List of Tables

List of Authors

Jørgen Drud Hansen, Jean Monnet Professor, Director of Jean Monnet European Centre of Excellence, Department of Economics, University of Southern Denmark.

Jan Guldager Jørgensen, PhD, Assistant Professor, Jean Monnet European Centre of Excellence, Department of Economics, University of Southern Denmark.

Teit Lüthje, PhD, Associate Professor, Jean Monnet European Centre of Excellence, Department of Economics, University of Southern Denmark.

Finn Olesen, Associate Professor, Jean Monnet European Centre of Excellence, Department of Environmental and Business Economics, University of Southern Denmark.

Philipp J. H. Schröder, PhD, Assistant Professor, Jean Monnet European Centre of Excellence, Department of Economics, University of Southern Denmark.

Morten Skak, Associate Professor, Jean Monnet European Centre of Excellence, Department of Economics, University of Southern Denmark.

Chapter 1
Economic Integration in Europe: Setting the Stage

Jørgen Drud Hansen and
Philipp J. H. Schröder

1.1 Introduction

DURING the first half of the twentieth century, Europe was devastated by two world wars. Some of the most important factors behind these extensive wars were nationalistic tendencies and territorial conflicts, and after the latest war, Europe was basically torn in two: a Western Europe associated with the Western world with the USA as the leading nation; and a Central and Eastern Europe annexed to the Soviet Union. In the Western European bloc there was a strong division between the individual countries, and there was only very limited trade and economic cooperation between them. But the traumatic events of the wars gave rise to new visions and hopes of a better and more harmonious future for Europe. Particularly the Chancellor of the new Federal Republic of Germany, Konrad Adenauer, and the Foreign Ministers of France, Robert Schuman, and Belgium, Paul-Henri Spaak, were central forces behind the process which, at the beginning of the second half of the century, became the starting point of the budding European Union (EU), an unprecedented cooperation between nation states.

The ultimate goal of these endeavours was to create a European identity based on common values and a common desire to develop a Europe free of wars. The philosophy was that lasting peace among the European countries was best furthered by economic prosperity. To achieve this goal, the founding fathers of the EU had to weave the countries of Europe into a fabric of economic interdependence; an interdependence that would eliminate conflicts by achieving mutual gains through specialization and foster economic growth by creating a dynamic framework for the European economies. The answer to this challenge was *economic integration*. In the strict sense of the concept, economic integration means the removal of trade barriers and the introduction of free movement of factors of production. But the concept is broader and also includes concerted efforts to address specific policy areas such as monetary stability, the survival of certain sectors, or assistance to underdeveloped regions.

From the very beginning, it was emphasized that European integration should be an ongoing process. Or, to quote from the preamble of the Treaty of Rome, which was the initial legal framework adopted in 1957, the founding members were determined:

- 'to lay the foundations of an ever closer union among the peoples of Europe',

which had as its main objectives:

- 'to ensure the economic and social progress of their countries and common action to eliminate the barriers which divide Europe';
- 'to strengthen the unity of their economies and to ensure their harmonious development by reducing the differences existing between the various regions and the backwardness of the less-favoured regions';
- [to pool] 'their resources to preserve and strengthen peace and liberty, and calling upon the other peoples of Europe who share their ideal to join in their efforts'.

About this book

The aim of this book is to highlight the motives, rationales, and experiences of the process of integrating the European economies. The book will identify the main areas of successful economic integration as well as areas where the economic integration process has failed. Themes central to the book are the impact of the *Single European Market* on trade and mobility of labour and capital, the *Economic and Monetary Union* (EMU) based on one common currency, the euro, and the prospects for an *Eastern enlargement* of the European Union with several Central and Eastern European countries.

The book addresses the integration issues by mixing theory and evidence and briefly introduces the relevant theoretical concepts in a non-technical way. Theory is used to derive a priori views on the effects of integration and supplemented by real world data to check the theoretical assumptions and predictions. Ample use of descriptive statistics helps to generate stylized facts about the integration process. It should be borne in mind, however, that stylized facts do not explain causalities as other factors may have played an important role. A causal analysis requires a more thorough examination than the mere comparison of facts with expected results. Stylized facts only illustrate whether the development corresponds with the defined goals of the integration.

The book examines the EU in both an *external* and *internal context*. In the external context, the position of the EU in the so-called *Triad*, consisting of the three main economic forces in the world economy, i.e. the EU, the USA, and Japan, is evaluated.

In the internal context, the differences in structure and wealth between individual member states are illustrated. This duality in the level of analysis is a main feature of the book.

To the extent possible, data sources have been limited to readily available statistics, the main source being *Eurostat*, the official statistical office of the EU. The book relies on standard economic theory, and many of the concepts can be found in standard textbooks. Occasionally, however, more specialized concepts are introduced, and each chapter will provide an overview of the main relevant theories. For a more theoretical introduction to the principles of integration and an in-depth analysis of the statistical material, the reader should consult the listed literature. Each chapter contains its own reference list and a section on suggested reading so that issues of particular interest can be pursued further.

The remainder of Chapter 1 provides the basic background to the historical and institutional framework of European integration. Section 1.2 introduces the main historic events leading to the foundation of the European Union, and Section 1.3 presents some of the economic policy areas central to the book. An overview of the institutional structures of the EU is given in Section 1.4, whereas Section 1.5 lists some key figures, such as population sizes and GDP. Finally, Section 1.6 summarizes the different chapters of the book.

1.2 A brief history of integration

IN the early years following World War II, three important initiatives were taken to liberalize trade in general: The General Agreement on Tariffs and Trade, the Organization for European Economic Cooperation, and the European Payments Union. Formally, these arrangements were outside the institutional framework of what were to become the EU, but all can be considered to constitute the beginning of global, and hence also European, economic integration.

The first initiative was the *General Agreement on Tariffs and Trade* (GATT), established in 1947, which aimed at reducing tariffs between most of the industrial countries in the world economy, including countries beyond the borders of Europe. The main principle behind the GATT was the 'most favoured nation' clause, which ensured that bilateral agreements lowering tariffs between two partner countries automatically extended to all other signatory countries. Throughout the last half of the century, the GATT was very active in reducing tariffs through several rounds of negotiations involving the partner countries. Recently, the GATT was transformed into the *World Trade Organization* (WTO) with a strengthened capacity of monitoring the participating countries' adherence to their commitments to liberalize trade.

The second initiative was the establishment of the *Organization for European Economic Cooperation* (OEEC) in 1948. The primary task of this organization was to coordinate and manage the financial assistance to the European countries under the Marshall

Plan, which was a concerted programme whereby the USA provided grants and loans towards the reconstruction of Europe. However, another objective of the OEEC was to liberalize trade, and it was quite successful in ridding Europe of trade barriers, partly because the grants and loans for reconstruction to some extent were conditional upon the elimination of quantitative restrictions on trade. The OEEC was succeeded by the global *Organization for Economic Cooperation and Development* (OECD).

The third initiative was the *European Payments Union* (EPU), which was established in 1950 (although some of its tasks had already been identified in a payments agreement from 1947). The main objective of the EPU was to secure *convertibility* of currencies so that trade in Europe was not restricted by a lack of specific foreign currencies. By introducing convertibility, the members achieved a *de facto* pooled trade balance and this meant that the multilateral trade balance became the binding constraint rather than the more limiting constraints of the individual bilateral trade balances.

These initiatives were complementary in the sense that they removed, or at least reduced, layers of effective trade barriers, and this stimulated trade considerably. What also characterized the GATT, the OEEC, and the EPU was that, by and large, simply by adhering to the principles of cooperation in a specific area, a country could participate in or become member of the agreement or institution. The cooperation was therefore fairly open with no extensive, institutional commitments on the part of the participating countries. The cooperation within the European Union, on the other hand, is totally different in the sense that it is based on strong commitments on a wide range of issues, backed by powerful institutions.

The first real predecessor to the European Union was the *European Coal and Steel Community* (ECSC) in which Belgium, Germany, France, Italy, Luxembourg, and the Netherlands participated. The ECSC was based on the Paris Treaty from 1951 and came into force that same year. The main task of the ECSC was to stabilize prices and coordinate supply and demand in the coal and steel market. Although the ECSC was a purely economic association, it was deeply rooted in political interests. At the time, coal and steel were perceived to be the most important resources facilitating economic growth, but notoriously, they were also the main ingredients of war machinery, so the challenge was to let Germany engage in the exploitation of its substantial natural resources and at the same time keep a close eye on its activities.

The next major step in the formation of the European Union was the establishment of the *European Economic Community* (EEC) and the *European Atomic Energy Community* (Euratom). The legal framework of the EEC and Euratom was the above-mentioned Treaty of Rome, which was signed in 1957 by the same six countries which had formed the ECSC.

The EEC was the most comprehensive of the three communities (ECSC, EEC, and Euratom) defining a wide range of important economic issues as areas of cooperation subject to common decision making. The aim of Euratom was limited to the non-military utilization of nuclear power, and the role of the ECSC was confined to two, very specific, areas.

The ratification of the Treaty of Rome was the decisive breakthrough for the European integration process, which has been progressing steadily ever since. Since 1957, several countries have joined this cooperation which is known today as the

European Union (EU). In 2000, the Union consisted of the following fifteen European countries: Belgium, Denmark, Germany, Greece, Spain, France, Ireland, Italy, Luxembourg, the Netherlands, Austria, Portugal, Finland, Sweden, and the UK. This list of members is expected to be extended further in the beginning of the twenty-first century by up to ten countries from Central and Eastern Europe. At present, accession negotiations have been initiated with Bulgaria, the Czech Republic, Hungary, Poland, Romania, Slovakia, Slovenia, Estonia, Latvia, and Lithuania, and several of the other Central and Eastern European countries have applied for membership. Finally, Cyprus, Malta, and Turkey have also applied to become members. For each enlargement, the new members have to adopt the so-called *acquis communautaire*, i.e. the existing legal body of the EU. This means that new member states must fully accept the treaties of the Union and the existing legislation and rules of cooperation.

A summary of the landmarks in the European integration process can be found in Table 1.1, where the treaties are referred to by their popular, rather than by their official, names. Apart from these main elements of the formal integration of Europe, there have naturally been other major breakthroughs, e.g. in the form of proposals

Table 1.1 Main historic events of the formation of the European Union

Institution	Treaty (year of ratification)	Year of implementation	Landmarks of economic integration
European Coal and Steel Community (ECSC)	Treaty of Paris (1951)	1951	Common policy for coal and steel production. Members: France, Germany, Italy, Belgium, the Netherlands, and Luxembourg
European Economic Community (EEC)	Treaty of Rome (1957)	1958	Customs union. Free mobility of factors of production. Members: as ECSC
Euratom	Treaty of Rome (1957)	1958	Non-military utilization of nuclear power. Members: as ECSC
First enlargement	Revised Treaty (1972)	1973	New members: UK, Denmark, and Ireland
Second enlargement	Revised Treaty (1979)	1981	New member: Greece
Third enlargement	Revised Treaty (1985)	1986	New members: Spain and Portugal
The Single Market	Single European Act (1986)	1986–92	Formation of the Internal Market
The European Union (EU)	Maastricht Treaty (1992)	1993	Plans for establishing the Economic and Monetary Union from 1 Jan. 1999
Fourth enlargement	Revised Treaty (1994)	1995	New members: Austria, Finland, and Sweden
The European Union (EU)	Amsterdam Treaty (1997)	1998	Obligations for increased efforts to improve employment

and reports, or so-called 'white books', which have influenced the development. Seen in retrospect, they have been forerunners of the revisions of the treaties. Examples are the *Werner Report* from 1970, which started the debate about the establishment of a monetary union, and the more recent *Agenda 2000*, which addresses the need for internal reforms of the EU prior to the integration of the Central and Eastern European countries into the EU. Documents and initiatives of relevance to the discussions of this book will be introduced in the relevant chapters.

1.3 Main economic policy areas of the European Union

It is remarkable for a supranational body such as the EU to be involved in the formulation of policies in areas ranging from tariffs to social security of workers, and from agriculture to monetary policy. Still, the main driving force behind the economic integration in Europe is the free movement of goods and services. The Treaty of Rome—in particular concerning the EEC—obliged the member states to establish a *customs union*, i.e. to remove internal tariffs and quotas and to establish a common tariff towards third-party countries. To some extent, the Treaty of Rome also provided for the free movement of persons and capital. However, trade was significantly hampered by various *invisible trade barriers*, such as discriminatory practices for public procurement, border control, and national technical standards for goods. Those barriers were effectively removed by the *Single European Act*, which provided for the establishment of a Single European Market defined as '*an area without internal frontiers in which the free movement of goods, services, persons and capital is ensured*' (Amsterdam Treaty, Article 14).

The establishment of the Single European Market, also called the Internal Market, or simply the Single Market, has significantly influenced the economic structure of the countries involved. The effects have primarily been felt in the area of trade, where there has been a rapid increase in the volume of internal trade between the EU member states. Furthermore, the exposure of national markets to competition from companies in other member states has led to a significant restructuring of firms and markets, resulting in increased company specialization and possibly also in increased focus on R&D. In a long-term perspective, the restructuring has led to a wave of cross-border mergers and acquisitions, making the know-how of individual companies more accessible to the entire Single Market. Also consumers have been directly affected by the Single Market, as the free movement of goods and services has reduced the geographic differences in prices for the same products. Overall, these structural changes have presumably increased efficiency and stimulated the technological development of the EU. An important aim of the integration has in fact been to create a more innovative economy in the EU.

Another main area of European economic integration is related to industrial policy, most importantly to the *Common Agricultural Policy* (CAP), which reflects the dual endeavour of securing the provision of food and, at the same time, ensuring fair standards of living for farmers. The CAP operates through a comprehensive regulation of prices and market conditions in the agricultural sector. Industrial policy also includes *competition policy*, which aims at securing fair competition in the European market.

Economic integration includes vital components of macroeconomic policy, such as exchange rate policy and monetary policy. Since 1979, the efforts to stabilize bilateral exchange rates have been institutionalized through the European Monetary System (EMS), and the bilateral exchange rates between a number of member states have thus been relatively stable for a number of years. The development towards monetary integration has been strengthened significantly through the establishment of the Economic and Monetary Union (EMU) with the main aim of introducing one common currency, the *euro*. Preparations for the EMU have been going on since the beginning of the 1990s, and as from January 1999, eleven EU countries (Belgium, Germany, Spain, France, Ireland, Italy, Luxembourg, the Netherlands, Austria, Portugal, and Finland) have irrevocably fixed their exchange rates as the decisive step towards the establishment of the EMU. In the summer 2000, Greece was admitted into the common currency as well, while Denmark, Sweden, and the UK await public referendums or parliamentary decisions. In any case, with the possible exception of the UK, these countries will probably continuously aim at keeping stable exchange rates vis-à-vis the euro, which means that *de facto*, important elements of monetary integration will apply also to them.

A common currency, or even just stable exchange rates in connection with free capital mobility, will reduce interest differentials, thus equalizing financing conditions for investments between countries. Economic theory indicates that monetary integration has clear efficiency gains, but at the same time presents arguments which imply that macroeconomic stabilization becomes more difficult, since monetary and exchange rate policies are no longer available as policy instruments to individual member countries.

Although the integration aspects introduced above have contributed to uniting the European economies in many ways, industrial structures and standards of living do not necessarily converge throughout the Union. Trade leads to *specialization*, and this specialization may enhance differences in industrial structures between individual regions in the EU. Free movement of factors of production opens up new possibilities for the location of economic activity, and this may lead to differences in economic growth from region to region. Capital is particularly mobile, whereas the mobility of the labour force is hampered for example by language and cultural barriers between countries. Differences in growth between individual regions influence differences in wealth, and in certain cases, the establishment of the Internal Market has widened the gulf in standards of living between the wealthy and the poor regions in the EU. Such differences in development, where the development in wealth of some regions lags behind, may threaten the entire integration process. This is also why all the Treaties contain more or less explicit objectives of furthering *the economic and social cohesion* between the different regions of the Union. This and other difficulties of integration will feature in coming chapters.

1.4 Institutional framework and distribution of power

THE most important EU institutions are the European Commission, the Council of Ministers, the European Parliament, the European Court of Justice, the European Court of Auditors, and the European Central Bank (ECB).

The *European Commission* administers the EU cooperation and has the right of initiative, e.g. to make proposals regarding the further development of the cooperation. The Commission is managed by a college of twenty EU Commissioners who are appointed for a five-year period with the sole purpose of safeguarding the common interests of the EU. Commissioners are nominated by the national governments, with the small countries having one member, and the large countries having two. The *Council of Ministers* is the decision-making body and consists of the relevant ministers of the governments of the individual member states. Thus, decisions on agricultural issues will be made by a Council of Ministers consisting of the Ministers of Agriculture of each member state. In most cases, decisions of the Council of Ministers will be made by qualified majority voting according to a system whereby the large countries have more votes than the small countries, but in very important cases, unanimity is required, which means that a decision can be blocked by a veto from just one country. The Council of Ministers makes decisions on specific areas and should not be confused with the *European Council*, which is a decision-making body on a superior level consisting of the heads of state or heads of government as well as the President of the Commission. The European Council provides the general political guidelines for the EU cooperation.

The *European Parliament* has the right of hearing before decisions are made in a number of areas, and in certain cases, e.g. concerning the Budget and appointment of the Commission, decisions can only be made after prior approval by the Parliament. The Parliament consists of 626 members elected directly in the individual member states. Each member state has been allocated a certain number of seats, and the election period of the Parliament is five years. Over the years, the Parliament has been criticized for being a somewhat toothless institution, and talk of a 'democratic deficit' has harmed the image of the EU. A first step in the direction of tackling these issues was taken in the Treaty of Amsterdam where the competences of the Parliament were strengthened, and the dismissal of the EU Commission in 1999 can be taken as a sign of this changing balance of power.

The *European Court of Justice* makes decisions on the interpretation of the Treaties as the legal basis for the EU cooperation and determines legal disputes between the

Commission, the member states, and individual firms in areas such as trade and competition. The *European Court of Auditors* carries out the audit of the EU Budget, i.e. examines the accounts of revenue and expenditure of the EU institutions. Finally, the *European Central Bank* (ECB) was established in connection with the introduction of the EMU, and this institution is responsible for the monetary policy of the monetary union.

An intricate problem relating to all these institutions is how to allocate power and representation among member states. Generally, the influence of the small countries is disproportionate to their population share. This appears from Table 1.2, which compares actual representation of each member state with the proportion of representation to which they would be entitled if the representation were to reflect the population share of individual countries. The major donors of power are the large countries, Germany, the UK, France, and Italy. What has caused such a skewed allocation of power? In any type of cooperation, the small partner will be concerned about the loss of decision power, since simple majority voting will always favour the large partner. Consequently, when joining a cooperation such as the EU, small countries will be more concerned about surrendering power, whereas a large country can exert considerable influence, even if it gives up some of its decision power in the institutions. The risk of being overruled is therefore smaller for a large country. Thus, if a large country finds that the partnership with a small country is of value from an overall point of view, the large country will be willing to accept a certain power bias in favour of the small country.

As an example, consider the top level institution, the Council of Ministers, where qualified majority requires 62 votes out of 87. This means that a minority of just 26 votes can block a decision. It is no coincidence that the small countries in terms of population, i.e. Belgium, Denmark, Ireland, Luxembourg, Austria, Portugal, and Sweden, which only constitute 12.5 per cent of the total population, muster exactly the 26 votes required to form a blocking minority.

The political system of the European Union is based on a division of power between the centralized EU institutions and the individual member states. Hence, the EU bears some resemblance to a federal system, as decisions are made both at a centralized federal level and at a decentralized member state level in accordance with a certain distribution of competences. But compared with actual federal states, such as the USA and the Federal Republic of Germany, the extent of the decision-making power at the federal level in the EU is much more limited. The limited competence of the EU institutions is explicitly derived from the Treaties and from the so-called *principle of subsidiarity*, which prescribes that decisions must be made at the decentralized level, unless significant advantages can be achieved by transferring the competence to the centralized level.

Table 1.2 Actual versus proportionate representation of member states

	Share of population per cent	Votes in the Council		Seats in the Parliament		Number of EU Commissioners	
		Actual	Reweighted	Actual	Reweighted	Actual	Reweighted
Belgium	2.7	5	2	25	17	1	1
Denmark	1.4	3	1	16	9	1	0
Germany	21.9	10	19	99	137	2	4
Greece	2.8	5	2	25	18	1	1
Spain	10.5	8	9	64	66	2	2
France	15.7	10	14	87	98	2	3
Ireland	1.0	3	1	15	6	1	0
Italy	15.4	10	13	87	96	2	3
Luxembourg	0.1	2	0	6	1	1	0
The Netherlands	4.2	5	4	31	26	1	1
Austria	2.2	4	2	21	14	1	0
Portugal	2.6	5	2	25	16	1	1
Finland	1.4	3	1	16	9	1	0
Sweden	2.4	4	2	22	15	1	0
UK	15.8	10	14	87	99	2	3
EUR15	100.0	87	(86)	626	(627)	20	(19)

Note: Reweighted figures are constructed in accordance with the weights of the population share in 1998. Figures in parentheses are the totals of the reweighted values and differ slightly from the actual totals because of rounding off.

Source: EU Commission (1998), Annexe: table 1. Authors' calculation.

1.5 Key statistics of the European Union

TABLE 1.3 shows area and population in the Triad compared to the world as a whole. In the Table, EUR15 consists of the fifteen countries which were members in 1996. The Triad does not amount to much in the overall picture if the measure is area or population. In total, EUR15, the USA, and Japan only take up about one-tenth of both area and population in the world. Internally in the Triad, EUR15 has the largest population and the USA the largest area. Population density is largest in Japan and smallest in the USA.

The size of the economies may also be measured by GDP in absolute terms. From the first column of Table 1.4, which illustrates GDP at current exchange rates, it appears that GDP of EUR15 is almost equal to that of the USA but nearly twice that of Japan. A comparison of individual member states shows that Germany is by far the largest economy as GDP of Germany constitutes around 25 per cent of total GDP in EUR15. Measured by GDP, the four largest countries, Germany, France, Italy, and the UK, constitute almost three-quarters of total GDP in EUR15.

Table 1.3 Area, population, and population density in the Triad, 1996

	Area, million sq. km.	Population (millions)	Inhabitants per sq. km.
USA	9.4	267	28
Japan	0.4	125	332
EUR15	3.2	372	115
World	136.3	5,687	42

Source: Eurostat (1997): table 3.2.

Table 1.4 also illustrates GDP per capita as a crude measure of standards of living. In the Triad, GDP per capita at current market prices is lowest in EUR15, with GDP per capita being 50 per cent and 54 per cent higher in the USA and Japan, respectively (see column 3). There are also significant differences between individual member states. Thus, GDP per capita in Portugal and Greece is approximately only half of the EUR15 average, whereas GDP per capita in Luxembourg is 92 per cent higher than the EUR15 average. Traditionally, Denmark, the Netherlands, and Germany are among the relatively wealthy EU countries, although the standards of living plunged in the unified Germany after the reunification of the relatively rich West Germany with the relatively poor East Germany.

However, price levels between countries may differ, and for that reason alone, GDP per capita at current exchange rates may be a poor indicator of standards of living. To correct for this bias, GDP is also measured at *purchasing power standards* (PPS), where 1 euro represents the same purchasing power everywhere. Table 1.4, column 4, illustrates GDP per capita at PPS. Generally, there is a positive correlation between price levels in the member states in euro and GDP per capita in euro, and consequently GDP per capita at PPS shows less inequality compared with GDP per capita at current exchange rates.

Although such quantitative assessments of differences in standards of living may be questioned, it is obvious that significant welfare disparities do exist and that the endeavours to develop *cohesion* among member states, regions or social groups must remain on the European agenda. The originally observed internal heterogeneity in the EU is mainly caused by differences in endowments of physical and human capital and differences in industrial structures. The question of whether or not economic integration has closed this gap will be addressed in subsequent chapters.

As a supranational body, the EU has its own budget, and the Amsterdam Treaty stipulates that this budget must balance. The main items of the Budget for 1999 are listed in Table 1.5, in which year total expenditure and revenue amounted to 85.6bn. euro. The most significant item under expenditure is the Common Agricultural Policy, which makes up around 48 per cent of total expenditure, whereas the EU structural funds, consisting of various subsidies to areas with low standards of living or social problems in general, make up around 36 per cent of total expenditure. It is

Table 1.4 GDP in the EU member states and in the Triad, 1999

	GDP		GDP per capita (EUR15 = 100)	
	Billion euro	EUR15 = 100	Market exchange rates	PPS
Belgium	230.6	2.9	107	110
Denmark	163.1	2.1	145	118
Germany	1,979.5	24.9	114	107
Greece	117.4	1.5	53	67
Spain	556.1	7.0	67	82
France	1,349.2	17.0	108	101
Ireland	84.7	1.1	107	112
Italy	1,091.9	13.7	90	99
Luxembourg	17.5	0.2	192	180
The Netherlands	369.3	4.7	111	112
Austria	195.1	2.5	114	111
Portugal	104.1	1.3	50	75
Finland	121.7	1.5	111	103
Sweden	222.9	2.8	119	102
UK	1,337.9	16.8	107	102
EUR15	7,941.1	100.0	100	100
USA	8,576.0	108.0	150	153
Japan	4,117.6	51.9	154	111

Source: EU Commission (1999), Annexe: tables 5, 8, and 9. Authors' calculation.

Table 1.5 The Budget of the European Communities, 1999

	Billion euro	Per cent
Expenditure		
Agriculture (CAP)	40.9	48
Structural Funds	30.7	36
Internal and external policies	9.1	11
Administration	4.5	5
Other	0.3	0
Total	85.6	100
Revenue		
Contribution based on GNP and VAT	69.6	81
Import duties and agricultural levies	13.8	16
Other	2.1	2
Total	85.6	100

Source: EU Commission (1999), Annexe: tables 81A and 81B. Authors' calculation.

particularly through the redistribution of funds, in the form of subsidies from rich to poor areas of the EU, that the objective of cohesion and solidarity is pursued. The remaining expenditures under the EU Budget are relatively small with the item internal and external policies consisting mainly of expenditures on subsidies stimulating research and development as well as financial aid to poor countries outside the EU. Other expenditures are insignificant, and contrary to common belief, expenditures on administration are very modest.

Approximately 81 per cent of revenue stems from direct contributions from the member states. The size of these contributions is determined partly by the gross national product (GNP) of individual countries. The specific rules governing the collection of value added tax in individual member states is thus of no importance for the contribution to the common EU Budget. Other significant sources of income are import duties and agricultural levies, which make up around 16 per cent of total revenue of the EU Budget.

The Budget only constitutes approximately 1.25 per cent of GDP of the EU as a whole. By way of comparison, the federal budget of the USA constitutes around 25 per cent of GDP of the USA. The federal element of the budgets of the EU member states is thus very modest. Responsibility for and financing of public sector activities is by and large referred to the individual member states, whereby they have maintained a much higher degree of autonomy than the constituent states of actual federations such as the USA.

1.6 **Plan of the book**

BELOW is a brief overview of the chapters of the book.

Chapter 2 illustrates the demographic development in the EU. Demography sets the overall framework for any economy and is therefore a central point of departure for economic analysis. However, the most important reason for devoting a chapter specifically to the demographic development of the EU is to outline the perspectives of future development in this area. For the first time in recent history, population figures seem likely to decline in all EU member states, as the current birth rates are unable to maintain the size of the population. In coming years, the age distribution will change markedly as the proportion of old people in the population will increase. This may have far-reaching economic and political consequences, e.g. for the financing of old age pensions, thus challenging the basic principles of the welfare state. It is these problems in particular that will be discussed in Chapter 2.

Chapter 3 analyses the labour market in the EU in general and offers a comprehensive overview of the European unemployment problem in particular. In an economically integrated Europe dominated by the principle of a free market economy, the development in employment largely depends on the *flexibility of the labour market*. Here, flexibility reflects the mobility of the labour force, geographically and between different types of jobs, as well as flexibility in wage determination. The lack of homogeneity of the European workforce combined with low labour market flexibility will be identified as the main cause of the European unemployment problem.

Chapter 4 describes the economic growth in the EU and examines whether integration has actually fostered economic prosperity in Europe. The chapter will highlight the need for more capital accumulation to raise standards of living and reduce unemployment in the European Union, and the possible impact of integration on real convergence, i.e. convergence of GDP per capita, will also be analysed in this chapter. The last section will examine whether the structural funds actually succeed in placing resources in those regions that are in need and whether this has an impact on growth.

Chapter 5 analyses various issues relating to the *industrial structure* of the EU. The chapter stresses the relation between economic growth and the reorientation of production from agriculture to services and briefly presents the common agricultural policy (CAP). This section will furthermore illustrate how the endeavours to protect the standards of living of farmers through price support schemes, regulation of production, and import restrictions towards third-party countries, harm the efficiency of the EU as a whole. The chapter also includes a description of industrial structures and technological developments. Looking at stylized facts, there is no clear evidence that industrial structures and industrial behaviour have changed markedly to become more dynamic, and empirical evidence furthermore shows that differences in industrial structures among member states seem to persist. Seen in that light, the European economies are not converging. The development in size and concentration of firms in individual industries is also examined and discussed with respect to the economic integration. The chapter explains how the enhanced competition following in the wake of the Internal Market seems to have eroded the market power of firms to the benefit of the consumers in the form of lower prices. Finally, the EU rules on state aid and the stance on tax harmonization are discussed.

Trade policy, trade patterns, and competitiveness are described in Chapter 6. An illustration of the importance of European integration for internal and external trade flows is accompanied by a description of the trade between the EU and third-party countries and internally between member states. The chapter demonstrates that *internal trade* has increased rapidly and that *intra-industry trade* in particular has gained importance. The question of whether integration has promoted specialization in Europe is examined, and it is found that although there is no specialization at industry level, there is still an impact from trade in that, increasingly, Europe engages in intra-industry trade. Finally, the concepts of competitiveness and revealed comparative advantages, which are essential to the evaluation of sustainable growth, are discussed.

Chapter 7 illustrates the development in foreign direct investment (FDI) in the EU, particularly from the mid-1980s when the development of the Internal Market was initiated, including an examination of the actual mobility of capital. The chapter identifies a drastic increase in direct investment, both internally between individual EU countries and externally between the EU and the rest of the world. Part of these direct investments have been in the form of mergers and acquisitions. Thus, the internationalization of firms through the establishment of multinational company networks has become a conspicuous trend in connection with the formation of the Single Market and globalization in general, and cause and effect of this development will be discussed.

Chapter 8 describes the monetary integration in the EU, starting with an account of monetary integration as it has developed from the *snake in the tunnel* arrangement of the 1970s over the EMS cooperation of the 1980s and 1990s, to the establishment of the EMU at the end of the 1990s. Based on the theory of *optimum currency area*, the advantages and disadvantages for the EU countries of a monetary union are discussed. The conclusion is that the common currency, the euro, may benefit firms and consumers, but that the cost may be increased macroeconomic instability. The chapter also contains a description of the potential of fiscal policy in the EU after the introduction of the so-called *Stability and Growth Pact*, which obliges those member states participating in the EMU to avoid disproportionately large government budget deficits. Finally, the goals and instruments of the European Central Bank as well as the monetary policy of the euro-area are discussed.

The twenty-first century presents the EU with a substantial new challenge in connection with the enlargement of the EU by up to ten Central and Eastern European countries. This challenge is the subject of Chapter 9. If all ten Central and Eastern European countries currently engaged in actual membership negotiations are admitted, the population of the EU will increase by more than 25 per cent, whereas GDP will increase by no more than 10 per cent as a consequence of the low productivity of these countries. Thus, extensive revisions of the agricultural and structural policies of the EU must be envisaged. In order to analyse these issues, the chapter also includes a description of the economic transformation process in Central and Eastern Europe.

The last chapter of the book summarizes the previous nine chapters and puts their analyses into perspective. It will present various dimensions of the concept of integration, which will then form the basis of a discussion of the relations between the economic and political integration process. Finally, the chapter will evaluate the state of the ongoing transformation of the individual national economies into one common EU economy.

Further reading

Several books on the European Union have been published in recent years. Below is a list of references to books which expand on the various issues touched upon in the Introduction. Economic integration from a predominantly theoretical perspective is addressed in W. Molle, (1998), *The Economics of European Integration*, 3rd edn., Dartmouth, Aldershot. The EU institutions and the political decision making process are outlined in H. Wallace, and W. Wallace (eds.) (2000), *Policy Making in the European Union*, 4th edn., OUP, Oxford. An anthology of important political economy issues of European integration is presented in F. Laursen (ed.) (1995), *The Political Economy of European Integration*, Kluwer Law International, European Institute of Public

Administration, Maastricht. The legal framework of the European Union is described in C. Vincenzi (1999), *Law of the European Union*, Financial Times, 2nd edn., London. Finally, the actual texts of the Treaties can be found in European Union (1997), *Consolidated Version of the Treaty on European Union and the Treaty Establishing the European Community*, Luxembourg.

References

EU Commission (1998), *European Economy*, no. 66.

—— (1999), *European Economy*, no. 69.

Eurostat (1997), *Basic Statistics of the European Union, Comparisons with Major Partners of the European Union*, 33rd edn.

Chapter 2
European Demographics: Trends and Problems

Jørgen Drud Hansen

2.1 Introduction

THE demographic developments will pose a challenge to European politicians in the future. Throughout the past decades, all EU member states have experienced a marked decline in reproduction, i.e. the birth rate of the population. The general expectation is that, also in future, the reproduction rate will be relatively low, and unless the EU experiences a significant immigration from non-member states, there is a prospect of a decrease in the population in coming decades. Although a net immigration from non-EU countries is expected, it will hardly be to such an extent that a decrease in population can be avoided.

It is not the prospect of a decline in the population as such that causes concern, but rather the accompanying shift in the age structure of the population. The share of older persons in the population is expected to increase significantly, and since elderly people display a low employment frequency, a relatively larger share of total output produced by other generations must be reserved for this age group in order to maintain their standard of living. The result may be that public finances in individual member states will come under increasing pressure and that basic principles of the welfare state, such as old-age pensions, taxation, and other elements, must be put on the political agenda.

The purpose of this chapter is to illustrate the demographic trends in Europe and specifically to highlight the prospects of a dramatic shift in age structure towards an increasing share of elderly people. Section 2.2 describes the composition and development of the population in the EU in recent years. Section 2.3 lists the main Eurostat projections for the development of the population in the EU in coming decades. This section also illustrates the consequences for the age structure if the development follows the pattern described in these projections. Section 2.4 discusses the economic implications of the expected shift in age structure towards a growing number of elderly people. The main conclusions of the chapter are summed up in Section 2.5.

2.2 The declining growth in population

I**F** a person was randomly selected from the world's total population, the probability of this person coming from an EU country would only be around 1/15. The probability of this person coming from the largest EU country in terms of population, Germany, would be around 1/67. And with a probability of only around 1/558, it is even less likely that the person would be Belgian. These main demographic figures will be highlighted in this section. The size of the EU population will be compared to that of the rest of the world and a comparison will also be made between individual member states. The section will furthermore present the long-term trends of the determinants of population growth in the EU.

The Union in a global context

At the beginning of 1995, the total population of the fifteen EU countries amounted to 372 million inhabitants, (see Table 2.1). This is equivalent to approximately 7 per cent of the total world population. The population of the USA amounts to 5 per cent and that of Japan 2 per cent of the world population. Thus the EU, the USA, and Japan, who form the Triad of the world economy, only embrace around 14 per cent of the total population of the entire world. In comparison, the population of the less developed countries makes up around 79 per cent of total world population. The populations of China, India, and Brazil alone account for 41 per cent of the world's population, which is approximately three times that of the Triad of the world economy. So whereas the Triad is big in economic terms, it is small in demographic terms.

A look at the population sizes of the member states

The population of individual member states as in 1998 is illustrated in Table 2.2. With a population of around 82 million, Germany is the largest of the member states in terms of population with a share of approximately 22 per cent. The populations of France, the UK, and Italy are basically of identical size, as each of these countries accounts for 15–16 per cent of the total population of the EU. Thus, the four largest EU countries, in terms of population, constitute more than two-thirds of the total population of the EU.

Table 2.1 Population of the major regions of the world, 1995

	Millions	Per cent of world population
World	5,687	100
More developed countries	1,171	21
of which:		
EUR15	372	7
USA	267	5
Japan	125	2
Russian Federation	148	3
Less developed countries	4,516	79
of which:		
China	1,220	22
India	929	16
Nigeria	112	2
Brazil	159	3

Note: The classification into more and less developed countries follows Eurostat.

Source: Eurostat (1999): table D-1.

Table 2.2 Population in member states, 1999

	Millions	Per cent of EUR15
Belgium	10.2	2.7
Denmark	5.3	1.4
Germany	82.1	21.8
Greece	10.5	2.8
Spain	39.4	10.5
France	59.1	15.7
Ireland	3.7	1.0
Italy	57.7	15.3
Luxembourg	0.4	0.1
The Netherlands	15.8	4.2
Austria	8.1	2.1
Portugal	9.9	2.6
Finland	5.2	1.4
Sweden	8.9	2.4
UK	59.6	15.8
EUR15	376.9	100.0

Source: EU Commission (1999), Annexe: table 1.

The demographic determinants in Europe

Total population is a *stock variable*, which is registered at a given point in time, e.g. 1 January each year. The difference between the number of births minus the number of deaths for the period in question constitutes the natural rate of growth of the population. But the natural rate of growth of the population is not the only determinant of the population size. This is also influenced by the net migration in the period, i.e. the number of people entering the country (immigration) less the number of people leaving the country (emigration). Thus, the total change in population (which is a flow variable which is measured for a specific period of time) is equal to the natural rate of growth of the population plus net migration.

A first impression of the actual development in population in the period 1960–98, in those countries forming the EU today, is represented in Figure 2.1 by a curve illustrating the size of the population. The three alternative curves drawn into the figure for the years after 1998 illustrate Eurostat's projections of the future development in population given different assumptions. These projections of population growth are described in more detail in Section 2.3.

In 1997, the total population in EUR15 constituted 374 million inhabitants. In the period 1960 to 1994, the total population in EUR15, excluding the former East Germany, increased from around 299 million to 355 million, i.e. by approximately

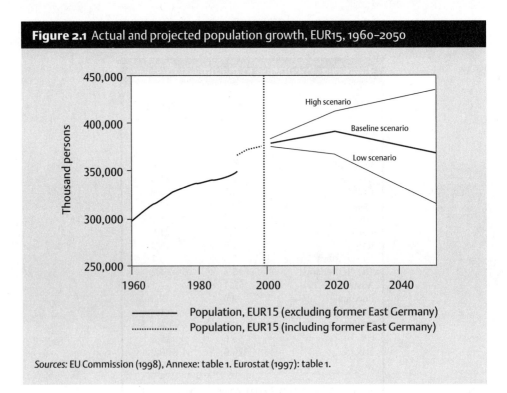

Figure 2.1 Actual and projected population growth, EUR15, 1960–2050

Population, EUR15 (excluding former East Germany)
Population, EUR15 (including former East Germany)

Sources: EU Commission (1998), Annexe: table 1. Eurostat (1997): table 1.

0.51 per cent p.a. It is apparent that, in absolute figures, the annual population growth has been decreasing. In the first half of the period, i.e. 1960–77, the population increased by 0.67 per cent p.a., whereas in the latter half of the period, i.e. 1977–94, the population increased by only 0.35 per cent p.a.

Table 2.3 illustrates the development in population growth in the EU for a number of periods distributed on the natural rate of growth of the population and net migration. Figures are indicated in number of persons per 1,000 inhabitants for the year in question. Total annual growth has decreased from almost 0.9 per cent in the 1960s to around 0.3 per cent in the 1990s. The data behind this change demonstrate a significant decrease in the rate of natural growth and a remarkable increase in net migration. Thus, in the latter part of the period, the lion's share of total population growth in the EU was constituted by net migration.

It appears from the table that net migration is relatively unstable compared with the development in the rate of natural growth. Violent events such as social unrest and war may cause significant migration. Thus, the net migration of recent years is *inter alia* related to the extensive changes in Eastern Europe and the Balkans.

The reasons for the marked decline in the rate of natural growth are illustrated in Figure 2.2, which shows the trends in the number of live births and the number of deaths per 1,000 inhabitants. The difference between these numbers expresses the rate of natural growth of the population per 1,000 inhabitants.

The number of births per 1,000 inhabitants has decreased significantly throughout the period, whereas the number of deaths has decreased only slightly. Thus, in recent years, the natural rate of growth of the population has almost stagnated.[1] The

Table 2.3 Components of population growth, EUR15, 1960–1997

Year	Annual average per 1,000 inhabitants		
	Natural growth	Net migration	Total increase
1960–4	7.9	0.6	8.6
1965–9	6.9	−0.1	6.8
1970–4	4.5	0.6	5.0
1975–9	2.6	0.8	3.4
1980–4	2.0	0.2	2.2
1985–9	1.7	1.3	2.9
1990–4	1.4	2.9	4.3
1995	0.7	2.2	2.9
1996	0.8	2.0	2.8
1997	0.8	2.1	2.9

Source: Eurostat (1999): tables A-2, A-3, and A-4.

[1] The number of births and deaths per 1,000 inhabitants in a specific year depends *inter alia* on the age structure of the population of that year. If, for instance, an unusually large number of women are of child-bearing age, then the number of births per 1,000 inhabitants will naturally be expected to be high. The age conditioned birth and death patterns, i.e. the average number of live births per 1,000 women of childbearing

Figure 2.2 Births and deaths in EUR15, 1960–1997

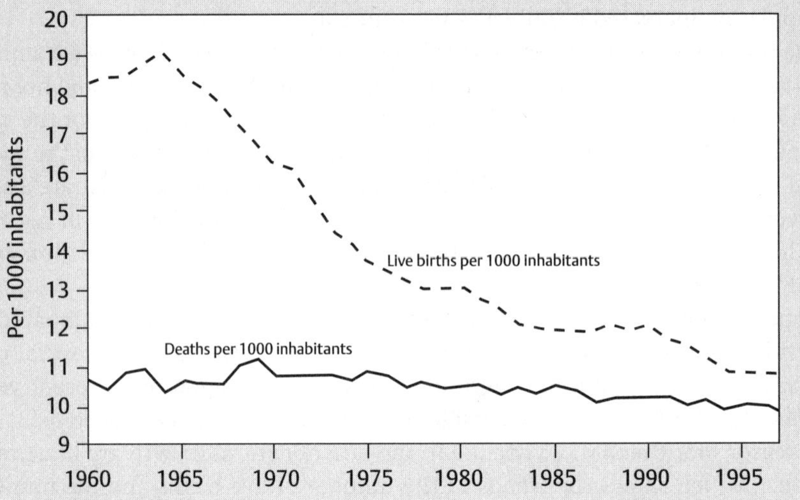

Source: Eurostat (1999): tables E-1 and G

declining birth rate is a general phenomenon for all developed countries, the background for this development being a mixture of cultural and economic changes following in the wake of the overall development in wealth. The increased equal rights between men and women to education and on the labour market is probably a main reason for the falling birth rates, as women are increasingly active on all levels of the labour market. A narrow economic analysis may offer a rationale for this change in demographic behaviour towards fewer children per family. Children may be perceived as a highly time-intensive activity of 'consumption', and with increasing real wages in the EU, the opportunity cost of choosing to have children has increased significantly.

2.3 The prospect of a declining population in the EU

A *population prognosis* is an estimation of the size of the population at some point in time in the future. The estimate is a forecast of the development of the current population based on assumptions about birth and mortality rates of individual age

age and the average number of deaths per 1,000 inhabitants per year in a life cycle, are relevant for the long-term natural rate of growth of the population.

groups as well as the pattern of migration, including the age structure of the migrants. Naturally, the result of such prognoses depends heavily on the selected assumptions on the development in fertility, mortality, and migration. Changes in these determinants will be reflected in the growth rate of the population and in this sense they will have a cumulative effect on the development of the population. Even modest deviations in fertility, mortality, and migration compared to the assumptions of the prognosis may thus result in the prognosis being completely wrong in the long run.

The UN has prepared a global population prognosis extrapolating the current population to the year 2025. The main results of this extrapolation, which are reproduced in Eurostat (Eurostat (1999), table D-1), show that the world population will increase from 5.6bn. inhabitants in 1995 to 8.0bn. inhabitants in the year 2025. In the same period, the population of the EU will only increase from 372 million inhabitants in 1995 to 382 million in 2025, and thus the EU share of the world population will fall from around 7 per cent to 5 per cent.

Eurostat also makes its own population projections. These projections are based on assumptions about *fertility* and *life expectancy* as both these measures are independent of the age structure of the population. Fertility indicates the expected average number of live births per woman outliving the childbearing age.[2] Life expectancy at birth expresses the average number of years a newborn baby is expected to live given existing mortality rates. In order to underline the sensitivity of the results to the selected assumptions of fertility and life expectancy, Eurostat makes projections in the form of a *high scenario* and a *low scenario*, expressing the extremes in terms of expected population growth. As an average of these extreme scenarios, a projection in the form of a *baseline scenario* is also made. The baseline scenario assumes a slight increase in fertility from the current level of 1.45 to 1.66 in the year 2050. Furthermore, an increase in life expectancy at birth of around 5–6 years is assumed, as well as a continued moderate net migration into the EU of around 500,000 per year (see Table 2.4).

In Figure 2.1, the expected development in population according to the baseline

Table 2.4 Demographic key assumptions used for the baseline scenario, EUR15				
	1995	2000	2020	2050
Fertility (children per woman)	1.45	1.55	1.65	1.66
Life expectancy at birth (years):				
Male	73.9	74.7	77.8	79.7
Female	80.4	81.1	83.6	85.1
Net migration per year (1,000)	762	679	592	592

Sources: EU Commission (1998), Annexe: table 1. Eurostat (1997): table 1.

[2] As the gender coefficient is close to ½, and as not all women outlive the childbearing age, fertility should be above 2 in order for the population to reproduce itself.

scenario is marked by the solid curve indicating the projected population size from the year 2000 to the year 2050. In the baseline scenario, the total population of the EU peaks in the year 2023, after which it will decline so that by the end of the projection period, in the year 2050, the total population will basically match the size of the current population.

The low scenario is the closest reflection of the current demographic conditions, i.e. fertility will remain at an unchanged low level, there will be an insignificant increase in life expectancy at birth, and the net migration will be at a slightly lower level than the current 500,000. In this scenario, the decline in population will start earlier, and by the year 2050, the total population of the EU will have fallen from the current level of 372 million to around 300 million.

The high scenario assumes an increase in fertility to a level of around 1.95, a higher increase in life expectancy at birth, and a net migration of around 800,000 per year. In the high scenario, the population size increases throughout the projection period, although the increase diminishes towards the end of the period.

The perspectives of the development of the population of individual member states are illustrated in Figure 2.3. There are significant differences between the member states in the sizes of the currently observed demographic parameters. In the baseline scenario, these initial differences have to some extent been maintained as assumptions for the projections at member state level. Consequently, the population decline will occur at different points in time in individual countries. It may come as a surprise that recent fertility levels are particularly low in Italy, Germany, and Spain, and based on this, the population of these countries is expected to start declining already ten to fifteen years into the twenty-first century.

A more detailed analysis of the results of the projections furthermore reveals a strong tendency towards an ageing of the population in all scenarios. The explanation of this shift is the assumption of a continued low level of fertility and a simultaneous increase in life expectancy at birth.

Figure 2.3 First calendar year of population decline, baseline scenario

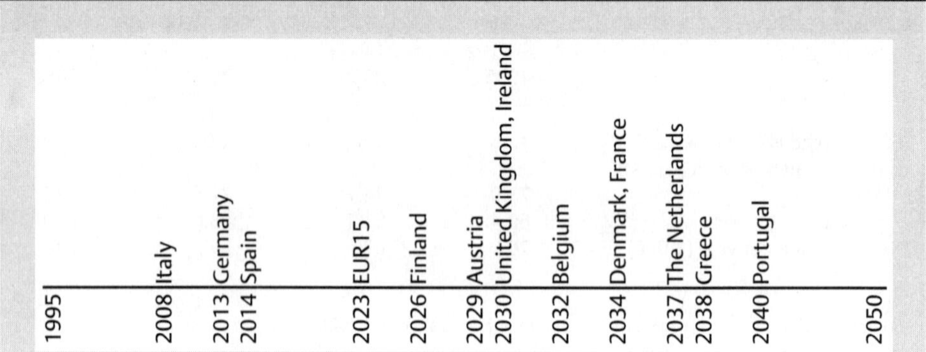

Sources: EU Commission (1998), Annexe: table 1. Eurostat (1997): table 1.

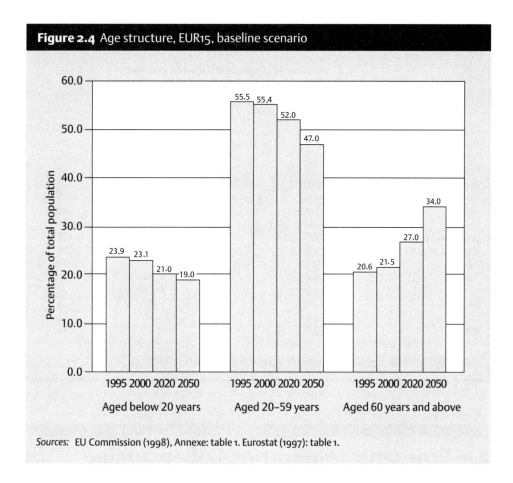

Figure 2.4 Age structure, EUR15, baseline scenario

Sources: EU Commission (1998), Annexe: table 1. Eurostat (1997): table 1.

Figure 2.4 illustrates the development in age structure in the baseline scenario for EUR15, and it appears from this figure that the share of elderly people (aged 60 years and above) will increase rapidly from 1995 to 2050. This increase should be compared to the moderate decrease in the share of 0–19-year-olds and significant decrease in the age group of 20–59-year-olds.

Table 2.5 illustrates the shift in age structure towards an increasing number of elderly in individual member states in the baseline scenario. For all countries, there is a prospect of a marked increase in the share of elderly people, and the member states will thus be hit by a vigorous *demographic shock*. Spain and Italy in particular are expected to have a large share of elderly (37 per cent aged 60 years and above) in the year 2050, whereas the share of elderly people will be relatively low in Denmark, Luxembourg, and Sweden (29 per cent aged 60 years and above).

Table 2.5 The ageing population in the member states, baseline scenario

	Percentage of population aged 60 and above			
	1995	2000	2020	2050
Belgium	21.3	21.8	28	32
Denmark	19.9	19.6	26	29
Germany	20.7	22.6	28	34
Greece	21.5	22.9	27	33
Spain	20.6	21.5	26	37
France	20.0	20.5	27	33
Ireland	15.3	15.6	22	32
Italy	22.2	23.8	29	37
Luxembourg	19.1	19.2	25	29
The Netherlands	17.7	18.2	26	30
Austria	19.8	20.1	26	33
Portugal	19.8	20.6	24	31
Finland	18.9	19.7	28	31
Sweden	22.1	21.9	27	29
UK	20.5	20.5	26	32
EUR15	20.6	21.5	27	34

Sources: EU Commission (1998), Annexe: table 1. Eurostat (1997): table 1.

2.4 Economic implications of an ageing population

As shown in the preceding section, Europe will be confronted with a dramatic increase in the share of elderly people. This demographic transition will have far-reaching consequences on vital parts of the economy. First, the public sector budget will be put under pressure. Individuals active in production are typically aged between 20 and 59 years, and a decrease in the share of the population in this specific age group may therefore automatically increase the burden of pensions and expenditures on care for the elderly to be carried by the economically active. Secondly, the demographic transition will lead to a lower aggregate rate of savings in the economy even if individual savings behaviour remains unchanged. The most important motive for individual savings is *intertemporal allocation* of consumption from the years where the individual earns an income to the age span where the individual plans to retire. The rate of savings is thus positive in the active years and negative in the inactive years. A change in the age structure towards a larger share of elderly people may therefore reduce the aggregate rate of savings. In standard macroeconomic texts, this age-dependent savings behaviour is outlined in the so-called *life-cycle hypothesis*.

Thirdly, the ageing population will influence the consumption pattern. Care for the elderly, public health, and old-age specific consumption, for example sheltered housing, will gain more importance in the composition of consumption compared with consumption in other areas. Finally, an ageing population may have negative consequences on the efficiency and development in productivity of the economy, as a consequence of the increasing average age of the labour force which is likely to be that labour market mobility will fall since the inclination to change jobs declines with age. Similarly, innovation and entrepreneurship also declines with age, and a development towards an increase in the number of elderly is thus likely to lead to a fall in the growth in productivity. However, these correlations are primarily based on speculation and it is difficult to document them empirically.

The most important macroeconomic effects of the change in the age structure are thus the impacts on the rate of savings and the public budget. These effects will therefore be discussed in more detail. Let us address the savings problem first. The fall in the savings ratio as a consequence of the shift in the age structure will lead to lower capital accumulation. However, as the population will decrease at the same time, the need for investment will be lower if wealth expressed in endowment of capital per capita remains unchanged. The demographic change as such will therefore not undermine the foundation for wealth through the effects on capital accumulation. However, the average age of the capital goods will increase (just as the average age of the population), and as new knowledge is built into every vintage of capital goods, old capital goods are less efficient than new. There may therefore be indirect negative effects on wealth of a decrease in the capital accumulation through the age effect on capital. However, it is of course extremely difficult to evaluate the importance of such effects.

The tax burden problem

The largest immediate problem arising from the demographic development is the prospect of an increased public budget deficit. In recent years, a number of estimations of the consequences of the demographic structural changes on public budgets have been made (see e.g. Franco and Munzi (1996, 1997)). Based on assumptions on the demographic development and the present social security system, *extrapolations* on public spending can be made of the development over time in public expenditure per capita of individual age groups. These extrapolations are then modified by including assumptions on changes in policies regarding public spending. Finally, assumptions are made on the economic development in general, after which public expenditures are related to GDP.

It is no surprise that individual estimations render varying results with respect to the increase in the level of spending depending on the actual assumptions forming the basis of the analyses. Franco and Munzi (1997) have compiled a series of national prognoses of the development in the age-related public expenditures related to GDP. The development in total age-related public expenditures for those EU member states

Table 2.6 Trend in total age-related public expenditure, 1995–2030

	Per cent of GDP		Change over the period
	1995	2030	1995–2030
Belgium	28.8	33.7–34.4	4.9–5.6
Denmark	35.0	41.5	6.5
Finland	43.0	49.1–49.9	6.1–6.9
Germany	25.0	31.2	6.2
Italy	28.3	32.1–33.2	3.8–5.0
The Netherlands	27.7	34.3–35.0	4.6–5.3
Spain	20.3	21.5–23.2	1.2–2.9
Sweden	33.0	35.7–36.8	2.3–2.7

Note: Where two sets of data are presented, the left indicates the lowest public expenditure scenario and the right indicates the highest public expenditure scenario.

Source: Franco and Munzi (1997): table 9.

where national prognoses are available is described in Table 2.6. Total age-related public spending includes expenditures on old as well as young age groups, i.e. reductions in public expenditure as a result of a smaller share of young, inactive generations have been included in the compilation.

According to these projections, Denmark, Finland, and Germany should expect an increase in expenditures of more than 5 percentage points, whereas the increase in Spain and Sweden will be limited to less than 3 percentage points. This variation in the results is partly due to differences in the demographic development, partly due to planned adjustments of pension schemes. A more thorough analysis of the expected development shows that it is only after the year 2010 that the effects on the public expenditures will be felt in earnest. In other words, all countries will have time to carry out structural reforms, which may seem appropriate given the demographic development.

The emerging perspective of an increase in public expenditures as a result of the ageing of the population is problematic given the commitments made by the member states regarding their fiscal policies. Through the Amsterdam Treaty, the member states are obliged to maintain healthy public finances, i.e. the member states must refrain from incurring excessive public deficits. This obligation was most recently confirmed in *The Stability and Growth Pact* (see Chapter 8). Thus, intervention is required to neutralize the effects of the tendency towards a deterioration of the public budget balance caused by the demographic changes. In principle, several possibilities exist. First, the level of taxation can be increased. However, this will distort the labour market, encourage early retirement, and lead the black economy to flourish. Secondly, public spending in other areas can be limited. However, for most countries, this solution will imply accepting an extensive reformulation of the tasks of the public sector. Thirdly, the *financing of old-age pensions* may be changed from a taxation-financed system to a funded scheme system. Finally, attempts can be made to change labour market participation so that the number of people in employment within individual age groups is increased. In the following, the pros and cons of changing the principles of the financing of old-age pensions to a funded scheme, as well as the possibilities of increasing employment in individual age groups, are discussed.

The pension problem

The taxation-financed system is often described as a *pay-as-you-go system* (PAYG), as the pensions of the current older generations are financed by the tax payments of the current younger generations. There is thus a continuous *intergenerational* transfer of consumption possibilities from the economically active to the older, inactive generation. The advantage of this system is that all persons of the older generation are covered by pensions, irrespective of earlier tax payments. Thus, an intergenerational *distributional solidarity* is built into the system. However, this distributional quality is also the weakness of the system, as the incentive for the individual to limit tax payments curbs the efficiency of the economy. This is because the principle of distributional solidarity means that there is no relation between the level of taxes paid and, later, the size of pensions received by the individual. Thus, in the active years, the individual is encouraged to adopt *free-ride behaviour* through efforts to avoid tax payments.

In a *funded scheme*, pensions are defrayed by a pension fund to which the individual has made contributions throughout the active years in the labour market. Pensions received are thus related to the contributions made by the individual to the fund, and the obligation to make payments to the fund does not distort the allocation to the same extent as the PAYG system. Furthermore, a funded scheme contributes to developing the capital markets of the economy since the payments are accumulated in the form of shares and bonds. The funded scheme creates volume and differentiation between various types of assets in the capital markets, leading to a more efficient economy (Holzman (1997)). On the other hand, there is no, or only very limited, distributional solidarity attached to the funded scheme.

An adjustment of the pension system from a PAYG system to a funded scheme will thus make it easier to finance the increasing pension costs caused by the demographic changes. However, if such a strategy is pursued, a transition problem will arise as, in the period of the transition, the economically active generations will have to continue paying high taxes to finance the pensions of the older generation at the same time as they will have to pay for the establishment of the pension fund. This *intergenerational distribution problem* calls for a gradual transition to a funded scheme. In this process, there is no need to phase out the PAYG system completely. If it is desirable to maintain a certain level of solidarity in the pension schemes, the PAYG system can to some degree be maintained as a social safety net.

In the long run it is unlikely that the choice of pension system will influence the aggregate savings ratio in the economy. In both systems, the private consumption of the older, inactive generation is financed by transfers. In a PAYG system, private consumption of the active generation is limited via taxation. In a funded scheme, private consumption of the active generation is limited through the contributions to the pension fund.

In the transition period, where the assets of the pension funds are gradually increased through the accumulation of the pension contributions, the aggregate savings ratio in the economy will be higher. The reason is the intergenerational transition problem, where the active generation in the period of transition will be hit by the double payment requirement of contributing to old-age pensions for themselves as well as for the contemporary older generations.[3]

Mitigating the tax increase through higher employment

The pressure of redistributing income to the inactive part of the population can be mitigated by increasing employment for a given share of the population. This can be done in two ways. First, by increasing the labour force, i.e. the number of persons in or seeking employment. Secondly, by increasing employment for a given share of the labour force, i.e. by reducing unemployment.

Table 2.7 illustrates the situation in the labour market in terms of labour supply and employment in the member states in 1997. The *activity rate* indicates the labour force as a percentage of the population aged between 15 and 64 years, whereas the *employment rate* indicates the number of people employed as a percentage of the population in that same age group. The difference between the activity rate and the employment rate is the unemployment rate, i.e. the number of unemployed aged between 15 and 64 years as a percentage of the labour force.

These key figures indicate that there are marked differences between the member states. The activity rate is thus particularly high in Denmark and Sweden compared with the other member states, whereas the activity rate is relatively low in Italy, Spain, and Greece. The main reason for this difference is that the participation of women on the labour market is much higher in Denmark and Sweden. In other words, Italy, Spain, and Greece have a larger potential than Denmark and Sweden for mitigating the effects of the ageing population through an increase in employment via increased participation of women in the labour market. An examination of current employment figures expressed in the employment rate also shows that all countries, and Spain in particular, can realize higher output through reduced unemployment. A more successful employment policy may therefore contribute to solving the problems which will arise because of the ageing of the population.

---

[3] In 1981, the pension system in Chile was radically changed from a conventional pay-as-you-go system to a funded scheme. This experiment has been the object of considerable interest as the Chilean economy consequently experienced a very positive development with strong growth based on a large increase in savings (see Holzman (1997)).

Table 2.7 Labour market participation, 1997

	Activity rate[a] per cent	Employment rate[b] per cent
Belgium	62.6	57.0
Denmark	79.8	75.4
Germany	70.6	63.6
Greece	60.9	54.8
Spain	60.8	48.0
France	68.0	59.4
Ireland	62.9	56.4
Italy	57.7	50.5
Luxembourg	61.5	59.9
The Netherlands	71.5	67.5
Austria	70.9	67.2
Portugal	68.2	63.4
Finland	72.8	61.9
Sweden	76.4	68.3
UK	75.1	89.7
EUR15	67.5	60.1

[a] The activity rate represents the labour force as a percentage of the population aged 15 to 64 years living in private households.
[b] The employment rate represents number of persons in employment as a percentage of the population aged 15 to 64 years living in private households.

Source: Eurostat (1998): table 1.

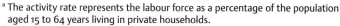

2.5 **Concluding remarks**

IN a global perspective, the most conspicuous trend in the demographic development in the EU in recent years is the perspective of a stagnation or very limited increase in the population in future. The result of this development is an ageing population. This will pose a challenge for the political foundation of the *welfare state*, first and foremost because it will be difficult to maintain the current methods of financing old-age pensions and care for the elderly in general. In large parts of the rest of the industrialized world, the demographic development follows the same pattern as in the EU. In a pessimistic article by Peterson (1998) in *Foreign Affairs* on the demographic tendencies, he talks about an advancing *floridarization* of the developed world, referring to the fact that Florida has become a society of old-age pensioners where more than 20 per cent of the population is aged 65 and above. In the coming decade, the share of elderly in a number of rich countries will reach levels similar to that of Florida.

The development of the population in the rich countries forms a sharp contrast to the development of the population in a number of less developed countries. The strong increase in population in these countries will hamper growth in wealth and thus the possibilities of a catch up of the standard of living with the EU countries. The consequence will be a constant, intense *migration pressure* on the EU countries.

Admittedly, a more intensive immigration into the EU will increase the labour force and thus mitigate some of the problems with the ageing population described above. On the other hand, such a development will challenge the welfare state in other ways due to the social and cultural tensions that will arise. This will pose significant demands on the political system to initiate educational, social, and cultural measures to facilitate the integration of immigrants. The problems that may be caused by this may prove to be more difficult to solve than the problems of making the EMU and the Single Market work.

Further reading

A formal exposition of demography, analysed in an economic framework, is presented in A. Razin and E. Sadka (1995), *Population Economics*, MIT Press, Cambridge, Mass. and London. Prospects for the world population in general and the European population in particular can be found in H. Birg (1995), *World Population Projections for the 21st Century: Theoretical Interpretations and Quantitative Simulations*, Campus Verlag, Frankfurt and St Martin's Press, New York, and D. Noin and R. Woods (eds.) (1993), *The Changing Population of Europe*, Blackwell, Oxford, and Cambridge, Mass. The economic prospects of the ageing population are dealt with in J. Stolnitz (ed.) (1992), *Demographic Causes and Economic Consequences of Population Ageing*, UN Economic Commission for Europe, United Nations Population Fund, Economic Studies, 3, New York.

References

EU Commission (1994), *European Economy*, 56.

—— (1997), *Statistics in Focus: Population and Social Conditions*, 7.

—— (1998), *European Economy*, 66.

Eurostat (1998), *Statistics in Focus: Population and Social Conditions*, 5.

—— (1999), *Demographic Statistics Data 1995–98*.

Franco, D., and Munzi (1996), 'Public Pension Expenditure Prospects in the European Union: A Survey of National Projections', in EU Commission, *European Economy, Reports and Studies*, 3.

—— —— (1997), 'Ageing and Fiscal Policy in Europe', in EU Commission, *European Economy, Reports and Studies*, 4, 'The Welfare State in Europe—Challenges and Reforms'.

Holzman, R. (1997), 'On Economic Benefits and Fiscal Requirements of Moving from Unfunded to Funded Pensions', in EU Commission, *European Economy, Reports and Studies*, 4, 'The Welfare State in Europe—Challenges and Reforms'.

Peterson, P. G. (1999), 'Grey Dawn: The Global Ageing Crisis', *Foreign Affairs*, 78(1), 42–57.

Chapter 3
Labour Markets: Europe's Big Headache

Finn Olesen and Morten Skak

3.1 Introduction

IT would be wrong to expect that the European labour markets can be integrated in the same way or at the same speed as the markets for trade in goods and services, or the financial markets. The reason is partly to be found in the fact that, more often than not, the 'commodity' labour can only be employed within a limited geographical area owing to requirements imposed by language and culture, and partly in the extensive 'mobility costs' which arise in connection with e.g. the change of residence necessary to shift the labour force across large geographical distances.

The year of 1993 introduced a new era for European labour market integration, as it marked the full implementation of the EU Single Market. The Single Market secured the free mobility of labour between member states by abolishing discrimination on grounds of nationality and by granting workers the right to move, seek employment, and reside freely within the territory of the member states. With freedom of establishment, it has furthermore become possible also for the entrepreneur or the doctor to move and practise freely within the EU.

The Amsterdam Treaty from 1997 provided the basis for a common employment policy and common rules for the labour market as well as the introduction of the European Social Fund. In practice, the coordination of the employment policies takes place by producing yearly reports on the employment situation in the member countries, followed by consultations. A fully harmonized EU regulation of the labour market conditions is, however, not imminent as there is agreement that differences in national practice, especially in the area of collective bargaining, must be taken into account.

The formation of the European Monetary Union has only enhanced the demand for flexibility in the European labour market. This issue will be examined in depth in

Chapter 8, but for the purpose of the present chapter, the core problem can be summarized as follows: Lack of competitiveness in a region leads to an increase in unemployment, but with a common currency, there are no possibilities of quickly re-establishing competitiveness through devaluation. In order to ameliorate the problem, excess labour must migrate to other regions with higher employment rates, or the labour market must secure a sufficient degree of wage flexibility to restore competitiveness through falling real wages. Similarly, labour force flexibility, in terms of retraining or changing trade or type of job, is also necessary.

The European labour market will be examined below, partly by comparing it with the labour markets in the USA and Japan, partly by comparing individual EU member states with each other. It will be demonstrated that, because of low flexibility, the labour market became Europe's big headache in the last quarter of the twentieth century, and a main objective of this chapter is to identify factors which illustrate the flexibility—or lack of it—in the European labour market. Section 3.2 opens with a brief overview of the development in employment and unemployment rates in the EU, the USA, and Japan. Section 3.3 summarizes labour market theories which offer an explanation for the development in the European labour market. Having introduced some of the relevant elements of theory, Section 3.4 identifies various ways of assessing labour market flexibility. Section 3.5 evaluates labour market policies, whereas Section 3.6 describes the effect of unionization on the labour market. Section 3.7 concludes the chapter and, following up on the introduction, attempts to make a general evaluation of the level and need for integration of the European labour market.

3.2 Job creation and unemployment

MAKING a general comparison of post-war Europe's ability to create employment with that of the USA and Japan, the development is not encouraging (see Figure 3.1). The EU has not been capable of creating nearly as many jobs as the other two industrialized regions, although the conditions must be said to have been fairly similar for all three areas. From the 1960s up to the early 1980s, job creation was significantly larger in the USA and Japan. Admittedly, from the mid-1980s and until 1992, the number of jobs in the EU increased significantly, but this favourable development was replaced by a more moderate development in the number of jobs up to 1997. The American labour market in particular impresses with a steadily high and long-term growth in the number of jobs. The relation between long-term growth, productivity, and total employment is the subject of Section 4.3 of Chapter 4, whereas here we will focus on developments in employment and unemployment.

The labour market is normally divided into three main sectors: agriculture, industry, and service. However, as the share of agriculture of total employment has diminished significantly over time, this sector will not be described in further detail in this

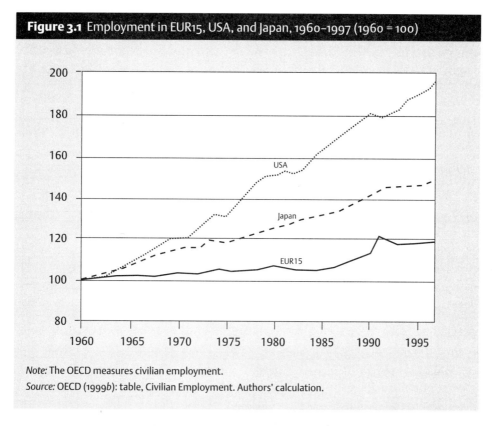

Figure 3.1 Employment in EUR15, USA, and Japan, 1960–1997 (1960 = 100)

Note: The OECD measures civilian employment.

Source: OECD (1999*b*): table, Civilian Employment. Authors' calculation.

chapter. Focusing on employment in the industrial sector (manufacturing and construction), the importance of this sector increased in all three regions until the early 1970s (see Figure 3.2). After this point in time, the number of jobs decreased in the EU, while employment in industry continued to increase in the USA and Japan. As trade in industrial goods takes place in an almost completely free international market with a significant degree of competitiveness between individual firms, the unfortunate European trend must be ascribed to a general lack of competitiveness of the labour force in European industry.[1] One of the reasons for this could be insufficient labour market flexibility in the EU in the period in question.

It is also worth noting that the Japanese industry has had the best performance in terms of job creation. While employment growth stagnated in the USA from the late 1970s, employment in the Japanese industry has continued to grow.

Shifting the focus from industry to the service sector, it appears from Figure 3.3 that, relatively speaking, the largest number of jobs have been created in this sector and that growth in this sector has been significant since 1960. Job creation has been

[1] This need not be inconsistent with the improvement in European competitiveness as measured by the change in the real effective exchange rate from 1980 to 1996 (see Ch. 6, Sect. 6.7). Some of this improvement has been reached by pushing workers out of the European industry in this period in order to raise labour productivity. See also Table 4.1 which demonstrates that labour productivity has grown faster in Europe than in the USA, although not as fast as in Japan.

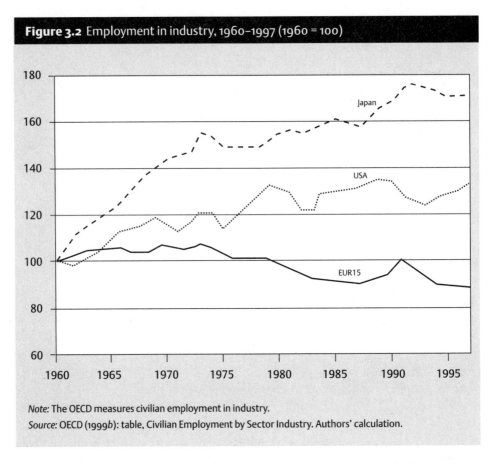

Figure 3.2 Employment in industry, 1960–1997 (1960 = 100)

Note: The OECD measures civilian employment in industry.

Source: OECD (1999b): table, Civilian Employment by Sector Industry. Authors' calculation.

the highest in the USA, while the EU displays the poorest performance. This development in Europe is even more unfortunate as it must be expected that future jobs will be created almost exclusively within the service sector.

Sluggish job creation in Europe

The shortage of jobs in Europe obviously has an influence on the unemployment figures, but they are also influenced by the labour market participation rate. For example, if the number of jobs is reduced by 5 per cent, but at the same time labour market participation falls by 5 per cent so that the labour force has shrunk by 5 per cent, then unemployment will remain constant. In this way not only job creation but also changing participation rates influence the rate of unemployment. Note that the unemployment rate is conceptually defined as the percentage of the labour force that does not have a job. Official definitions might differ. The general concept is that unemployment is the difference between two large factors measured in gross terms, the supply of labour on the one hand, and the demand for labour on the other.

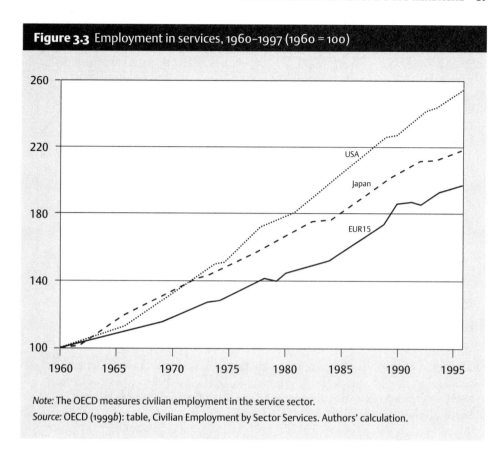

Figure 3.3 Employment in services, 1960–1997 (1960 = 100)

Note: The OECD measures civilian employment in the service sector.

Source: OECD (1999*b*): table, Civilian Employment by Sector Services. Authors' calculation.

Although participation rates react to changes in the demand for labour, they are fairly stable in the short run.[2] The unemployment rate is thus highly sensitive to the business cycle and in general a good indicator of the state and strength of the economies. And this is why—given a non-decreasing labour market participation—a low job creation rate in Europe results in a very high rate of unemployment.

Figure 3.4 illustrates unemployment in per cent since 1960 in the EU, the USA, and Japan. Throughout the 1960s, unemployment was low in EUR15, lower in Japan, and the highest in the USA. For all three regions, the first oil crisis, in 1974, is strongly reflected in the unemployment figures, most markedly in the EU and USA, less so in Japan. The latter is quite remarkable, as the Japanese economy at the time was highly dependent on imported energy. Also the second oil crisis towards the end of the 1970s had an influence on the unemployment figures. In the case of the EU, the consequence was that the unemployment rate continued to grow and in fact surpassed

[2] Since the early 1960s, the long-term trend in participation rates has been an increase in the participation rate for women and a fall for men. In Europe, this led to a fall in the overall participation rate at the beginning of the period which gradually turned into stagnation and then into an increase from the beginning of the 1980s. In the USA, the overall participation rate has increased markedly and then stagnated from the beginning of the 1990s. In Japan, an increase in female participation rates from the second half of the 1970s has turned an overall falling trend into an increase.

Figure 3.4 Unemployment in per cent of civilian labour force, 1960–1997

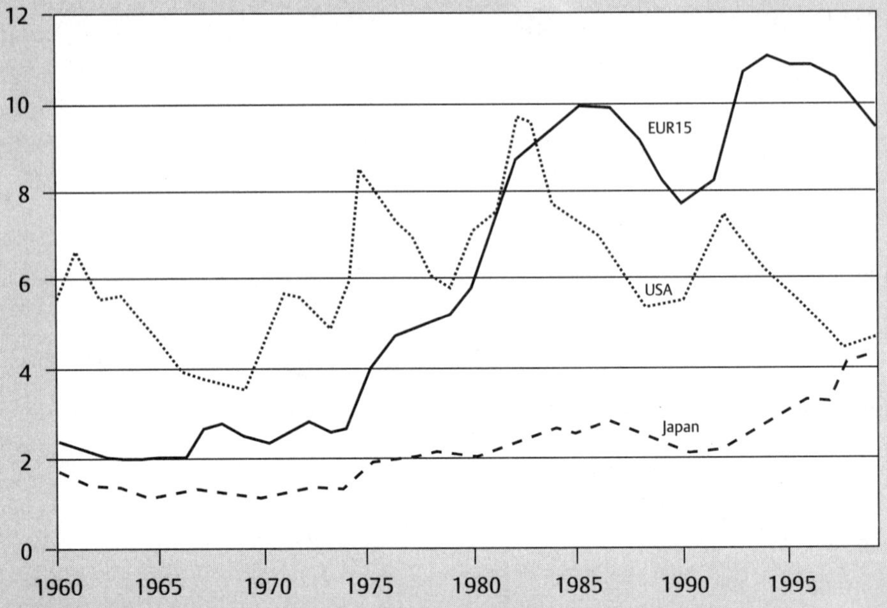

Note: Unemployment rate in EUR15 as defined by Eurostat, for USA and Japan as defined by OECD.
Source: EU Commission (1999): table 3.

the American rate. In the last part of the 1980s, unemployment fell only to see another increase, and the development shows a EUR15 reaching two-digit unemployment rates while the USA managed to return to the level of the 1960s. In the case of Japan, unemployment has been growing, but until recently the rate has been fairly low compared with the USA and the EU.

The overall conclusion of the above is that, in the period in question, the European economies displayed a relatively poor performance resulting in low growth in the number of jobs and high unemployment rates. Let us turn to economic theory to illustrate the problem.

3.3 Labour market theory

THERE is a plethora of economic theories on the functioning of the labour market. In the following, two schools of thought, which supplement each other in explaining the reasons for the development in unemployment in recent years, will be explained.

One school can be summarized in the acronym *NAIRU*, while the other is covered by the concept *hysteresis*.

NAIRU

NAIRU, derived from *Non-Accelerating Inflation Rate of Unemployment*, signifies the unemployment rate at which inflation neither increases nor decreases, i.e. an equilibrium rate of unemployment. The NAIRU school holds the opinion that there is a constant NAIRU, and that the economies will return to this rate of unemployment in the long run. If the actual unemployment rate rises above NAIRU, demand for goods and services as well as labour will be low. In most countries, wages react more to changes in demand than prices, which means that real wages will fall, and this fall in real wages will gradually increase the demand for labour and reduce unemployment. Similarly, if there is a high rate of employment in an economy, with an unemployment rate below NAIRU, this will lead to an increase in real wages and a subsequent reduction in employment until the unemployment rate again reaches the stable, long-term level. The higher the wage flexibility is in the labour market, the faster the adaptation will be, and the fewer will be the deviations from the long-term equilibrium, both in size and time.

Looking again at Figure 3.4, the movements in the unemployment rate in the USA appear to be consistent with the assumption of a constant NAIRU—in the case of the USA presumably between 5 and 6 per cent. The EU, however, has seen a long-term increase in the unemployment rate since the first oil crisis, and after a temporary decrease in the late 1980s, the rate reached two-digit figures and was still close to 10 per cent at the end of the century. At a first glance, the trend in Europe thus seems incompatible with the theory of a stable NAIRU.

In order to fit the European development into NAIRU theory, it is necessary to have a look at what determines NAIRU. In a market economy based on constrained optimization by individual agents, changes in the composition of production will happen continuously, and similarly, individuals will often move from one position in the labour market to another. Because of differences in the workforce with respect to education, geographical location, job preferences, availability of information on vacancies, and so on, there will always be a number of wage earners who are between jobs. With a constant and possibly low unemployment rate, there will thus be a number of persons who are without jobs—experiencing so-called frictional unemployment—for shorter or longer periods, while others will be re-employed immediately. In an efficient labour market, there will only be few and short spells of unemployment in this *matching process*, while low labour market efficiency will keep many unemployed for extended periods. Among other factors, the duration and purchasing power of unemployment benefits are of significance for this matching process as a lasting, high level of benefits reduces the economic strain of unemployment thereby reducing the incentive to look for a new job.

If the economy is in a transition process, where the sectoral structure changes, some firms will expand while others contract and as a consequence, many people will experience structural unemployment at the same time as new jobs are created. Due to the differences in qualifications required for the new and the old jobs, so-called bottlenecks will arise. In this way, structural changes may increase the unemployment rate consistent with stable inflation, in other words, NAIRU may increase. In the next section, we will examine whether the European economy has features which indicate that NAIRU has increased since the oil crises.

It must be conceded that it can be difficult to believe that in any given situation, the economy will automatically return to its long-term unemployment rate. In recessions, this process may take so long a time that there will be a call for a political decision to increase total demand and/or support the market mechanism by adopting measures to increase labour market flexibility. If, alternatively, there is a sustained boom due to structural factors, unemployment may remain low for so long that it is less appropriate to talk about a fixed long-term unemployment rate. The NAIRU school of thoughts has come under increasing criticism in recent years. For a general introduction to this criticism, see e.g. Galbraith (1997). Furthermore, by using American data, Coen et al. (1999) have demonstrated that the NAIRU theory probably also lacks reasoning when it comes to illustrating the conditions in more regional labour markets. However, proponents of NAIRU, such as Layard, Nickell, and Jackmann (1991), point out that in the very long run, e.g. over a century, the unemployment rate shows neither an increasing nor decreasing trend. There must therefore be forces which, in the long run, make an economy move towards its long-term equilibrium, NAIRU. If, on the other hand, it takes ten years or more for an economy to adjust itself to this equilibrium, it may not only be costly economically, it may also be politically unacceptable to wait for this. Later, we will therefore look at circumstances which may slow down or prevent the process of the economy returning to NAIRU.

Hysteresis

Hysteresis implies that an economy does not return to its original equilibrium after it has been exposed to some exogenous—but temporary—shock, e.g. an upswing in raw material prices. The theory of hysteresis (see Blanchard et al. (1986)), is closely connected to the concept of labour market insiders and outsiders (see Lindbeck and Snower (1988)), according to which the wage earners can be divided into two groups: one consisting of those who influence the wage determination process (called the *insiders*); and another group consisting of those wage earners who are without influence on the wage determination process (called the *outsiders*). The insiders are not necessarily identical with those in employment, but include some (short-term) unemployed who still influence the wage determination process, and similarly, the outsiders are not simply the unemployed. When the outsiders lose influence on the wage determination process, the reason may be that unemployment leads to a loss of job skills. But taking into consideration such factors as the compensation that the employer will have to pay for making a worker redundant and the costs of training a new employee, as well as the possible harassment by the existing workforce when underbidding outsiders are hired, it is possible for insiders to make wage demands without having to pay much attention to the competition from outsiders. It is also true that the incentive of the unemployed to compete for jobs with insiders deteriorates the higher the level of the unemployment benefits and the longer the benefits can be maintained. All in all, these are factors which indicate that the insiders are the wage determiners of society.

Fluctuations in society's total demand for goods will be reflected in the demand for labour. Experience shows that such fluctuations will have a smaller effect on wages than on employment. If an economy is exposed to a continuous slowdown, such as that following the oil crises, the rate of unemployment will increase. It follows that a number of wage earners, who lose their jobs, will become outsiders and lose influence on the wage determination process. When the economy booms, the reduced number of insiders will drive up wages to their own advantage but to the detriment of the outsiders, as the wage increase will lead to a reduced increase in employment, or no increase at all. Given the higher wages, firms will shift to more capital-intensive production methods.

Looking again at the development in European unemployment depicted in Figure 3.4, a summit-shaped development in the unemployment rate can be identified. After the first oil crisis, unemployment rose and stabilized at a higher level. After the second oil crisis, unemployment rose again to reach a new and even higher level. This development fits well with the hysteresis theory, according to which the explanation is that the falling demand following the first oil price shock pushed many workers into extended spells of unemployment. These workers lost their insider position and became outsiders with no influence on wage negotiations. When real oil prices fell again, and demand expanded, insiders took advantage of this to raise wage demands which would benefit themselves but not help the outsiders re-enter the labour market, and instead of falling, the rate of unemployment stagnated. The second oil price shock raised unemployment further and pushed even more workers into an outsider position. In the last part of the 1980s, the level of unemployment began declining again, which immediately resulted in a demand for higher wages by the insiders, and as a consequence, inflation also rose. In actual fact, the fear of inflation was rather pronounced among European governments following the oil crises, and as a result, a more restrictive economic policy was implemented, which led to a renewed increase in unemployment.

Research (see Brunello (1990)), also indicates hysteresis-compatible movements in the Japanese labour market, whereas the American labour market seems to be affected by hysteresis to a lesser degree. This leads to the question: what are the differences between the EUR15 and, in particular, the USA which imply that the EU is strongly affected by hysteresis whereas the USA is not? In the following, various measures of labour market flexibility, which may offer some answers to this question, will be examined.

3.4 Is the European labour market flexible?

Tʜɪꜱ section will take a closer look at different aspects of labour market flexibility, opening with some general comments on the issue and proceeding to highlight aspects of the macroeconomic dimension of the wage determination process in particular. The section concludes with some comments on the working-time flexibility, migration, and job mobility, or the lack of it, of the labour force.

The need for more flexibility

For quite some time, the economic policy debate has focused on the structure and way of functioning of the labour market. Would it be possible to change the institutional framework of the labour market in order to increase its efficiency? Increasing efficiency makes it possible to significantly reduce unemployment without increasing the rate of inflation at the same time. According to the proponents of the NAIRU school, it should be a primary objective of the political decision-makers not only to reduce the cyclical unemployment of the EU countries, but also to reduce the rate of the structural unemployment through an increase in employment, primarily in the private sector. The buzzword in the labour market policy debate has become the need for increased labour market flexibility.

How can efficiency be increased? Primarily by enhancing workers' incentive to supply their labour, i.e. to seek and compete for jobs, thus strengthening the market mechanism on the labour market. There are several means to achieving this aim. Below is a brief introduction to five of them, all of which have continued to influence economic policy in Europe in one way or another since the early 1990s.

First, attempts can be made at liberalizing the wage determination process. This can, for example, be done by decentralizing collective bargaining and removing any minimum wage requirements. Secondly, the tax burden can be relieved to increase the supply of labour, as, all other things held constant, this will make it more attractive to work, also for the unemployed. An added bonus may be a decrease in the level of activity of the black economy. Thirdly, it is important to adjust effective marginal taxation where this concept may include not only unemployment benefits but also items such as social and housing benefits. The actual increase in income achieved by joining the labour force and getting a full-time job has often been quite modest, particularly for the lowest paid. It is therefore highly necessary to reduce the effective marginal taxation to enhance the incentive to work. Fourthly, the benefits can be made less advantageous, partly by reducing the level of the unemployment benefit, partly, and not least, by reducing the period of time in which the unemployed are eligible for unemployment benefit. The intention is to give the unemployed an even larger incentive to find a job. Finally, the period of notice could be shortened. This would mean a more immediate reflection of the actual state of the business cycle in the development in unemployment, which again might have a positive influence on the wage determination process through a reduction in the upward wage pressure of the insiders. Similarly, employers might be more prone to hiring new staff at the beginning of a boom.

If the labour market becomes more efficient, e.g. because of the measures mentioned above, unemployment in the EU in general, and structural unemployment in particular, can be reduced. This will in turn reduce serious long-term unemployment as well as youth unemployment. Furthermore, unskilled workers—typically those labelled outsiders above—will gain a stronger footing on the labour market thus reducing their risk of becoming unemployed. Finally, there will also be a positive effect on geographical mobility, primarily within individual countries, but presumably also to a lesser degree between individual EU countries.

However, making the structure and way of functioning of the labour market more efficient will not only have an immediate effect on the size, composition, and duration of unemployment. The consequences will be more far-reaching. Indeed, increased labour market efficiency will have a positive effect on production also in the long run. A better-functioning economy will obviously also have an improved growth potential, as the size and quality of the labour force is the most significant factor of production. Describing the European labour market is therefore of vital importance, not only to understand the current integration but also to estimate the more distant future of the European Union.

Macro-wage flexibility

A high degree of wage flexibility at the macro-level means that real wages are highly sensitive to changes in the rate of unemployment. If this holds, it is possible to quickly reverse an increase in unemployment, as a fall in real wages will increase the demand for labour. However, based on an earlier OECD survey—Elmeskov and MacFarlan (1993)—this flexibility does not appear to be present in European economies to any large extent. Thus, only Sweden and Germany seem to have an elastic response to changes in unemployment, whereas the other EU countries seem to display rather inelastic behaviour in this respect.[3]

Looking at Japan and the USA, Japan reacts fairly strongly to an increase in unemployment—in concrete terms with a semi-elasticity of −1.63 indicating that an increase in the unemployment rate of 1 percentage point will reduce the real wage growth by 1.63 per cent—whereas the USA seems to be at the same level as most European economies (with a semi-elasticity of −0.60). This may be one of the reasons why the Japanese labour market was so relatively unaffected by the oil crises. The difference between the USA and the EU is, as just mentioned, negligible in this

---

[3] Whereas the reaction to an increase in total unemployment in Sweden and Germany is expressed in a semi-elasticity of −1.59 and −1.26, respectively, countries like Italy, the UK, and France react to changes in unemployment with a semi-elasticity of between −0.54 and −0.58.

respect. The explanation for the American ability to create jobs and thereby rather quickly return to the unemployment rate existing before the oil crises must therefore be found in other aspects of labour market flexibility.

Another way of illustrating macro-wage flexibility is by drawing real-wage Phillips curves for the USA, Japan, and the EU. This is done in Figure 3.5 for the period 1987–99. The figure clearly shows that there is no stable short-run relationship where an increase in unemployment and a fall in the real wage inflation go hand in hand. The three economies are also seen to fluctuate around three different unemployment rates. The EU consistently has the highest unemployment rate, but this is not reflected in a lower real wage growth than in the other two economies, which have even witnessed a fall in real wages for a couple of years. All in all, the conclusion must be that macro-wage flexibility, illustrated in this way, is lower in the EU countries than in the USA and Japan.

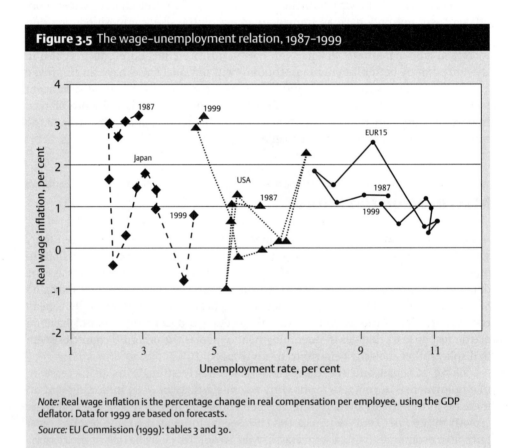

Figure 3.5 The wage–unemployment relation, 1987–1999

Note: Real wage inflation is the percentage change in real compensation per employee, using the GDP deflator. Data for 1999 are based on forecasts.

Source: EU Commission (1999): tables 3 and 30.

Nine-to-five flexibility?

High working-time flexibility implies the ability to quickly react to a reduction in the demand for labour by reducing the number of working hours. The equivalent would be to increase the number of working hours per person in periods where the economy booms.

Judged by the correlation between unemployment rates and involuntary part-time work (see OECD (1994)), particularly Japan, but also the USA, seem more flexible than most of the European countries. Unless it is possible to agree on a voluntary reduction in the number of working hours on an individual basis when the demand for labour weakens, a mandatory distribution of working hours may become necessary. It must be assumed that this form of flexibility will also have a positive effect on the labour market in general, as a compulsory division of labour will help maintain the qualifications of many employees who might otherwise be made redundant. Bearing the above insider–outsider discussion in mind, a mandatory distribution of working hours must have the added advantage of creating fewer outsiders during a recession. However, the empirical evidence does not indicate a uniform reaction pattern in individual countries. For example, Sweden and Germany have a tradition for mandatory part-time work when the demand for labour decreases, whereas other European countries make very little use of this labour market policy instrument. Again, the overall conclusion is that flexibility in the EU countries is low, also in terms of working-time flexibility.

Migration and job mobility

There is hardly any doubt that increased integration of the EU in and by itself will increase intra-EU mobility in every way, including in the labour market. But undoubtedly, cultural and linguistic barriers will significantly slow down this development. Looking at migration between the European countries (see Figure 3.6), it is only about one-fifth of intra-USA mobility between the four large regions of the USA. This is no surprise, and there is also no doubt that it will take many years for intra-EU mobility to reach the American level.

In general, however, one should use caution when making such comparisons of mobility. Statistics on mobility in a certain area are influenced by the number of regions making up the area. The more regions an area is divided into, the more borders will there be to cross, and the higher will the registered level of mobility be. In principle, comparisons should only be made of migration in areas which are alike in terms of population and geographical size and furthermore divided into the same number of regions.

Studies of inter-regional mobility (see OECD (1999c)), in the USA as well as inside individual European countries, where there are no language barriers, indicate that

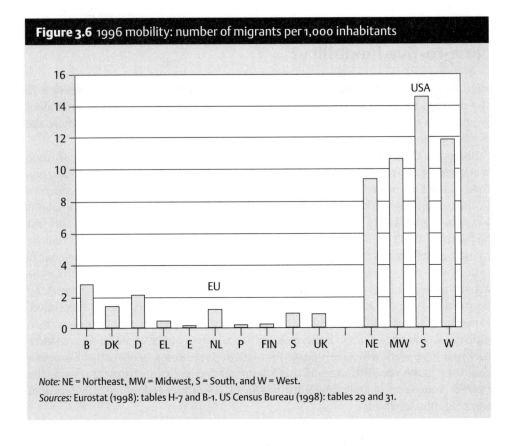

Figure 3.6 1996 mobility: number of migrants per 1,000 inhabitants

Note: NE = Northeast, MW = Midwest, S = South, and W = West.
Sources: Eurostat (1998): tables H-7 and B-1. US Census Bureau (1998): tables 29 and 31.

mobility is much lower in Europe. An explanation may be that the USA is a nation of immigrants, today sustained by immigration from e.g. Mexico. In the Europe of the future, the low mobility may be increased by the immigration from the East and the South.

A core feature of a free market economy is the mobility of the factors of production. However, geographical mobility is only one aspect. Labour mobility across sectors is equally important. The faster and less problematic the factors of production can move from one sector of production to another, the easier it will be for the economy to adapt to changes in demand, not least changes in the composition of demand for goods and services.

At a given level of employment, it is thus imperative that the labour force can move from sectors of diminishing demand to sectors of increasing demand. As it appears from Figure 3.7, the number of job movements is quite significant, even if the net changes are small. Based on a quick comparison of the gross job losses and gross job gains of individual countries in the figure, there is no indication that mobility measured in this way is lower in the EU than in the USA. Of the European countries, Denmark, France, and Sweden display high mobility—the sum of gross job gains and gross job losses approaches 30 per cent of total employment—whereas this job-to-job mobility is relatively low in Germany and the UK.

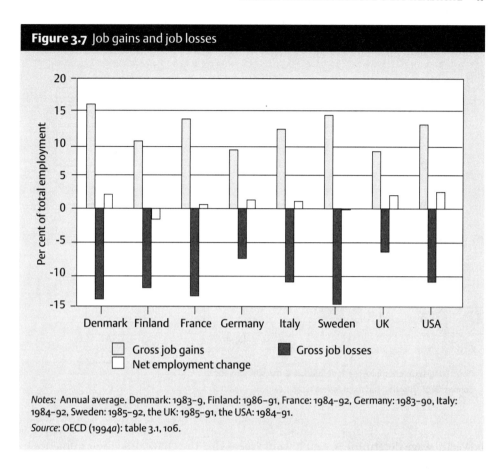

Figure 3.7 Job gains and job losses

Notes: Annual average. Denmark: 1983–9, Finland: 1986–91, France: 1984–92, Germany: 1983–90, Italy: 1984–92, Sweden: 1985–92, the UK: 1985–91, the USA: 1984–91.

Source: OECD (1994*a*): table 3.1, 106.

The need for this kind of mobility differs from country to country as well as over time, but from an overall perspective, the European economies seem to be fairly flexible with respect to job-to-job mobility of the production factor labour.

Unfortunately, high job flexibility in a labour market may still mean that part of the labour force is kept out of work for extended periods, with the ensuing risk of losing previously acquired job skills and reduced possibilities of acquiring new ones. The degree of this division of the labour market is expressed by the number of long-term unemployed.

As is evident from Figure 3.8, the share of long-term unemployed of the total number of unemployed is significantly higher in the EU than in Japan or the USA. The figures for 1997 may of course be negatively influenced by the weak economic growth in Europe at the time, but for many years, figures for the European countries have been marred by a relatively large number of long-term unemployed. As a consequence, the European labour market appears to have lost a large share of its human capital due to a combination of weak and receding business cycles and an inflexible labour market. Based on the insider–outsider and hysteresis theories, the long-term unemployment figures of the EU indicate that the barriers between insiders and outsiders are relatively high in the European Union, implying that insiders become

Figure 3.8 Long-term unemployment, 1997

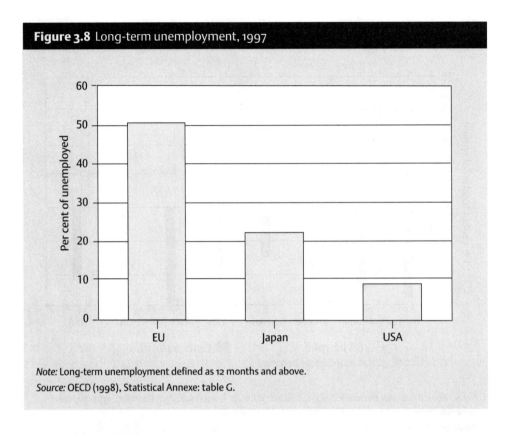

Note: Long-term unemployment defined as 12 months and above.

Source: OECD (1998), Statistical Annexe: table G.

powerful wage determiners. And it would seem that they have used their influence to create better working conditions for themselves rather than paving the way for employment for outsiders as well.

In summary, the above description of various measures of labour market flexibility has demonstrated that the European labour market is less flexible than the Japanese and American labour markets. For each measure identified, it has been possible to find individual regions in Europe measuring up to the USA and Japan in terms of flexibility, but for the EU in general, there is a clear tendency to a lack of flexibility.

Some alternative views

Various observers have offered alternative explanations of the cause of the, often prolonged, significant rate of unemployment experienced by most Western countries. For example, Davidson (1998) ascribes this unemployment within the OECD area to a significant fall in the rate of investment, which in particular has been caused by the transition from a fixed exchange rate system to more or less freely floating exchange rates after 1973. It is an indisputable fact that reduced investment rates give rise to unemployment, but obviously, this fact does not prevent the unemployment rates from deteriorating further in scope as well as in time if the labour market is inflexible at the same time.

This last aspect may be particularly problematic when viewed in a European context as individual EU countries may have different perceptions of the concept of flexibility. It is thus pointed out in, e.g. Casey *et al.* (1999), that there is a marked difference in perception in the UK and Germany. While flexibility, in a British context, is perceived as being almost exclusively synonymous with a deregulation of the institutional conditions on the labour market and the possibility of reducing the wage costs, the German perception is significantly broader in content, including organizational change, innovation and investment, and internal training of young and adult workers.

3.5 Labour market policies

HIGH unemployment rates during a period of recession do not necessarily imply that the labour market policy pursued is wrong. But based on the above comparisons between the EU and the USA and Japan it is tempting to ask if there are any differences in the labour market policies of these regions which may offer part of the explanation for the consistently higher unemployment rates of the EU. Since a detailed comparison of the labour market policy of the EU to those of the USA and Japan is beyond the scope of this chapter, only a few comments concerning this issue will be made.

Empirical evidence suggests that the level of unemployment benefits is relatively high in the EU compared with the USA and Japan (see e.g. OECD (1994*b* and 1996)), although the level has been quite low in a few European countries, like the UK and Italy. At the same time, it is possible to receive unemployment benefits for relatively long periods in the EU. In all fairness it should be pointed out that exactly these factors have been the object of considerable debate throughout the 1990s. As a consequence, the unemployment benefit systems have been made more stringent in some EU countries in recent years in order to obtain an increased level of flexibility in the European labour market.

The unemployment benefit level forms part of the labour market policy, and from a labour market policy point of view, the disadvantage of a high unemployment benefit level is that the downward pressure on real wages is reduced as a consequence of an increase in unemployment. The possibility of receiving unemployment benefit for extended periods may furthermore contribute to reducing the job search intensity of the unemployed, thereby increasing the number of long-term unemployed. There is no doubt that the unemployment benefit level in Europe is relatively high because social policy considerations strongly offset the labour market policy priorities.

The unemployment benefit level makes up the more passive part of labour market policy, but attempts have been made to introduce more active elements through e.g. educational programmes, special measures to reduce unemployment among young people, subsidized employment, and labour market assistance for the handicapped. Such active labour market policy measures clearly take up a larger share of the national budgets in the EU than in the USA and Japan (see the Statistical Annexe of OECD Employment Outlook). Obviously, a significant part of the explanation for this is that the unemployment rate is higher in the EU, and as a consequence, politicians are in favour of taking active measures to take care of the unemployed. It is furthermore in keeping with the general and widespread political objective of the welfare state as a practically possible ideal.

3.6 Unionization and the free market

FINALLY, another explanation for the lower European labour market flexibility could be the way in which the wage earners are organized.

As it appears from Figure 3.9, it is far more common for employees in the EU to belong to a union than it is in Japan and the USA. This is particularly the case in the Nordic countries, but also in Belgium, whereas further south, the degree of unionization is lower, especially in France.

However, it applies for most employees that their wage and working conditions will follow the collective agreements whether or not they themselves are members of a union. The collective agreements entered by trade unions thus cover a larger number of employees than is evident from the degree of unionization. In Japan, the opposite is true. If the influence of the trade unions is calculated by the degree of coverage of the collective agreements, there is a marked difference in influence between the EU on the one hand and Japan and the USA on the other. With the exception of the UK, the influence of the trade unions on wage determination and working conditions in general is very significant in the EU, whereas they only exert limited influence in the USA and Japan.

The fact that the trade unions have powerful influence on the labour market conditions in the EU does not necessarily mean that the explanation for the lack of flexibility in this market has been found. Trade unions give members a possibility of forcing through higher wages, but at the risk of loss of employment. The extent to which this possibility is used depends on the priorities of the employees. Some economists hold the opinion that it is best for an economy to have small and weak trade unions, or no trade unions at all, while others are of the opinion that when the trade unions become powerful and negotiations centralized, as is the case for some European countries, the trade unions and industry will consider the overall macroeconomic context and the implications for the level of unemployment in their bargaining process. No conclusions will be drawn here as to whether or not the European trade unions should be blamed for the unsatisfactory development in the European labour

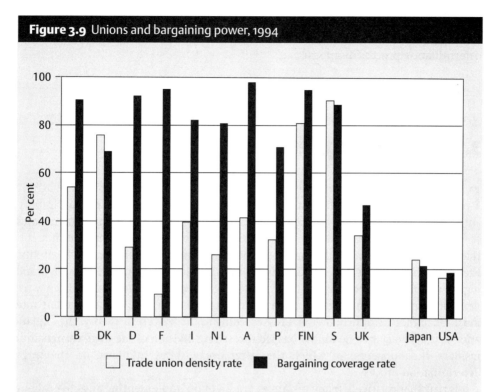

Figure 3.9 Unions and bargaining power, 1994

☐ Trade union density rate   ■ Bargaining coverage rate

Notes: Trade union density rate is defined as percentage of workers belonging to a trade union. Bargaining coverage rate is defined as the percentage of workers who are covered by collective agreements. All data refer to 1994 except: trade union density in Denmark (1993), Finland (1995), Germany (1993), Italy (1992), the Netherlands (1993), Portugal (1990), and Sweden (1992). Collective bargaining coverage in Finland (1995), France (1995), Italy (1993), Japan (1995), and Portugal (1993).

Source: OECD (1997): table 3.3, 71.

market. But it is a fact that labour market flexibility is relatively poor in the EU which, at the same time, has very influential trade unions.

One might fear that the formation of the European Monetary Union will make trade unions in individual countries more aggressive, as the inflationary pressure in a country will have only insignificant effects on total inflation in the Union. The trade unions will therefore not expect the European Central Bank to pursue a more restrictive monetary policy as a consequence of their wage demands. In order to avoid this more aggressive behaviour, there may be a need for institutions whose aim will be to ensure that wages are determined at an overall European level. However, the fear may be exaggerated as the common currency introduces a transparency which makes it easier to compare wage as well as price levels between member countries. A high level of inflation in a country may quickly lead to changed flows of goods, possibly combined with the transfer of place of production, which will lead to a fall in the demand for labour and an increase in unemployment in that country. If the trade unions become aware that although there may not be a reaction from the Central

Bank, there will be an immediate market reaction, they will gain nothing from a more aggressive behaviour and the need for an institutional integration of the wage determination process disappears.

3.7 Concluding remarks

Iᴛ has been demonstrated above that the European economies have been relatively poor at creating jobs in the last part of the twentieth century, and that an important part of the explanation for the continuously high European unemployment rates seems to be an inflexible labour market. According to the NAIRU school of thought, the explanation is that NAIRU has been increased due to the absence of flexibility. Factors such as the lack of working-time flexibility, low geographical mobility, and high unemployment benefit levels for relatively long periods have reduced the wage flexibility and thus, in order to avoid increasing inflation, the unemployment rate must reach increasingly higher levels. According to the hysteresis theory, the explanation is that the lack of flexibility has led to a strong division of the wage earners into insiders and outsiders, of which the latter are without influence on the wage determination process.

It is true that relatively many resources are spent on implementing an active labour market policy in the different EU member countries, where policies have been strongly influenced by social policy considerations, in particular distributional effects. This has made it easier for the individual and for society in general to tolerate high unemployment rates, but at the same time, flexibility has been reduced and this has consolidated the situation. One should bear in mind, however, that the unemployed labour force is an idle factor of production, and it must therefore be assumed that such policies have led to a reduction in production and total welfare.

As touched upon in the introduction, the formation of a common currency area increases the need for a flexible labour force, but geographical mobility in Europe is low, even where there are no language barriers. Apart from the formation of the Single Market, the common currency will increase wage and price level transparency and consequently also labour market integration. In the long run, it cannot be ruled out that higher levels of trade and communication, e.g. via the increasing use of the internet, will give the Europeans a common language, English, which may increase mobility. But all in all it must be concluded that a truly integrated European labour market is still very far away. Based on this conclusion, the member countries will continue to have a large need for other kinds of labour market flexibility.

It must be expected that institutional integration on the labour market will be relatively slow and take the form of common minimum requirements of the protection of the working environment, health, and safety. Currently, there are directives covering areas such as organization of working time, protection of young people at work, part-time work, and equal treatment of men and women. When it comes to collective bargaining, there is no immediate prospect of having that at a European level.

In connection with the formation of the Single Market, there is fear that the member countries will compete in making *social devaluations* in a *race to the bottom*. By reducing the level of labour force protection and cutting social benefits, a country may attract capital at the expense of fellow member countries. This will increase the country's employment and wage levels and attract labour from other countries. As a result, income per head may increase, but so may inequality and insecurity. It was demonstrated in Section 3.4 that geographical mobility in the European labour market is low, and this means that wage differences between countries may persist. One country may therefore opt for high wages and low social security, while other countries may choose lower wages but higher social security. The need for institutional integration emanates from a broad political desire to further social security for all European wage earners and pre-empt a race to the bottom.

Further reading

Any macroeconomics textbook has a detailed description of the structure and way of functioning of the labour market, and traditionally, they will also have a thorough analysis of the multiple aspects of unemployment. Standard textbooks include M. Burda and C. Wyplosz (1997), *Macroeconomics, a European Text*, OUP, Oxford; or R. Dornbusch *et al.* (1998), *Macroeconomics*, McGraw-Hill, New York. For a more in-depth discussion and analysis of the labour market, it is advisable to consult textbooks in this area, e.g. R. Layard *et al.* (1991), *Unemployment, Macroeconomic Performance and the Labour Market*, OUP, Oxford; or G. Borjas (1996), *Labour Economics*, McGraw-Hill, New York. OECD's yearly *Employment Outlook* touches upon several of the aspects dealt with in this chapter. Finally, the European Commission, *Employment in Europe*, is a yearly publication focusing on labour market developments in Europe.

References

Blanchard, O. J., and L. H. Summers (1986), 'Hysteresis and the European Unemployment Problem', *NBER, Macroeconomics Annual*, 1, 15–78.

Brunello, Giorgio (1990), 'Hysteresis and "The Japanese Unemployment Problem": A Preliminary Investigation', *Oxford Economic Papers*, 42, 483–500.

Casey, Bernard, *et al.* (1999), 'Flexibility, Quality and Competitiveness', *National Institute Economic Review*, 168 (April), 70–81.

Coen, Robert M., *et al.* (1999), 'The NAIRU and Wages in Local Labor Markets', *American Economic Review*, 89 (May), 52–7.

Davidson, Paul (1998), 'Post Keynesian Employment Analysis and the Macroeconomics of OECD Unemployment', *Economic Journal*, 108, 817–31.

Elmeskov, Jørgen and MacFarlan, Maitland (1993), 'Unemployment Persistence', *OECD Economic Studies*, 21.

EU Commission (1993), *European Economy*, 54.

—— (1999), *European Economy*, 66.

Eurostat (1998), *Demographic Statistics* (data 1995–8, detailed tables).

Galbraith, James K. (1997), 'Time to Ditch the NAIRU', *Journal of Economic Perspectives*, 11, 93–108.

Layard, Richard, Stephen Nickell, and Richard Jackmann (1991), *Unemployment, Macroeconomic Performance and the Labour Market*, OUP, Oxford.

Lindbeck, Assar, and Dennis Snower (1988), *The Insider-Outsider Theory of Employment and Unemployment*, MIT Press, Cambridge, Mass.

OECD (1994*a*), *Employment Outlook*.

—— (1994*b*), *The OECD Jobs Study. Facts Analysis Strategies*.

—— (1996), *Employment Outlook*.

—— (1997), *Employment Outlook*.

—— (1998), *Employment Outlook*.

—— (1999*a*), *Employment Outlook*.

—— (1999*b*), *Maxdata—OECD Statistical Compendium*, ed. 01#1999 (1960–99, database: OECD—employment—annual labour force statistics).

—— (1999*c*), *EMU Facts, Challenges and Policies*.

US Census Bureau (1998), *The Official Statistics*, Statistical Abstract of the United States.

Chapter 4
Economic Growth: Prospects and Challenges

Teit Lüthje

4.1 Introduction

HAS European integration created a more dynamic Europe with high economic growth, increasing standards of living, and a growing number of jobs? This question will be examined in more detail in this chapter. Economic theory offers several arguments which support the view that economic integration can increase efficiency and stimulate economic growth. The free movement of goods, services, capital, and labour encourages specialization and thus a more efficient allocation of resources, and increased competition between producers increases productivity for the benefit of consumers. A large market provides the opportunity of increasing sales through the introduction of new products and new technologies, and the establishment of the Internal Market increased the incentive of firms to defray costs of research and development. Finally, technological know-how will be diffused between countries as a result of an increase in trade and of a more extensive network of multinational companies within the Internal Market.

It is not given, however, that an increase in productivity benefits employment. The implication of higher productivity is that a given output will be produced using less resources. If employment is to increase at the same time, it partly requires a larger aggregate demand and partly that there is limited factor substitution, where labour is replaced by capital. Whether these conditions can be fulfilled in practice depend on the wage formation process and labour market flexibility in general (see Chapter 3). If real wages increase in connection with an increase in demand, firms get an incentive to introduce labour-saving technologies, and there will thus be a smaller effect on employment or, possibly, no effect at all.

It is nevertheless important that the capital stock is continuously expanded in order to keep pace with increasing employment. This is the only way to equip new jobs with the same amount of capital as existing jobs and a precondition for the wage level of new jobs to keep up with the existing real wage level. The EU Commission (1993) has underlined the need for investment-driven growth in order to reduce unemployment, and at the same time emphasized the importance of labour market flexibility in order to avoid a forced introduction of labour-saving technologies. This growth strategy is described in more detail in this chapter.

Another theme of the chapter relates to the geographic distribution of growth in the EU, i.e. the question of convergence of standards of living between member countries. Not only does economic integration influence total growth, it also defines the growth areas and thus influences the differences in standards of living between the regions of the EU. According to the neoclassical paradigm of economic theory, production conditions are basically the same everywhere. Based on this assumption, the free movement of goods, services, and factors of production will equalize prices of goods and factors, and the market forces will therefore gradually reduce differences in standards of living between the regions of the EU. However, new literature on economic geography emphasizes that proximity is as important as internal and external economies of scale in economic analysis. Accordingly, the most likely result of the free movement of goods and resources will be that economic activity will have a centre–periphery structure where the production in the centre will profit from local know-how spillover and at the same time gain easy access to a differentiated market for labour and intermediate products. There is thus no reason to assume that the market forces will reduce differences in standards of living.

Section 4.2 opens with an overview of the growth performance of the EU in the Triad. Focus will then shift to the individual EU member states. Section 4.3 describes the growth-oriented policy with particular emphasis on the fight against unemployment in the EU, whereas Section 4.4 describes growth in the individual EU countries. The growth in standards of living in the EU and the use of structural funds will be analysed in Section 4.5. Section 4.6 elucidates the European endowment of human capital, and Section 4.7 rounds off the chapter with a summary of the main conclusions.

4.2 World trends in economic growth

ECONOMIC growth is a measure of the long-term increase in production in the economy and is normally measured by the annual real growth rate of the gross domestic product (GDP). Economic growth depends both on the rate of growth in inputs, such as labour and capital, and on technological progress, and is of vital importance to the development in the average standard of living, which is typically measured by real GDP per capita. The growth rate in real GDP per capita equals the growth rate of real GDP minus the growth rate of the population.

The European performance in the Triad

Figure 4.1 illustrates annual change in real GDP in per cent for EUR15, the USA, and Japan. It appears that until 1992, and particularly in the 1960s, Japan experienced a markedly higher growth rate than the USA and the EU, whereas growth rates in the USA and EU have been fairly similar in the illustrated period.

Figure 4.2 compares standards of living in the same period for the EU, the USA, and Japan as measured by GDP per capita. In the figure, GDP per capita for EUR15 equals 100. For a more reliable comparison between the three areas, GDP per capita is measured in purchasing power standards (PPS), so that the GDP units represent the same purchasing power in the three areas.

The catch-up of the Japanese economy with both the EU and the USA during the observed period is remarkable. In 1960, standards of living in Japan were only around 50 per cent of EU standards, whereas at the end of the century, Japanese standards of living were approximately 10 per cent higher than in the EU. The differences in standards of living in the EU and the USA, on the other hand, have remained fairly constant.

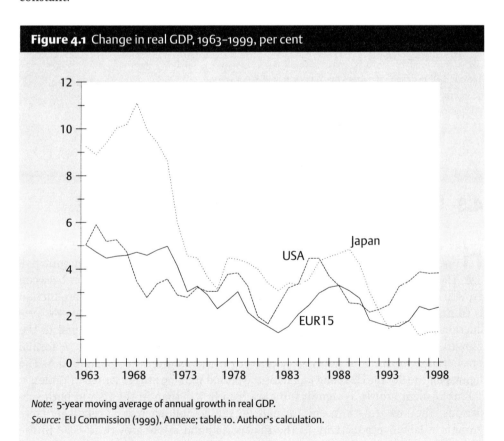

Figure 4.1 Change in real GDP, 1963–1999, per cent

Note: 5-year moving average of annual growth in real GDP.
Source: EU Commission (1999), Annexe; table 10. Author's calculation.

Figure 4.2 Convergence in the Triad, 1960–1999

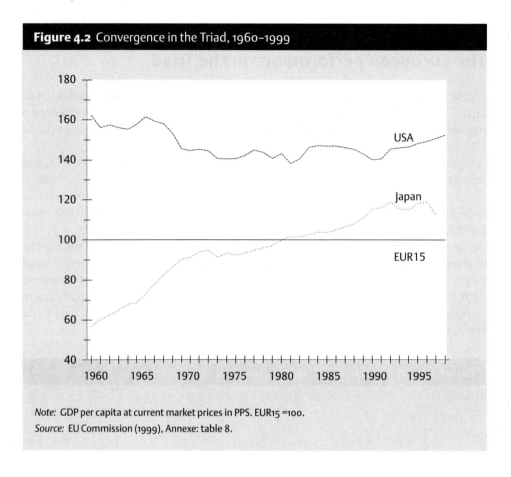

Note: GDP per capita at current market prices in PPS. EUR15 =100.
Source: EU Commission (1999), Annexe: table 8.

4.3 Economic growth and employment

HAS economic growth in the EU led to an increase in employment? And can unemployment in the EU be reduced through a growth-oriented economic policy? These questions will be examined in more detail below. The relation between growth in production and growth in employment is not simple. Increased production is contingent upon an increase in employment and/or labour productivity, i.e. production per person employed. The growth rate in production is thus equal to the growth rate in employment plus the growth rate in labour productivity. A formal presentation of this in a neoclassical growth model is given in Appendix 4.A. The figures for the EU, the USA, and Japan for the period 1961–99 are presented in Table 4.1.

Employment growth is significantly lower in EUR15 than in the USA in both sub-periods. The low growth in employment in the EU follows from a relatively large growth in labour productivity in the first period and a low growth in GDP in the

Table 4.1 GDP, employment, and labour productivity, 1961–1999

	Average annual growth rate, per cent		
	Real GDP	Employment	Labour productivity
1961–1991			
EUR15	3.3	0.4	2.9
USA	3.3	1.8	1.5
Japan	6.2	1.0	5.2
1992–1999			
EUR15	1.9	0.2	1.7
USA	3.6	1.8	1.8
Japan	1.0	0.2	0.8

Notes: 1961–91 excluding former East Germany. The growth rate in labour productivity is calculated as a residual between the growth rates in GDP and employment, respectively.

Source: EU Commission (1999), Annexe: tables 2 and 10. Author's calculation.

second period. In the case of Japan, growth in employment is modest in the first period as a result of the fact that the strong growth in GDP is matched by an almost equally strong growth in labour productivity. In the second period, growth in employment in Japan is also modest as a result of low growth in GDP. Of the Triad economies, the USA has thus been the most successful in creating new jobs. The weak growth in the employment rate in the EU has far from been able to absorb the growth in the labour force and as a result, the European Union has ended up in a serious unemployment problem.

What is the background for the strong growth in labour productivity in the EUR15 countries? In order to answer this question, it is necessary to add more nuance to the growth analysis by dividing the growth in labour productivity into three components (see Appendix 4.A for a formal analysis). The components are:

- Total factor productivity
- Hours worked per person employed
- Capital per person employed

Total factor productivity reflects the general level of technological know-how. More precisely, the growth in total factor productivity expresses the growth in production at a given inflow of labour and capital. It follows that the growth in total factor productivity influences the growth in labour productivity. Changes in the number of hours worked also influence labour productivity. Generally, the number of hours worked per person in the EU has been reduced, and if other factors remain unchanged, this will lead to a reduction in production per person employed, i.e. a fall in labour productivity. Finally, capital per person employed influences labour productivity. The amount of labour in production can be reduced by introducing more capital intensive methods. Growth in capital per person thus increases labour productivity through the introduction of labour saving technologies.

As already mentioned, a closer analysis of the growth in labour productivity requires that the three factors listed above are examined individually. Such an analysis has been carried out by the EU Commission (2000). Table 4.2 presents some of the main findings of this work and shows the importance of these three factors for the growth in labour productivity in the EU in the period 1961–99. All three sub-periods have seen significant growth in labour productivity, mainly because of growth in total factor productivity, i.e. improved technological know-how. However, more than one-third of the growth in labour productivity can be explained by the substitution of labour by capital. This has curbed the positive effects on employment of the economic growth in the EU. It furthermore appears from the table that this substitution has more than offset the positive effect on employment of the reduction in working hours. There has been a pressure to reduce labour stimulated by wage rigidities and the lack of flexibility on the European labour market, as explained in Chapter 3.

As displayed in Table 4.1, the USA has been better at creating new jobs than the EU, where developments have been characterized by nearly jobless growth in comparison. This indicates that the labour market in the USA is more flexible than in the EU. On the other hand, a high degree of flexibility can lead to significant income and wage differences, and as shown in an analysis published by OECD (1996) the favourable development in employment on the American labour market goes hand in hand with a high degree of earnings dispersion and a high incidence of low-paid jobs. Although the unemployment problem thus appears to have been solved in the USA, from a distributional point of view, the solution has its disadvantages.

Given the preferences of European politicians, the question therefore is whether it is possible to achieve *job-creating growth* in the European Union without creating low-salary jobs. The solution to this dual problem consists of furthering investment in a way which, on the one hand, creates the basis for well-paid jobs and, on the other,

Table 4.2 Determinants of growth in productivity in EUR15, 1961–1999

	Average annual growth rates		
	1961–73	1974–95	1996–9
Total factor productivity	3.4	1.5	1.0
+ Hours worked per person employed	−0.5	−0.4	−0.2
+ Capital per person employed	1.5	0.8	0.5
= Labour productivity	4.4	1.9	1.3

Notes: The figures in the table express the effect on labour productivity of growth in total factor productivity, changes in working hours, and substitution between capital and labour. For a more formal analysis, see Appendix 4.A.

Source: EU Commission (2000): 56.

does not lead to factor substitution. This strategy for job-creating growth is outlined in a report by the EU Commission (1993). Its main elements are presented below.

A strategy for investment-driven growth in employment

A prerequisite for the creation of new, well-paid jobs is capital, and from this point of view, the unemployment in the EU is a consequence of scarce capital and insufficient investment. In order to analyse this issue in more depth, a few formal considerations are necessary. First, let us look at the relation between investment and growth, given that labour is not a scarce resource. Let us assume that investment creates new jobs without leading to a substitution of labour by capital to any large extent. Behind this assumption is a more basic—although questionable—presupposition that the labour market is flexible so that no bottleneck situations will arise resulting in wage increases. More precisely, it is assumed that the capital/output ratio is constant, where the capital/output ratio, R, is equal to K/Y where K is the capital stock, and Y is GDP. It follows that:

$$Y = \frac{1}{R} K.$$

As net investment, I^N, makes up the change in the capital stock, ΔK, the change in GDP, ΔY, can be expressed as:

$$\Delta Y = \frac{1}{R} \Delta K = \frac{1}{R} I^N.$$

Dividing by Y on both sides of the equals sign, the following expression for the growth rate is derived:

$$\frac{\Delta Y}{Y} = \frac{1}{R} \frac{I^N}{Y}. \tag{1}$$

The GDP growth rate is thus proportional to the share of net investment in GDP. An increase in the share of investment by 1 percentage point of GDP thus increases the growth rate of GDP by $1/R$ percentage point.

Net investment equals the difference between gross investment, I, and reinvestment, I^{Re} (investment replacing depreciated capital). Relation (1) can thus be rewritten as follows:

$$\frac{\Delta Y}{Y} = \frac{1}{R} \left(\frac{I}{Y} - \frac{I^{Re}}{Y} \right). \tag{2}$$

In the above-mentioned EU Commission report (1993) it is estimated that the capital/output ratio is 3.4 and that the share of reinvestment in GDP is 12.6 per cent. In the following exercises it is assumed that these structural growth variables are

Figure 4.3 Illustration of real growth rate and share of investment, per cent

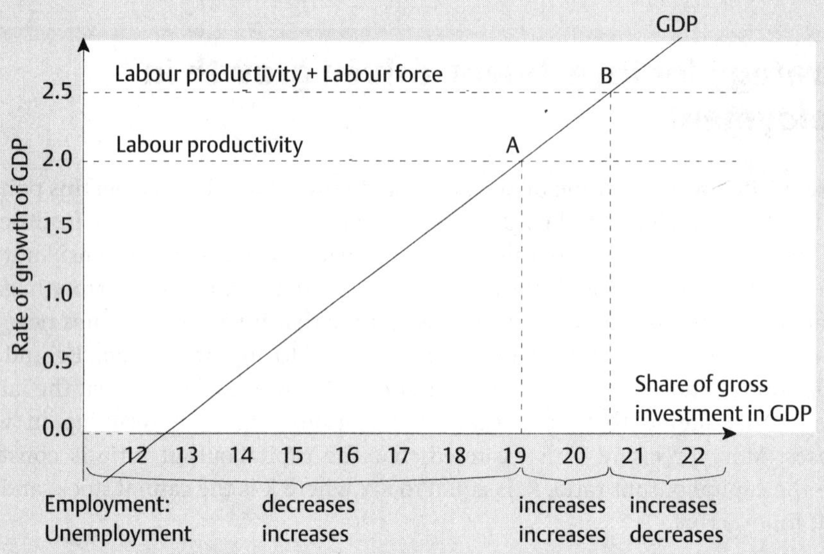

Note: GDP, labour productivity, and labour force are all measured in percentage change.
Source: The figure is based on EU Commission (1993): 102–4. See text for further explanation.

constant. Inserting them into relation (2) gives the lineary relation between the growth rate of GDP and the share of investment in GDP illustrated in Figure 4.3.

The relation implies that an increase in the share of gross investment in GDP by 3.4 percentage points will increase growth in GDP by 1 percentage point. If the share of gross investment in GDP only equals the share of reinvestment in GDP, i.e. 12.6 per cent, the economic growth equals 0. Positive net investment is a prerequisite for positive economic growth. If the target growth rate is 2 per cent, the share of gross investment in GDP must equal 19 per cent.

Assume now that labour productivity increases by around 2 per cent p.a., which corresponds roughly to the development witnessed in the 1970s and 1980s (see Table 4.2). If the growth in labour productivity increases by 2 per cent, the real growth rate must increase by more than 2 per cent for employment to rise and, as shown above, this requires that the share of investment in GDP is higher than 19 per cent. In Figure 4.3, the economy should be placed further north-east than A on the GDP-line through A and B.

From increased employment to reduced unemployment

An increase in employment is not tantamount to a reduction in unemployment. Reducing unemployment also depends on the growth in the labour force. The influx into the labour force depends on the population growth as well as on the development in the participation rate, which expresses the share of the population already in, or seeking, employment. It follows from Chapter 2 that from 1960 to 1994, the total population of the EUR15, excluding the former East Germany, increased by a little more than 0.5 per cent p.a. The growth rate of the population has been decreasing, but at the same time, the participation rate has increased, particularly in southern Europe. Although there is uncertainty about the future development in the participation rate, there may be a potential for a further increase in coming years. In the following, it is therefore assumed that the labour force increases by 0.5 per cent p.a.

In order to achieve a fall in unemployment, the growth in GDP must exceed the sum of the growth in labour productivity and the growth in the labour force (the economy lies to the north-east of B in Figure 4.3). If the growth in GDP is larger than the growth in labour productivity but smaller than the sum of the growth in labour productivity and in the labour force (the economy is between A and B in Figure 4.3), employment as well as unemployment will increase. To follow up on our numerical exercise: if the labour force increases by 0.5 per cent p.a., and labour productivity increases by 2 per cent, the growth in production has to exceed 2.5 per cent in order to force a decrease in unemployment. Such a situation is illustrated by point B in Figure 4.3. As it appears from earlier calculations, a growth rate of 2.5 per cent requires a share of investment in GDP of around 21 per cent.

But is this the case in Europe? The answer to this question is given in Figure 4.4, which shows the development in the share of investment in GDP for EUR15 in the period from 1960 to 1999. From the 1960s until the early 1980s, the share of investment in GDP was higher than the 21 per cent mentioned above. With the exception of a brief boom at the end of the 1980s, the share of investment then fell to a level of around 19–20 per cent. There were clearly considerable expectations that the formation of the Internal Market would stimulate investment significantly and thus provide a basis for job-creating growth. The removal of the barriers to free movement of capital should make the capital market more efficient, and this should in turn stimulate investment. Furthermore, the envisaged increase in trade and specialization should lead to a restructuring, both internally in individual firms and between industries (see Chapter 6), which in itself is a catalyst of investment. However, the actual development from the mid-1980s onwards does not indicate that such a development has taken place, even if the stylized facts presented here obviously can neither confirm nor refute that the Single Market has promoted investment.

The above calculations nevertheless indicate that the current share of investment in GDP in the EU is too low to ensure continuous and stable job creation. The conclusion must therefore be that it is necessary to increase the level of investment. To help

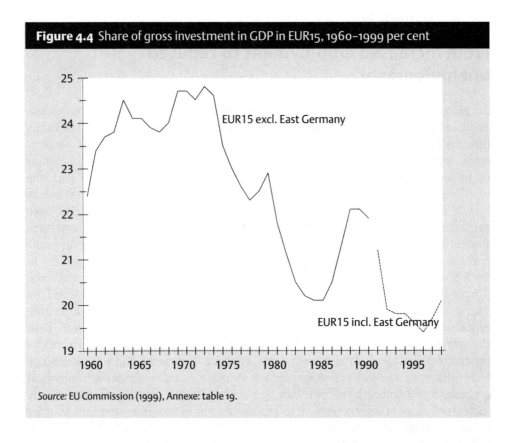

Figure 4.4 Share of gross investment in GDP in EUR15, 1960–1999 per cent

EUR15 excl. East Germany

EUR15 incl. East Germany

Source: EU Commission (1999), Annexe: table 19.

increase investment, it is important to create an environment with favourable financing conditions and low real interest rates. In the long run, this can be done by strengthening private and public savings. Furthermore, investing can be made more advantageous by changing the depreciation rules in the taxation legislation and/or by introducing various subsidies, e.g. aimed at investment in research and development. In addition, a more flexible and well-functioning labour market will stimulate investment and thus lead to an increase in economic growth. However, the investment rates of the 1960s seem a long way away.

4.4 Investment and growth – a member state perspective

THE relation between investment and growth in the fifteen EU countries is illustrated in the following. As a start, Table 4.3 shows each country's annual growth rate in real GDP from 1961 to 1999. Note that, again, high growth rates are observed

Table 4.3 Average annual growth in real GDP, 1961–1999 (1990 prices)

	1961–70	1971–80	1981–90	1991–9	1961–99
Belgium	4.9	3.4	1.9	1.8	3.0
Denmark	4.5	2.2	2.0	2.6	2.8
Germany[a]	4.4	2.7	2.2	1.4[b]	2.7
Greece	7.6	4.7	1.6	2.1	4.0
Spain	7.3	3.5	3.0	2.3	4.1
France	5.6	3.3	2.4	1.6	3.3
Ireland	4.2	4.7	3.6	6.5	4.7
Italy	5.7	3.6	2.2	1.2	3.2
Luxembourg	3.5	2.6	4.5	5.3	3.9
The Netherlands	5.1	3.0	2.2	2.7	3.3
Austria	4.7	3.6	2.3	1.9	3.2
Portugal	6.4	4.7	3.2	2.5	4.2
Finland	4.8	3.4	3.1	1.8	3.3
Sweden	4.6	2.0	2.0	1.4	2.5
UK	2.9	1.9	2.7	2.0	2.4
EUR15	4.8	3.0	2.4	1.8[b]	3.0

[a] 1961–91 excl. East Germany.
[b] 1992–9.

Source: EU Commission (1999), Annexe: table 10. Author's calculation.

for the early years, whereas growth rates are more modest for recent years. It appears from Table 4.3 that growth does not depend on the size of the country. Thus, for the entire period 1961–99, in large countries like Germany and the UK, the growth rate is lower than the average growth rate for EUR15 as a whole. This simple observation underlines that, in itself, creating a larger European economy through the Internal Market and the EMU is unlikely to have any major influence on the long-term real growth rate in GDP.

Figure 4.5 illustrates the share of investment in GDP and the growth rate for the EUR15 countries, excluding Ireland and Luxembourg. As it appears from the figure, there is considerable variation in the share of investment in GDP between individual EU countries, from around 25 per cent in Portugal to just above 15 per cent in Sweden. Similar, although less broad, variations are found in the average growth rates. Overall, the figure seems to confirm the assumption that, in the long run, economic growth is investment-driven: the higher the share of investment is, the higher is the growth rate. This relation is illustrated by the straight line in Figure 4.5.

When interpreting the empirical correlation of Figure 4.5 it is important to remember that the causality runs both ways. On the one hand, a higher level of investment may increase the growth rate as a result of an increased production capacity of the economy. On the other hand, increased growth may necessitate an expansion of the capital stock and thus create demand for investment (in line with the principle of acceleration). Nevertheless, in the long run, it is the impact of

Figure 4.5 Growth and investment in EUR15 countries, 1991–1998, per cent

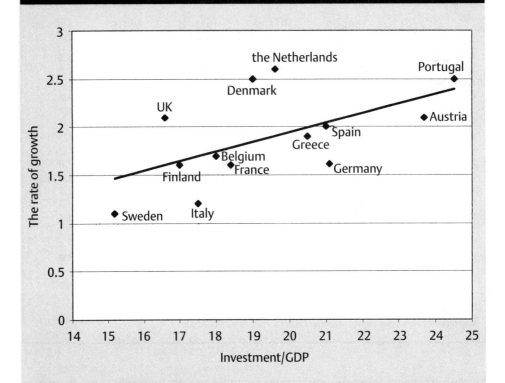

Notes: Average annual growth rates of GDP at 1990 market prices. Ireland and Luxembourg are excluded. Growth rates were 7.7% for Ireland and 4.9% for Luxembourg and the share of investment in GDP 17.1% for Ireland and 22.5% for Luxembourg. Germany 1992 to 1998. The straight line is based on a simple linear regression between the two variables.

Source: EU Commission (1998), Annexe: tables 10 and 19. Author's calculation.

investment on the production capacity which is the important factor, and in this perspective, it is the share of investment in GDP which determines the rate of growth.

Although Figure 4.5 indicates that there is a positive relation between investment and growth, it also indicates that other factors influence growth. There are several possible reasons for the variation in the positions of the individual countries around the regression line. First, the examined period, 1991–8, is relatively short, and specific developments in the business cycles of individual countries may therefore influence observations. Secondly, labour market conditions may differ, and this may lead to differences in the capital/output ratio. Finally, developments in total factor productivity may vary between countries. Growth in total factor productivity depends, *inter alia*, on the level of education, i.e. investment in human capital, as well as on the level of research and development, and as it will appear from Section 4.6, these levels differ between the individual member states.

4.5 Convergence of living standards

So far, we have examined growth in GDP. However, the development in standards of living depends on growth in GDP per capita. Concerning this, the EU cooperation builds on a fundamental objective of a harmonious and balanced development in economic activities and a high degree of convergence of economic performance, i.e. each country and region should have its fair share of the welfare growth. The following will therefore examine the distribution in standards of living across countries and regions. Figure 4.6 illustrates standards of living for all EUR15 countries measured by GDP per capita. The figure shows the average standard of living for each country as a whole as well as the average standard of living in the country's poorest and richest region, respectively. The table ranks the countries, from left to right, according to the level of standards of living for the country as a whole. The regional distribution follows the NUTS1 classification. NUTS is derived from 'The Nomenclature of Territorial Units for Statistics'. Each NUTS1 region consists of a number of NUTS2 regions, and each NUTS2 region in turn consists of a number of NUTS3 regions. The small EU countries, Denmark, Ireland, and Luxembourg, only make up one region at the NUTS1 level.

Denmark and Luxembourg have the highest level of GDP per capita, whereas Portugal, Greece, and Spain are the relatively poorest countries in the EU. The spread in GDP per capita between regions is remarkable. Note for example the large difference in income per capita between the richest and poorest regions in both Germany and France. It is also noteworthy that standards of living in the richest region in Germany are above those in Luxembourg and Denmark, and that the poorest region in Sweden is richer than the richest region in Spain. However, caution should be used when making such comparisons, as the definition of the regions may influence results significantly. If the definition is very narrow, the likelihood of identifying very poor and very rich regions is larger, and a large regional spread in GDP per capita will be recorded.

However, these differences in standards of living, both between countries and between regions of individual countries, have changed over the last forty years. Figure 4.7 compares the average annual real growth rate in GDP per capita for the period 1961–99 with GDP per capita of individual member countries in 1960. The figure shows that the growth rate in GDP per capita is inversely related to GDP per capita at the beginning of the period. In other words, countries with a low GDP per capita in 1960 have experienced a relatively higher growth in the following forty-year period than countries with a high GDP per capita. As a result, the differences in welfare between the EU countries have been reduced in the period in question, as the poor countries have been catching up with the rich. The road towards less inequality has, however, not been smooth and as it will appear from the following, there have been periods where the poor countries have been unable to follow the growth of the rich countries.

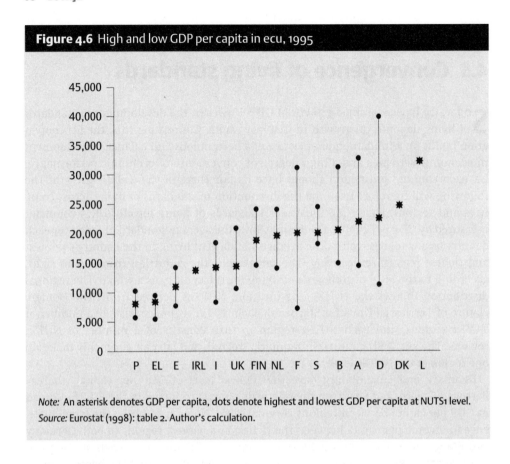

Figure 4.6 High and low GDP per capita in ecu, 1995

Note: An asterisk denotes GDP per capita, dots denote highest and lowest GDP per capita at NUTS1 level.
Source: Eurostat (1998): table 2. Author's calculation.

Integration and convergence of standards of living

This section will elucidate the importance of economic integration for the convergence of the standards of living among the EU countries. According to traditional trade theory (see also Chapter 6), international trade will contribute to equalizing real wage levels between countries of labour with similar qualifications. In the same way, free movement of the factors of production will contribute to equalizing wages. Add to this that between open economies there will be a transfer of technological know-how to less advanced regions. By introducing the technology of the relatively rich countries, the relatively poor countries can achieve an increase in their standards of living. However, as a country catches up with the technologically leading countries, the scope for technology transfers will be reduced.

The question is whether membership of the EU in itself has had an impact on the convergence process. The answer to this question is blurred by the fact that the circle of EU members has been expanded several times. In order to get a clearer picture covering the current fifteen member states, the period 1960–99 is split into five sub-periods, each examining a period with a given number of member countries, i.e.

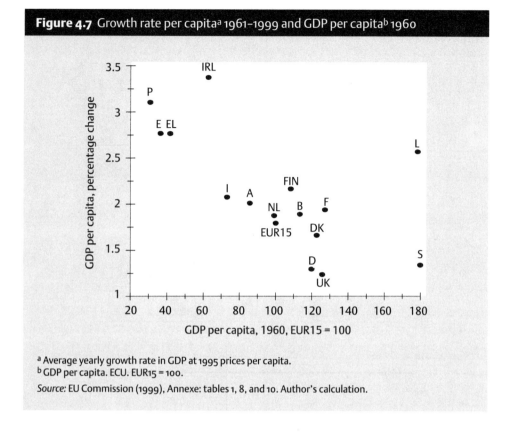

Figure 4.7 Growth rate per capita[a] 1961–1999 and GDP per capita[b] 1960

[a] Average yearly growth rate in GDP at 1995 prices per capita.
[b] GDP per capita. ECU. EUR15 = 100.

Source: EU Commission (1999), Annexe: tables 1, 8, and 10. Author's calculation.

EUR6 for 1960–72, EUR9 for 1973–80, EUR10 for 1981–5, EUR12 for 1986–94, and finally EUR15 for 1995 onwards. For each sub-period, the development is illustrated in Figure 4.8 for *Ins* (member countries in the particular sub-period) as well as *Outs* (countries which were not members at the time). GDP per capita of individual countries is related to GDP per capita of all EU member countries in the sub-period in question. This obviously means that the average will change concurrently with the increase in the number of member countries. Each sub-figure thus illustrates the development in GDP per capita of each country in relation to the EU average. For reasons of clarity, Luxembourg is not included in the figure but it is included in the analysis related to the figure, in line with the other EU countries.

In the period 1960–72, five of the EUR6 countries moved towards the overall average of the countries and only one country moved away from the average. Of the Outs, all nine countries showed a converging development. The UK was below the EUR6 average at the start of the period, but above at the end of it. However, as the average divergence decreased, convergence still took place. The increase in standards of living in the poor countries, Greece, Spain, and Portugal, was particularly significant, and it becomes clear that convergence is a phenomenon which is not narrowly related to the EC area, but more generally to European integration. With the exception of Ireland, a review of the other sub-figures does not alter this conclusion.

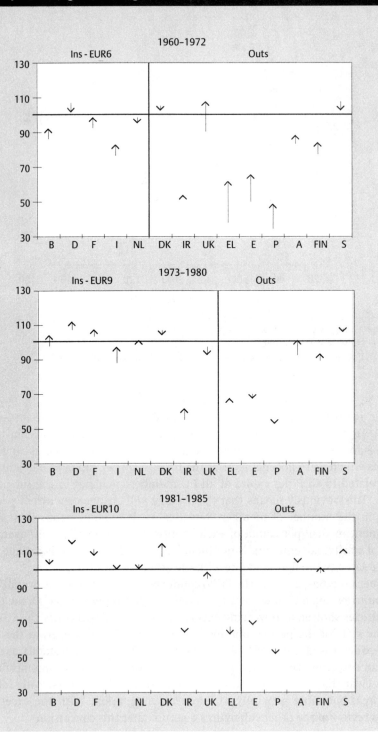

Figure 4.8 Convergence among the EUR15 countries, 1960–1999

Figure 4.8 Continued

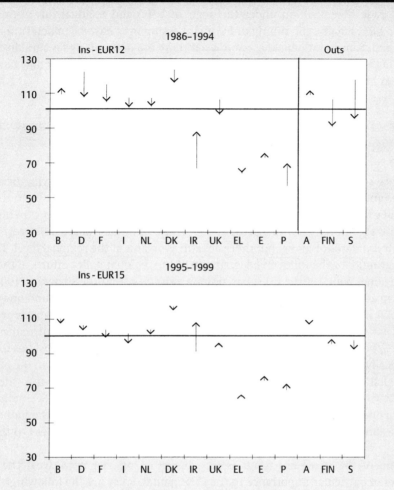

Notes: Ins are those countries which were members of the European Union in the sub-period in question. *Outs* are defined as countries which were not members in the sub-period in question, but became members before 1995. GDP per capita at current market prices in PPS. EUR = 100. 1961–91 excl. East Germany. Luxembourg is an outlier and therefore not listed. GDP per capita in Luxembourg in various years is 1960: 139.2; 1972: 129.9; 1973: 144.0; 1980: 121.7; 1981: 125.2; 1985: 130.1; 1986: 145.8; 1994: 163.9; 1995: 163.0; and 1999: 160.4.

Source: EU Commission (1999), Annexe: tables 1 and 6. Author's calculation.

The overall conclusion which can be drawn from Figure 4.8 is that growth in the fifteen current member states has been converging for the past forty years as growth in GDP per capita has been largest in the poor countries. It is not at all clear, however, if actual membership of the EU is the main reason for this convergence. First, it is possible that membership of the EU has simply not had any significant impact. Secondly, a number of sub-periods are short, and the time difference between the business cycles of the countries may therefore influence results. Thirdly, significant economic integration has taken place concurrently with the EU cooperation, e.g. through trade liberalization under the aegis of WTO and regional integration via EFTA and EEA. Finally, the timing of EU membership may have been determined by special conditions in individual economies. If there is a particularly favourable development in the economy of a country which is not a member of the EU, it may be more difficult to convince the population of the advantages of membership.

Structural funds and their impact on growth

Experience so far does not indicate that differences in standards of living between countries and regions of the EU will be fully eliminated in the foreseeable future. A successful example is Ireland which, from a very low starting point, has experienced comparatively strong growth. Portugal and Spain have also had a relatively high growth in standards of living, but are still problems at the regional level. This is the background for the following description of the regional policy efforts of the EU.

The regional policy of the EU is based upon subsidies from the structural funds to projects in economically weak areas. The structural funds make up around one-third of the total EU budget. Although the total budget of the EU only constitutes around 1¼ per cent of GDP of the entire EU, and the structural funds thus only constitute around 0.4 per cent of total GDP of the EU, the significance of these subsidies for the economically weak areas is larger than will be immediately apparent from the budget figures. First, the subsidies are limited to problem areas, and compared to the economic activity in these areas, the subsidies are of a considerable size. Secondly, the regional policy of the EU builds upon the principle of co-financing, i.e. the individual member state must contribute with resources of its own as a supplement to the EU subsidy.

The aim of the structural funds is to achieve six priority objectives. The four objectives of particular importance to the EU regional policy are the following:

- Development and structural adjustment of those regions where development is lagging behind, the definition being a GDP per capita below 75 per cent of the EU average (objective 1).
- The conversion of industrially declining regions (objective 2).
- Facilitating the development and structural adjustment of rural areas (objective 5b).
- Promoting the development and structural adjustment of regions with an extremely low population density (objective 6).

Table 4.4 shows total distribution of the structural funds as well as distribution per capita for the individual EU countries for the period 1994–9. GDP per capita in 1994 is also listed, as well as structural funds as a percentage of accumulated gross investment in the same period.

In the examined period, structural funds furthering the first objective made up the

Table 4.4 GDP per capita 1994 and structural funds and gross investments 1994–1999 [a]

	GDP per capita at current market prices in PPS (ecu)	Structural funds (mill. ecu)	Structural funds per capita (ecu)	Ratio of structural funds to investment, per cent
Belgium	19,148	1,267	124	0.5
Denmark	19,808	173	33	0.1
Germany	18,365	16,433	200	0.7
Greece	10,896	13,980	1,329	13.6
Spain	12,687	29,380	745	4.9
France	17,917	8,202	139	0.6
Ireland	14,808	5,620	1,501	7.8
Italy	17,369	17,224	299	1.8
Luxembourg	27,984	21	49	0.1
The Netherlands	17,483	950	60	0.2
Austria	18,615	664	82	0.3
Portugal	11,707	13,980	1,410	11.4
Finland	15,487	819	158	0.8
Sweden	16,311	539	61	0.3
UK	16,674	7,758	131	0.8

Notes: All figures are in 1994 prices.
[a] Excluding objective 2 expenditure from 1997 to 1999.

Sources: Armstrong (1998): 382. EU Commission (1999), Annexe: tables 1, 5, 6, 19, and 24. Author's calculation.

main part of total funds and were concentrated in the poor regions of a relatively small number of countries, in particular Greece, Portugal, Spain, Italy (NUTS1 regions of southern Italy), Ireland, and Germany (NUTS1 regions of former East Germany). These areas received more than 88 per cent of the total budget for this objective. It is no surprise that the subsidy per capita (see column 3), is largest for the relatively poorest countries and for countries with both rich and poor regions.

Resources from the structural funds are primarily used to subsidize investment of private companies and public authorities (e.g. to develop infrastructure). The structural funds thus contribute to financing investment in line with savings in the area, and as a result, the level of investment in the poor areas will presumably be increased. It is, however, difficult to estimate the effect of the structural funds, as the subsidies are rationed and only awarded to projects after prior application. The extent to which a project would have been carried out without structural fund resources is thus an open question.

It is possible, however, to get an impression of the importance of the structural funds by relating the allocations from the structural funds to the gross investment of individual countries (see the last column of Table 4.4 from which it appears that Greece, Spain, Portugal, and Ireland display a relatively large share of investments financed by the structural funds). With the exception of Greece, these countries have experienced a somewhat higher growth than the EU average, which has led to a convergence towards the average EU standards of living. Between them, Greece, Spain, and Portugal received more than 58 per cent of total structural funds under the first objective mentioned above in the period in question, but in spite of this, only Spain has managed to pass the threshold of 75 per cent of GDP per capita by 1999.

The overall conclusion is that the desired convergence of standards of living has started, although there is no doubt that a higher rate of convergence is politically desirable.

4.6 The European endowment of human capital

Accorting to traditional neoclassical growth theory, countries with similar technology will converge towards the same standards of living. As illustrated above, this seems to be only partly true in the case of the EU, and even in those cases where convergence does take place, the development is often very slow. This indicates that other factors than the share of investment in GDP are of importance for the growth rate. The concept of human capital introduced by the so-called 'new' growth theory is an attempt to take this into account. Human capital denotes the knowledge and experience possessed by the labour force and is a vital input into research and development. It generates new goods and methods of production underpinning technological progress. An economy well endowed with human capital is likely to experience a high growth rate. This section is dedicated to these factors behind the technological development in the EU.

Human capital

As explained above, a central factor behind a country's economic growth is its endowment of human capital. In the following, university-level education, the number of researchers, and expenditure on research and development will be used as indicators of the EU's endowment of human capital. The ratio between the figures listed in Table 4.5 indicates the relative degree to which the EU is endowed with human capital compared with the other two economies in the Triad. It should be pointed out that there is no obvious method of measuring human capital correctly, and the indicators used here are only a few, simple measures out of many possible. In Table 4.5, the most direct measure of human capital could be the percentage of the population aged 25-64 with university-level education. No figures are available for

Table 4.5 Human capital and research and development

	University-level education[a], 1996	Researchers[b] in business enterprises, 1995	GERD[c] as a percentage of GDP, 1996
EU	12[d]	2.31	1.8
USA	26	5.91	2.7
Japan	n.a.	5.76	2.8

[a] Per cent of the population aged 25–64 with university-level education according to the International Standard Classification of Education. The content and duration of educational programmes classified at this level will of course differ inside as well as between countries.
[b] Or university graduates per thousands of the labour force.
[c] Gross Domestic Expenditure on R&D.
[d] Calculated as the weighted average using population size as weights.
Source: OECD (1999): tables 2.6.1, 3.1.1, and 4.1.2.

Japan, but it would appear that only half as many have reached university-level education in Europe as in the USA. If the majority of technological inventions take place in business enterprises, the number of researchers in this sector is highly relevant. Again, the European level seems to be less than half the level of the USA and Japan. Taking a positive view, there seems to be much room for improving the human capital in Europe.

Judged by the ratio of gross domestic expenditure on research and development (R&D) to GDP, the picture remains the same: the EU is lagging behind. However, the size of expenditures allocated to R&D is one thing. How efficiently these expenditures are translated into technological changes is quite another. Expenditures on R&D measure the technological *input* of a country and include innovative as well as imitative activities, whereas the number of patents measures the technological *output* of a country and only includes innovative activities. The number of patents is thus the measurable *result* of the R&D efforts of a country. The technological output is the object of analysis of the next section.

Technological changes

The following measures the technological output of the EU countries in the form of the number of patents. Not all innovations can be patented, however, and besides that, the number of patents does not necessarily indicate the value of individual innovations. The number of patents can thus only be used as a rough measure of the innovative capacity of a country.

In Table 4.6, the number of patents granted to EU countries, the USA, and Japan — and still in force in the year 1998 — is related to population and GDP. Patents may stay in force for up to twenty years from the issue of the patent only, so the number of patents in force does not convey the actual outcome of human research activities. At

Table 4.6 Patents in force in 1998			
	Ratio of patents to population	Ratio of patents to GDP	Ratio of patents to GERD[b]
EU[a]	100	100	100
USA	147	105	75
Japan	251	216	149

[a] Includes all signatory states to the European Patent Convention, i.e. EUR15, Switzerland and Liechtenstein.
[b] Gross Domestic Expenditure on R&D in 1990.

Sources: Japanese Patent Office and European Patent Office (2000): Graph 1.1 and 4.3.1. EU Commission (1999), Annexe: table 1. Author's calculation.

the same time, statistics on newly granted patents or patent applications are blurred by the fact that many European inventors file an application with their national patent authority first, and only later consider the appropriateness of transferring the application to the European Patent Office (EPO), which means that the same invention may show up in both national and EPO statistics. Moreover, as some inventors decide not to apply to the EPO but only keep a national patent, the number of applications received and patents granted by the EPO is small compared to the Japanese Patent Office and the US Patent Office.

Looking at Table 4.6, it becomes clear that the result of human research and development, measured by patents in force, is comparatively low in the EU when related to the population. If the ratio of patents to GDP is used, the differences between the EU and the USA and Japan are somewhat reduced because of higher overall productivity in the EU countries.

The last column of Table 4.6 relates the number of patents in force in 1998 to expenditure on research and development in 1990. Patents in force in 1998 are of course the result of innovation activities carried out in many years up to 1998, and 1990 is only one of these years. However, resources used on research and development do not change so much over the years that it invalidates the index shown. The column indicates that the EU is more efficient at transforming research and development efforts into patents than the USA, and it appears that Japan is by far the most efficient country at turning research and development into patents.

Of the patents granted by the EPO to inventions made outside the EU, Japanese inventors receive 20 per cent and American inventors 26 per cent (1999 EPO figures). Of patents granted in Japan, European and American inventors only obtain 5 per cent each, whereas Japanese inventors received 20 per cent, and European only 16 per cent, of patents granted in the USA. This seems to confirm the impression of a Europe lagging slightly behind in technological progress. It should be borne in mind, however, that the differences may partly be caused by differences in practice and patent legislation between countries.

It is difficult to determine exactly how large a part the European integration process has played in the technological development. An increase in the number of patents may be connected to technological progress brought about by the improved access of the individual countries to the knowledge pool of all member countries. However, as international competition sharpens because of globalization and trade liberalization (see Chapter 6), it is possible that it has become increasingly important to patent new inventions in order to stand up to this competition. If this is the case, it is not the flow of innovations, which has increased, but only the incentive to register the individual innovation as a patent.

4.7 Concluding remarks

THE objective of this chapter has been to illustrate problems of economic growth in the European Union. In the first part of the chapter, this was done through a neoclassical growth analysis, where investment is a determining factor for growth. However, it appeared that the increased level of integration in connection with the formation of the Internal Market did not lead to a higher share of investment in GDP. Growth in the EU has therefore been relatively small in general, and as there has been a simultaneous increase in labour productivity as a consequence of a substitution of labour by capital, a serious unemployment problem has arisen.

At country level, some convergence of standards of living has taken place, although not at a speed which would seem politically desirable. A remarkable feature of this development has been that several countries have demonstrated the highest convergence rate in their standards of living before EU accession, and that, with the exception of Ireland and Portugal, former *Outs* countries have hardly experienced any convergence after joining the European Union.

The results of a number of model simulations confirm, however, that European integration has in fact had an impact on total production of the member countries (see EU Commission (1996)). GDP of EUR12 in 1994 was estimated to be between 1.1 per cent and 1.5 per cent higher than the level would have been if the Single Market had not been established. This is a difference corresponding to around 70 bn. ecu. The actual growth rate has, however, not been influenced to any significant degree. The EU Commission estimates that growth in GDP has increased by 0.1 per cent as a result of integration. Seen in relation to the growth rates in Figure 4.1 and Tables 4.1 and 4.3, this must be said to be a very marginal increase in the growth rate, and in the short run, a change of this magnitude has no significance at all. However, changes in growth rates have a cumulative effect, and in a very long perspective, even an increase in the growth rate by 0.1 per cent p.a. will be of significance.

In summary it can be concluded that there is no clear indication that the integration, which has taken place under the auspices of the EU so far, has had any significant impact on economic growth in general or on the improvement of the standards of living when compared to economic growth in Western Europe outside the EU.

4.A Appendix

In the following neoclassical growth model, real GDP, Y, is determined by input of capital, K, labour, L, in a Cobb–Douglas production function:

$$Y = A\,K^{\theta}\,L^{1-\theta},\ 0 < \theta < 1. \tag{A 1}$$

θ denotes output elasticity with respect to capital, and hence $(1 - \theta)$ denotes output elasticity with respect to labour. K is the capital stock and L the total number of working hours, i.e. $L = hN$, where h is the number of working hours per person employed and N the number of persons employed. Transforming (A1) into relative changes gives:

$$\frac{\Delta Y}{Y} = \frac{\Delta A}{A} + \theta\,\frac{\Delta K}{K} + (1 - \theta)\,\frac{\Delta N}{N} + (1 - \theta)\,\frac{\Delta h}{h}. \tag{A2}$$

The rate of growth in real GDP, $\Delta Y/Y$, is thus determined by the growth rate of total factor productivity, $\Delta A/A$, capital, $\Delta K/K$, employment growth, $\Delta N/N$, and working hours per person employed $\Delta h/h$, respectively.

The growth rate in labour productivity is defined by:

$$\frac{\Delta AP}{AP} = \frac{\Delta Y}{Y} - \frac{\Delta N}{N}. \tag{A3}$$

Inserting (A2) in (A3) gives:

$$\frac{\Delta AP}{AP} = \frac{\Delta A}{A} + (1 - \theta)\,\frac{\Delta h}{h} + \theta\left(\frac{\Delta K}{K} - \frac{\Delta N}{N}\right). \tag{A4}$$

The right-hand side of (A4) illustrates the decomposition of the growth rates in labour productivity, in total factor productivity, in working hours per person employed, and in capital per person employed (see Table 4.2).

Further reading

An introduction to growth theory can be found e.g. in R. Dornbusch, S. Fischer, and R. Startz (1998), *Macroeconomics*, McGraw-Hill, New York. For more advanced surveys, refer to R. J. Barro and X. Sala-i-Martin (1995), *Economic Growth*, McGraw-Hill, New York, and G. Silverberg and L. Soete (eds.) (1994), *The Economics of Growth and Technical Change*, Edward Elgar, Cheltenham. A detailed analysis of the convergence process at a regional level as well as the regional policy of the EU can be found in R. Martin (1998), *Regional Policy in the European Union*, Centre for European Policy Studies, Brussels.

References

Armstrong, H. W. (1998), EU regional policy, in El-Agraa, in M. Ali (ed.), *The European Union—History, Institutions, Economics and Policies*, Prentice-Hall Europe, London.

Barro, Robert J. and Sala-i-Martin, Xavier (1995), *Economic Growth*, McGraw-Hill, New York.

Eurostat (1998), *Statistics in Focus—regions*, 1998–1.

EU Commission (1993), *European Economy*, 54.

—— (1996), *Economic Evaluation of the Internal Market*, 4.

—— (1998), *European Economy*, 66.

—— (1999), *European Economy*, 68.

—— (2000), *European Economy*, Supplement A, 'Economic trends', 1/2 (April).

Japanese Patent Office and European Patent Office (2000), *Trilateral Report 1999* (www.euro-patent-office.org/tws).

OECD (1996), *Employment Outlook*, July.

—— (1999), *Main Science and Technology Indicators, 1999–2*.

Solow, Robert M. (1956), 'A Contribution to the Theory of Economic Growth', *Quarterly Journal of Economics*, 70 (1) 65–94.

The Economist (1997), 'Labouring the point', October, 106.

Chapter 5

Industrial Structures: Specialization, Efficiency, and Growth

Jørgen Drud Hansen and
Jan Guldager Jørgensen

5.1 Introduction

COMPETITION between firms in most sectors in the EU has increased because of the formation of the Single Market in particular and global liberalization of trade and capital movements in general. As a result, firms increasingly engage in cross-border activities, and this has led to a radical industrial restructuring in the EU.

This chapter highlights the changes in industrial structures which have taken place in the EU in recent years and looks at developments in the main sectors as well as in company size and market concentration on individual markets. The central theme of the chapter is a description of the structural changes which have taken place since the creation of the Single Market and their impact on efficiency and growth. Structural changes influence efficiency and growth in different ways. First of all, the level of specialization increases, not only between countries, but even more so between individual firms. Secondly, free access to a larger market has an impact on Research and Development (R&D). Thirdly, trade liberalization limits the market power of firms, and as a consequence, price distortions resulting from imperfect competition will decrease and efficiency will increase. These issues will be examined in more detail in the following sections.

Section 5.2 examines the distribution of production on main sectors (agriculture, industry, and services) with particular emphasis on the diminishing importance of agriculture. As the agricultural policy is a central policy area in the EU, the *Common*

Agricultural Policy (CAP) is the subject of a special analysis in Section 5.3. Section 5.4 looks at the sectoral structure of manufacturing, using a classification of industries according to their technology content, and questions whether manufacturing in the EU has become technologically more dynamic since the formation of the Single Market. Section 5.5 analyses the extent to which the industrial structures in manufacturing have converged between member states. This question is of relevance to the analysis of the pros and cons of a common currency, as differences in industrial structures can lead to diverging business cycles between countries. Section 5.6 looks at the development in company size, whereas Section 5.7 describes the development in market concentration since the formation of the Single Market and analyses the impact of these changes on price determination. State aid and tax harmonization are the issues of Section 5.8, and Section 5.9 concludes the chapter with an overall evaluation of the industrial restructuring which has taken place in the years following the formation of the Single Market.

5.2 The sectoral distribution

THE most general classification of the industrial structure contains only three main sectors: agriculture, industry, and services. Table 5.1 describes the distribution of production in these three sectors based on Eurostat's division of sectors according to the so-called *NACE classification* (General Industrial Classification of Economic Activities within the European Community).[1] The composition of each of these three sectors is very heterogeneous. Agriculture, for example, also includes forestry and fishery, and apart from the traditional manufacturing goods, such as chemical products and textiles, industry also includes agricultural and industrial machineries, food, beverages and tobacco, clothing, leather and footwear, fuel and power products, and building and construction. Services include recovery and repairs, wholesale and retail trade, lodging and catering, inland transport, communications, credit and insurance, and general government services.

Table 5.1 shows the distribution in main sectors for the Triad. Comparing the EU, the USA, and Japan, it should be noticed that the data for EUR15 are from Eurostat, whereas OECD data are used for the USA and Japan. The agricultural sector formed a very small part of total gross value added at market prices in 1997 in both the EU, the USA, and Japan, with a share of 2.1, 1.6, and 1.7 per cent, respectively. But with respect to the other two main sectors, industry and services, the differences are more pronounced. In both 1988 and 1997, the relatively largest service sector was found in the USA and the smallest in Japan, while the opposite was true for the industrial sector, in that industry was relatively small in the USA compared to Japan.

---

[1] NACE is derived from the French version: 'Nomenclature générale des Activités économiques dans les Communautés Européennes'.

Table 5.1 Gross value added at market prices, 1988 and 1997						
	Agriculture		Industry		Services	
	1988	1997	1988	1997	1988	1987
EUR15	3.1	2.1	35.3	30.5	61.8[a]	67.4
USA	1.8	1.6	28.8	25.2	69.4	73.2
Japan	2.6	1.7	39.0	35.6	58.5	62.7

[a] 1989.

Sources: Eurostat (1996): table 1. Eurostat (1999): table 1. OECD (2000): 150–1 and 290–1.

The development in distribution in main sectors in EUR15 is also illustrated in Table 5.1, demonstrating a shift from agriculture and industry to services in the period from 1988 to 1997. This trend, which is general for most industrialized countries, reflects that there is a link between economic growth and the composition of demand in the economy. The increase in real income created by economic growth changes the composition of demand from goods with low-income elasticity to goods with high-income elasticity. Food, for example, is generally characterized by low-income elasticity, and as a consequence, food will gradually form a smaller part of the composition of consumption in growing economies. In the long run, production and resources adapt to the development in demand, and that is why the share of agriculture in production and employment is declining.

The service sector, on the other hand, is increasing, because services generally have a high-income elasticity. The service sector is very heterogeneous. It includes both human capital-intensive service activities such as education, medical care, and administration, and labour-intensive service activities such as retail sale, hairdressing, and personal care. In many ways, the size and composition of the service sector reflects the economy. Education and research, as emphasized in Chapter 4, have a strong impact on economic growth, and growth, on the other hand, influences the allocation between individual services as the income elasticity for individual types of services varies. Labour market policy and labour market efficiency may also influence the service sector, as described in Chapter 3. On a highly flexible labour market with large wage dispersion, the service sector plays the role of an absorber of employment if demand weakens. The reason is that entry barriers for labour-intensive service activities, such as personal care or the establishment of a hot-dog stand, are very low. If unemployment benefits are pared, working in the service sector may be preferable to staying unemployed. This may keep the unemployment rate low, but the cost is higher inequality.

The service industry has been profoundly affected by the Single Market, globalization, and the introduction of information technology (see EU Commission (1993)). Before the formation of the Single Market, service activities in general were non-tradable because of high trade costs and/or because of discriminatory practices of the member states. The Single Market has removed the institutional obstacles to mobility of services and placed a wide range of service industries, e.g. telecommunications, banking, insurance, and air freight, in a much more competitive environment. This has stimulated efficiency and reduced price distortions to the benefit of the consumers. However, other kinds of services, e.g. personal care, are to a large extent still non-tradable, because production and consumption is a simultaneous process restricted to the same location. For those industries, distance makes up an effective barrier to competition and limits the market size to the local area.

The dwindling agricultural sector

There is a disproportion between the significant attention paid to the agricultural sector in EU forums and public media in general and its share of production in the EU. The reason for this paradox is firstly that agriculture used to play a much larger role in production, and traditionally the conditions of this sector have been the subject of keen public interest. Secondly, the agricultural sector is essentially regulated by the CAP, which gives rise to discussions about both the current administration and the long-term considerations on the development of this sector.

Agriculture's share of employment in the EU exceeds its share of production, and labour productivity, measured by value added per person employed, is therefore lower in agriculture than in the economy as a whole. This is revealed by Table 5.2, which shows that relative labour productivity in agriculture is less than half of that of the economy as a whole. It should be kept in mind that the low, relative labour productivity in agriculture illustrated in the table is the result of many years' increase in real output per person employed, combined with a significant decrease in the relative price of agricultural products. However, the table seems to corroborate the hypothesis that overall labour productivity may be raised by an outflow of labour from the agricultural sector.

Looking at the distribution in main sectors inside the EU, it becomes evident that there are significant differences between member states. This appears from Table 5.3, which describes the distribution of gross value added at market prices in individual

Table 5.2 Relative labour productivity in main sectors, EUR15, 1997

	Share of value added	Share of employment	Relative labour productivity
Agriculture	2.1	5.0	0.42
Industry	30.4	29.4	1.03
Services	67.5	65.3	1.03

Source: Eurostat (2000): 218–23 and 297–8. Authors' calculation.

Table 5.3 Distribution of gross value added at market prices by sector, 1997, per cent

	Agriculture	Industry	Services
Belgium	1.2	28.8	70.0
Denmark[a]	3.2	27.2	69.6
Germany	1.0	31.8	67.2
Greece[a]	8.1	23.0	68.9
Spain	3.3	31.1	65.6
France	2.4	27.5	70.1
Ireland	4.5	40.9	54.6
Italy	2.7	31.1	66.3
Luxembourg	0.8	21.1	78.1
The Netherlands	3.0	28.5	68.5
Austria	1.4	32.3	66.3
Portugal	4.1	33.6	62.3
Finland	3.9	34.8	61.3
Sweden	1.8	28.9	69.3
UK	1.5	31.6	66.9
EUR15	2.1	30.5	67.4

[a] Estimated by Eurostat as these countries only supply figures on gross value added at factor costs.

Source: Eurostat (1999): table 1.

member states in 1997. Relatively large agricultural sectors are found in Greece, Ireland, and Portugal, whereas the industrial sector is relatively large in Ireland, Finland, and Portugal, and the service sector is relatively large in Luxembourg, France, and Belgium.

In general, the share of agricultural production in the member states varies inversely with wealth. This correlation appears from Figure 5.1, which compares the agricultural share of value added to production per capita in individual member states in 1997. The figure shows production per capita in GDP per capita measured in PPS, thus adjusting for any over- or under-estimation of the currencies of individual countries in relation to their purchasing power. It is characteristic of all the poor countries that the share of the agricultural sector is high.

The general tendency towards a correlation between the relative size of the agricultural sector and real income confirms the assumption that the share of consumption constituted by food declines when real income increases, and that the composition of demand on the home market to some extent is reflected in the composition of production. However, trade may break this pattern, as trade disconnects a country's production from its consumption. This is true of e.g. Denmark, Ireland, and the Netherlands, which have a relatively large share of production in agriculture, whereas Sweden and the UK have a relatively small share compared to their wealth. These differences are due to the fact that Denmark, Ireland, and the Netherlands

Figure 5.1 GDP per capita and share of agriculture in gross value added, 1997

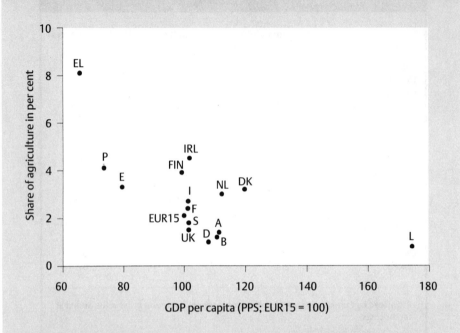

Notes: GDP per capita index at current market prices. Gross value added at market prices with [a] from Table 5.3 applying to DK and EL.

Sources: EU Commission (1999), Annexe: table 9. Eurostat (1999): table 1.

have significant agricultural exports, whereas Sweden and the UK have significant agricultural imports.

Naturally, the correlation between the share of agricultural production and wealth also manifests itself over time. This is illustrated in Figure 5.2, which compares the development in the share of agriculture of gross value added in 1980 to that in 1997 for each member country. The figure clearly indicates the dwindling importance of agriculture in the creation of value added. During the examined period, all member states have experienced real growth in production per capita at the same time as the share of agriculture of gross value added has declined. It also appears from the figure that the share of agriculture of gross value added has declined, particularly in those countries which had a relatively large agricultural sector in 1980 (Greece, Ireland, Portugal, and Finland).

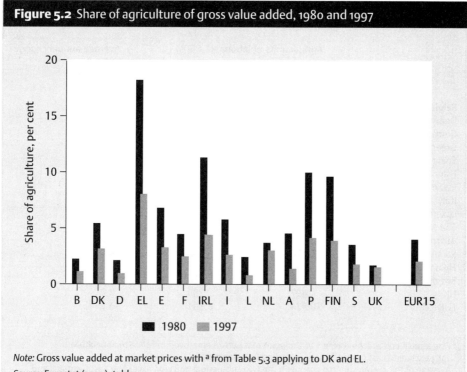

Figure 5.2 Share of agriculture of gross value added, 1980 and 1997

Note: Gross value added at market prices with ᵃ from Table 5.3 applying to DK and EL.
Source: Eurostat (1999): table 1.

5.3 The common agricultural policy

THE dwindling importance of agriculture is in no way due to lower efficiency measured by physical output per unit input of labour. On the contrary, technological developments and an increased input of real capital have led to an increase in labour productivity measured by physical output per unit of labour, e.g. tonnes of grain, litres of milk, or kilos of meat. The fact that value added per unit of labour is still relatively low is due to an unfavourable price development for the sector, the reason being that the strong growth in physical output combined with the low income elasticity for food has led to a fall in prices for agricultural products relative to prices of other goods and services. Viewed separately, this reduces the value added per unit of labour. The result has been a significant migration of labour from agriculture (see Table 5.4).

The agricultural labour force has decreased by some 3-4 per cent per year since 1983 in the EU as a whole, but migration from agriculture has been particularly large in Portugal, Austria, and Finland. To a large extent, the migration has consisted of

Table 5.4 The agricultural labour force, 1983–1997

	Annual units of labour[a] (1,000s)		Average annual change 1983–97
	1983	1997	(per cent)
Belgium	109	77	–2.5
Denmark	128	83	–3.0
Germany[b]	946	660	–2.5[c]
Greece	917	581	–3.2
Spain	1,615	1,032	–3.1
France	1,671	1,006	–3.6
Ireland	276	218	–1.7
Italy	2,655	1,664	–3.3
Luxembourg	8	5	–3.3
The Netherlands	248	220	–0.9
Austria	250	137	–4.2
Portugal	1,110	562	–4.7
Finland	315	173	–4.2
Sweden	130	86	–2.9
UK	497	389	–1.7
EUR15[b]	10,874	6,891	–3.2[c]

[a] One annual unit of labour refers to the input of a person employed full-time in agriculture.
[b] 1983 excluding East Germany, 1997 including East Germany.
[c] Average of the average annual change in the two sub-periods 1983–93 excluding East Germany and 1993–7 including East Germany with the number of years as weights.
Source: Eurostat (1998): table 4. Authors' calculation.

individual farmers retiring from the labour market due to age, so in these cases, there has not been a need for special labour market measures, such as retraining or providing subsidies enabling farmers to move to areas with jobs in other sectors.

The migration of labour from agriculture curbs the increase in agricultural production which in turn limits the deterioration of the terms of trade for this sector. Thus, in the long run, a sufficiently large migration will help ensure that the income development of farmers follows that of other sectors. Yet, for the last decades, the *Common Agricultural Policy* (CAP) has aimed at securing 'reasonable' income levels in the agricultural sector by providing various subsidies (Articles 32 to 38 in the Amsterdam Treaty provide the full set of objectives for the CAP). This has weakened the short-term impact of the market mechanism on migration, which has led to a slowdown in migration from agriculture and encouraged maintaining economic activity in rural areas. As will appear from the following, the disadvantage is a significant loss of efficiency, which will affect consumers and taxpayers in particular.

The CAP consists of a comprehensive system of regulations shielding the Internal Market from competition from third countries in the agricultural sector at the same time as it ensures that individual farmers operate under similar market conditions inside the EU. This means that the EU's trade in agricultural products with third countries is regulated by a series of customs and import restrictions and export sub-sidies. This disconnects the price level for agricultural products in the EU from the world market prices. Furthermore, prices are guaranteed for most agricultural prod-ucts, and these guaranteed minimum prices are maintained through EU financed *intervention buying*, where the agricultural produce is either put into intervention storage or exported with subsidies.

This price support mechanism impedes migration from the agricultural sector and stimulates increased production. The low increase in demand for food from con-sumers in the EU, the strong growth in productivity, and the incentive to increase production created by the guaranteed price system, have resulted in a considerable excess production of both vegetable (grain, sugar) and animal (butter, beef, veal) produce.

As a consequence, the agricultural subsidies have become very costly for the EU. Recent reforms have been aimed at reducing production in different ways. Firstly, guaranteed prices have been lowered and approached world market prices. To allevi-ate the effects of this on income, area payment has been introduced, i.e. subsidies which are not determined by actual production but only by the size of the area cultivated. Secondly, measures, which directly regulate production, have been adopted, e.g. production quotas for milk and compulsory set-aside schemes for farm land. Finally, pension schemes, aimed particularly at older farmers encouraging them to cease production, have been introduced.

The result of the CAP reforms is that the share of the EU budget being spent on agriculture has stagnated at a level of some 40bn. ecu, or approximately half of the total EU budget (see Table 5.5).

The CAP creates a significant efficiency loss in the EU. The social loss relates only to a limited extent to the expenditures under the EU budget, but stems from the loss imposed on consumers as a consequence of higher consumer prices of food compared with the food price level on the world market. To this should be added a loss to society as the agricultural sector retains resources which could contribute more effi-ciently to production in other sectors. The disconnection from world market competition has distorted trade in agricultural products from cheap imports from countries outside the EU to expensive trade in agricultural products inside the EU. In relation to the traditional customs union theory, CAP has thus resulted in a pronounced degree of trade diversion resulting in a welfare loss.

It is difficult to estimate the size of the welfare loss quantitatively, *inter alia* because the price level of agricultural products on the world market would increase if the CAP were terminated. Without subsidies, including intervention buying and subsequent subsidized exports, the EU's production and exports would decrease and prices con-sequently increase on the world market. However, the significant EU expenditures on the CAP and the marked difference between EU agricultural prices and world market prices point to a significant welfare loss.

Both this and the previous section have emphasized the dwindling importance of agriculture in production and demonstrated that the share of agriculture in gross value added has decreased in all member countries. Productivity is higher in both industry and services than in agriculture, and this structural transition has

Table 5.5 CAP budget expenditures, million ecu

	CAP expenditures million ecu	Per cent of	
		EU Budget	EUR12 GDP[a]
1973	3,769	81.2	—
1975	4,587	73.8	—
1980	11,596	72.2	—
1985	20,546	72.8	—
1986	23,068	66.2	0.65
1987	23,939	67.5	0.64
1988	27,532	65.1	0.68
1989	25,869	56.4	0.58
1990	27,234	58.4	0.57
1991	33,443	59.1	0.65
1992	38,462	61.2	0.72
1993	37,135	56.1	0.69
1994	40,751	58.2	0.73
1995	40,247	55.9	0.62[b]

[a] East Germany not included for the years 1986–90.
[b] Per cent of EUR15 GDP.

Sources: EU Commission (1998a), Annexe: table 5 and 79a. EU Commission (1995), Annexe: table 5. Authors' calculation.

contributed to economic growth. But the future growth potential coming from a restructuring of resources from agriculture to industry and services will be more restricted as, by now, the share of resources attached to agriculture is rather limited.

The CAP has to some extent delayed the migration from agriculture, and this has impeded economic growth. The resulting loss of efficiency is the price paid to ensure a 'fair' standard of living for farmers and to maintain economic activity in rural areas. However, the cost of the CAP has proved to be untenable. It is this fact which has motivated reforms of the CAP, although the main principles remain the same and the problem with the high level of expenditures remains unsolved. The latest attempt to change the CAP more profoundly, at the European Council meeting in Berlin in March 1999, also turned out quite disappointingly as it was decided to take only limited steps towards reducing the gap between EU and world market price levels for agricultural products for the next five to six years.

5.4 Is European industry becoming more innovative?

FROM a theoretical point of view, it may be argued that there is a positive correlation between market size and the incentive for firms to create innovations through research and development (R&D). R&D costs are *sunk costs*, which means that the costs related to individual innovations are defrayed once and for all or, in other words, that R&D costs are independent of the subsequent product runs in the firm. As product runs often increase with market size, the yield of the innovation also increases. Hence, the incentive to make innovations increases with market size. These lines of reasoning, based on sunk costs and accumulation of technological know-how, have been demonstrated by Sutton (1991), among others.

If a firm makes product innovations, where the innovation consists of developing new products, it may expect larger sales of the new product on a large market. In the case of process innovations, where new technology leads to lower production costs per unit of a certain product, total cost savings will again be larger on a large market, as this normally implies larger sales.

The formation of the Internal Market was *inter alia* motivated by the desire to encourage a more dynamic development of manufacturing industry in Europe. In order to examine whether or not manufacturing in the EU has in fact become more dynamic, two areas in particular will be analysed. Firstly, we will look at the development of the industrial structures using the OECD (1997a) classification into *high-* and *low-technology-intensive industries*. Secondly, the development in R&D in individual industries will be illustrated.

Table 5.6 illuminates developments in the manufacturing industries in the EU in the period 1986 to 1994. It appears that the overall distribution in high- and low-technology-intensive industries has been almost constant in the examined period. Within individual industries, changes have in general also been fairly limited, i.e. less than 1 percentage point of total value added in manufacturing. In the group of low-technology-intensive industries, the share of textiles has decreased by approximately 1.5 percentage points, whereas the share of food has increased almost as much. Thus, the development in the sectoral structure does not show a clear tendency towards a more dynamic industrial structure. When compared to the USA and Japan (see Figure 5.3), the development in the EU is equally disappointing.

In 1986, the USA and Japan had a significantly higher share of value added in high-technology-intensive industries than the EU. This difference enhanced slightly in subsequent years, so in general, the EU has not gained ground in the high-technology-intensive industries during the global specialization process.

Although it does not seem that industrial structures in the EU have moved in a more technology-intensive direction, individual industries in general may have become more focused on R&D. However, this conclusion is not supported by the

Table 5.6 High- and low-technology-intensive manufacturing industries in the EU

	Share of value added per cent	
	1986	1994
High-technology-intensive industries:		
Chemicals	7.9	7.3
Drugs	1.8	2.5
Non-electrical machinery	8.2	7.9
Computers	1.6	1.2
Electrical machinery	5.1	5.0
Electronic equipment	4.8	4.8
Transport: Aircraft + Motor vehicles + Other transport	9.4	9.7
Instruments	1.9	1.8
Other manufacturing	1.1	1.1
Total high	41.9	41.3
Low-technology-intensive industries:		
Food	12.8	13.8
Textiles	8.0	6.5
Wood	3.6	3.9
Paper	7.1	7.7
Petroleum	4.5	4.3
Rubber and plastic	3.7	4.5
Non-metallic minerals	4.6	4.8
Ferrous metals	4.1	3.4
Non-ferrous metals	1.6	1.5
Metal products	7.5	7.8
Transport: Shipbuilding	0.6	0.5
Total low	58.1	58.7
Manufacturing total	100.0	100.0

Note: OECD (1997a) classification into high- and low-technology-intensive industries.

Source: OECD (1999). Authors' calculation.

evidence presented in Table 5.7, which compares *R&D intensity* for high-technology-intensive industries in the four largest member countries of the EU to that of the USA for 1988 and 1994. The R&D intensity expresses R&D costs of an industry in per cent of the value of production of that industry. Table 5.7 shows an ambiguous pattern, not only between individual member countries, but also between individual industries.

The presented data do not seem to support the thesis that European industry has become more innovative. Firstly, the share of technology-intensive industries in manufacturing has remained more or less constant since the establishment of the Internal Market. Secondly, the development in R&D intensity from the late 1980s to the mid-1990s shows a mixed picture, both of individual industries and of individual member states. However, the quality of the data, as well as the classification of industries according to technology intensity, may be questioned and it is therefore difficult

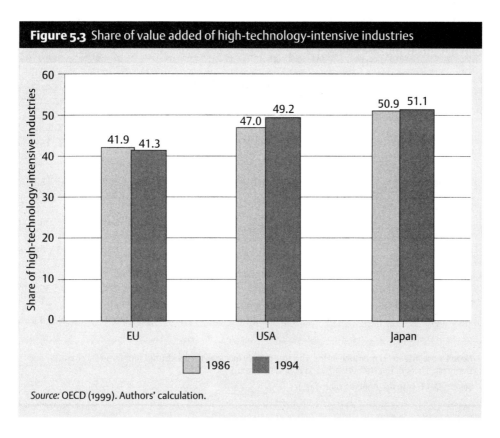

Figure 5.3 Share of value added of high-technology-intensive industries

Source: OECD (1999). Authors' calculation.

to be very conclusive. It should also be kept in mind that technological progress does not depend on R&D intensity in the economy only. *Diffusion of technology* also plays a significant role in levelling out gaps in technological know-how at firm level as well as between countries. Multinationals are major agents in the diffusion of technology, and as the Internal Market has acted as a large stimulus to multinational activities (see Chapter 7), the Internal Market may indirectly have contributed to technological progress in the EU through a swift diffusion of technology.

5.5 Has the industrial structure converged?

A**LTHOUGH** the economic integration of the EU amalgamates the economies of the member states, it is an open question whether this development increases or reduces differences in industrial structures. *International trade theory* does not offer any unequivocal answers to this question. Integration leads to specialization, and this again leads to increased trade. To the extent that the specialization essentially manifests itself in *inter-industry specialization*, the result will be larger divergence of the

Table 5.7 R&D intensity for total manufacturing and for R&D-intensive industries in manufacturing

	Business enterprise R&D costs in percentage of value of production									
	France		Germany		Italy		UK		USA	
	1988	1994	1988	1995	1988	1995	1988	1995	1988	1994
Industrial chem.	8.2	10.3	10.6	9.1	3.6	3.1	8.2	7.3	7.6	8.0
Pharmaceuticals	25.0	27.5	19.0	15.8	15.6	14.2	28.1	33.3	21.1	23.7
Fabr. metals and machinery	10.3	12.1	9.5	9.8	5.3	5.6	8.7	8.0	16.2	13.4
Comps./off. mach.	10.8	11.3	11.1	17.6	15.4	12.3	18.2	5.9	55.4	49.5
Electr. mach.	4.3	4.6	11.3	11.6	4.0	3.4	9.3	8.6	3.9	5.9
Communic. equip.	29.3	34.2	18.4	14.8	16.6	25.3	15.9	13.9	24.6	15.0
Motor vehicles	8.6	12.6	10.0	13.6	8.6	10.9	9.0	9.7	17.5	16.5
Aerospace	40.1	37.6	53.4	43.4	36.2	39.1	21.4	22.1	50.6	36.1
Scientific instrum.	5.0	4.4	3.6	4.2	1.1	1.3	3.5	3.7	11.7	21.0
Total manufact.	5.8	6.8	6.4	6.2	2.7	2.7	5.3	5.4	8.9	8.0

Note: Of the fifteen EU member states, the source only includes the illustrated four large EU countries and Denmark, Finland, the Netherlands, Spain, and Sweden.

Source: OECD (1997*b*), Annexe: table I.12.1.

industrial structures. If, on the other hand, specialization primarily takes the form of *intra-industry specialization*, the effect on the industrial structures is uncertain. If there are significant external economies of scale between firms in the same industry, they will settle in a certain area, and there will be a tendency towards increased divergence. This view has been expressed by Krugman (1991), who demonstrated that there is a higher geographic concentration of industries in the USA than in the EU. According to Krugman, this difference is due to the fact that economic integration has been a reality for a longer time in the USA than in the EU.

Studies of actual developments in the EU after the formation of the Internal Market do not give rise to unequivocal conclusions with respect to convergence or divergence of the industrial structures of the EU countries. An overall measure of differences in industrial or sectoral structures appears by making up an *index of divergence*. The basis of the computation of an index of divergence for a country in relation to a reference country is a comparison of the share of activity in an industry in one country with the share of activity of the same industry in the reference country. The index of divergence is expressed in the sum of the absolute value of the differences for all industries. Thus, the index of divergence for member state i compared with Germany (D), $I_{i,D}$, is defined by the formula:

$$I_{i,D} = \sum_{j=1}^{n} |a_{ij} - a_{Dj}|,$$

where n signifies the number of industries, a_{ij} is the share of activity measured by share of value added in member state i for industry j, and a_{Dj} is the share of value added in Germany in industry j. If the industrial structures are completely identical, i.e. $a_{ij} = a_{Dj}$ for any j, then $I_{i,D} = 0$. If, on the other hand, the sectoral structures are completely different, i.e. either $a_{ij} = 0$ or $a_{Dj} = 0$ for any j, then $I_{i,D} = 2$. The index will thus assume a value in the interval 0 to 2, and the size of the index will then reflect the degree of divergence.

Table 5.8 illustrates the indices of divergence of individual member states compared to Germany for 1986 and 1994, respectively. The countries included in the table were either members of the EU at the time, or participated in the Internal Market via membership of the European Economic Area (EEA). Calculations are made for an industrial structure of twenty-eight industries.

For 1994, the differences in industrial structures as indicated by the indices of divergence are relatively small for France, the Netherlands, Austria, and the UK compared to Germany. The indices reveal significantly larger differences in industrial structures between Greece and Portugal compared to Germany. Furthermore, as described in Section 5.2 above, Greece and Portugal have a relatively large agricultural sector measured by share of gross value added.

Table 5.8 compares the indices of divergence for 1986 and 1994, i.e. at the beginning and end of the period which saw the removal of trade barriers in the Single Market. However, the figures do not reveal a clear tendency in the development. For

Table 5.8 Indices of manufacturing divergence of EU member states relative to Germany

	1986	1994
Belgium	0.53	0.53
Denmark	0.60	0.63
Germany	0.00	0.00
Greece	0.81	0.86
Spain	0.52	0.55
France	0.34	0.27
Italy	0.47	0.48
The Netherlands	0.41	0.42
Austria	0.31	0.34
Portugal	0.75	0.89
Finland	0.60	0.57
Sweden	0.39	0.48
UK	0.31	0.44

Note: The source has no data for Ireland, Luxembourg, and EUR15.

Source: OECD (1999). Authors' calculation.

France and Finland, the development converges with the industrial structure in Germany, whereas other countries, such as Portugal, Sweden, and the UK, seemingly demonstrate a clear development towards increased divergence from Germany.

One should be careful about drawing too solid conclusions on structural differences based on indices of divergence. The computed values indicated in such indices are sensitive to sectoral distribution. All other things held constant, a more detailed sectoral distribution will lead to a higher value for the indices of divergence. Keeping this reservation in mind, the figures in Table 5.8 reveal significant differences between the EU countries in industrial structures in manufacturing, and there is no clear tendency towards a reduction in these differences.

On the Internal Market, demand for individual manufacturing products is not location-specific, but generally manifests itself throughout the Internal Market. Production capacity, on the other hand, is unevenly distributed, as appears from the indices of divergence in Table 5.8. Thus, the impact of *asymmetric industry-specific shocks*, where developments in demand for products of individual industries are significantly diverse, will differ in individual countries due to differences in industrial structures. This will also make the asymmetric industry-specific shock manifest itself as an asymmetric country-specific shock, i.e. shocks which affect developments in activities differently in individual countries. As described in Chapter 8 on monetary integration, such cases of asymmetric country-specific shocks may create a need for individual countries to control their own currency in order to let monetary and exchange rate policies compensate for the asymmetric development.

5.6 Firm size in European manufacturing

THE Internal Market has significantly changed external conditions for firms, and this may lead to intra-firm restructuring. This section focuses specifically on the possible effects on firm size. Eurostat defines a firm as the smallest, autonomous legal business unit, consisting of one or several plants, engaging in production activities. In other words, the characteristics of a firm is that it has its own balance sheet and can be party in a court case. Frequent measures of firm size are either output, as in value added, or input, as in employment. Both measures are subject to criticism. Value added is influenced not only by the physical production but also by prices. And measuring size by employment only disregards other types of input, as well as heterogeneity of input of labour.

Some theoretical considerations

Economies of scale and market size are the most important determinants of firm size. Economies of scale are cost savings resulting from a long-run increase in production where *all* types of input in the firm are adjusted efficiently. This is reflected in a downward-sloping long-run average cost (LAC) curve. The size of the production, when the economies of scale are exhausted, defines the *minimum efficient scale* (MES) of the firm.

There is little empirical evidence of long-run decreasing returns to scale (Pratten (1988), EAG (1997)), and expanding the scale beyond MES will thus take place at constant unit costs reflecting constant returns to scale (see Figure 5.4). The slope of the LAC curve defines the cost gradient which describes the extra costs of output below MES. In an extensive analysis of the European industries by Pratten (1988), cost gradients have been investigated by estimating the supplementary costs, s, for output at half the level of MES. The supplementary costs typically make up 2–5 per cent of unit costs at MES, and in about 70 per cent of all cases, the supplementary costs are below 10 per cent of average MES costs (see Pratten (1988)).

These results confirm that, whereas economies of scale are essential, the addition to average costs of production below, but not too far from, MES is modest. If competition in the market is weak, high profit margins may allow firms to exist also in the long run at scales below MES. Flat cost gradients are thus consistent with high variance in the size distribution of firms.

The Internal Market may affect firm sizes in various ways. Firstly, the increased competition within the Internal Market may lead to firms exiting, thus leaving larger

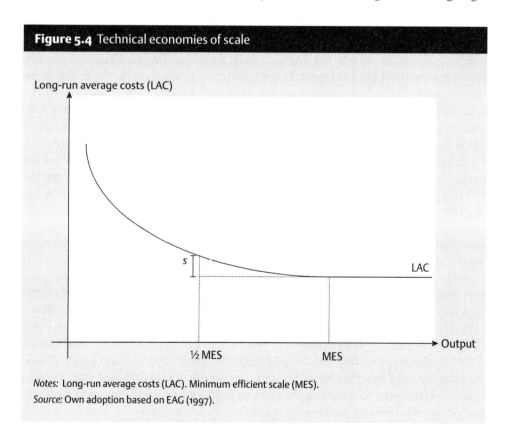

Figure 5.4 Technical economies of scale

Notes: Long-run average costs (LAC). Minimum efficient scale (MES).
Source: Own adoption based on EAG (1997).

market shares to the remaining firms in the market. This consequence of the Internal Market is expected where economies of scale are very strong, i.e. where the MES is large compared with the size of the national markets. From a social point of view, this will lead to improved welfare, mainly because of the better utilization of economies of scale. For industries where economies of scale are traditionally modest, firm size is not constrained by the size of the national market, and the reasons for the possible effects on firm size must therefore be found elsewhere.

Secondly, the Internal Market reduces fixed trade costs, e.g. trade costs induced by border controls (EAG (1997)). This reduces MES and allows entry of smaller firms, which points to a decrease in average firm size.

Thirdly, the reduction of X-inefficiency in the more competitive market may lead to the exit of mainly small, cost-inefficient firms. X-inefficiency signifies extra costs caused by negligence and bad management in general (Leibenstein (1966)). Both small and large firms may suffer from X-inefficiency, but small firms have the added disadvantage of cost inefficiency caused by deficient utilization of economies of scale. Small firms are therefore more likely to exit than large firms when X-inefficiency is eliminated. The endeavours of small firms to survive through rationalization may prove to be unsuccessful, because not only must they eliminate X-inefficiency, they must also be able to raise output in order to utilize economies of scale (EAG (1997)). It therefore seems logical that average firm size increases.

Fourthly, the effects of the Internal Market may also depend on the *structure of fixed costs*, which is divided into exogenous and endogenous fixed costs (Sutton (1991), Davies *et al.* (1996), EU Commission (1996)). Exogenous fixed costs are fixed costs which cannot be changed by the firms, typically fixed costs incurred by the firm every period for inputs of physical capital, and these costs fundamentally represent economies of scale. Endogenous fixed costs are fixed costs which can be influenced by the firm, typically R&D or advertising costs, e.g. with the aim of altering consumer preferences by creating a brand name. If there are only exogenous fixed costs, MES is a well-defined concept corresponding to the level where economies of scale are exhausted, i.e. the minimum of the total average cost curve. If the market size allows the existence of firms of the size given by MES in equilibrium, an increase in market size will lead to entry of new firms, which may also be of the size given by MES, i.e. the firm size may remain unchanged. If R&D or advertising are important strategic variables for the firm, i.e. endogenous fixed costs exist, an increase in market size will strengthen the incentive to increase R&D and advertising costs. In this case, the most likely outcome of an increase in total fixed costs will be an increase in firm size.

Fifthly, the Internal Market may stimulate a *focusing strategy* of firms leading them to concentrate on their core competences. In a small market, it may be more rational for a firm to serve a broader spectrum of the market utilizing *scope economies*. When the market size increases, the competitive pressure may induce firms to increase cost efficiency by reducing their segment of products and trying to increase their market shares on the more limited number of product variants (see e.g. Caves (1989)). Thus, the effect on firm size may be ambiguous. On the one hand, firm size may increase because of larger product runs on the variants produced. On the other hand, firm size may decrease because of the reduced number of variants.

Empirical evidence

The above reasoning, which is anchored in economic theory, leaves the question of how the Internal Market will influence firm size in the EU open, and it may therefore not come as a surprise that the empirical evidence is ambiguous.

Evidence on the development in firm size in various member states from 1985 to 1992 is furnished by the EU Commission (1996) (see Table 5.9). The figures show average firm size in manufacturing measured by gross value added in 1990 prices.

On average, firm size measured by value added has increased in the four member states, but there are large variations from member state to member state, and the UK has even experienced a small decrease in firm size. The figures are at a very aggregated level as they include all manufacturing industries. Table 5.10 shows the percentage change in average firm size (value added) for manufacturing classified according sector sensitivity to Internal Market measures.

The figures do not give any indication of differences in impact of the Internal Market on sensitive or non-sensitive sectors. In order to identify possible effects, the data need to be even less aggregated. In reports from the EU Commission (1996) and EAG (1997), a group of industries classified as R&D- and advertising-intensive, and non-R&D and advertising-intensive, was investigated. It is argued above that the potential for an increase in firm size induced by an increase in market size may be larger for advertising and R&D-intensive sectors because of the endogenous nature of such fixed costs. This is confirmed, both for those sectors which are R&D- and advertising-intensive and for those that are advertising-intensive, but not for those sectors which are only R&D-intensive. The reason for this mixed evidence, given the theoretical expectations, may be the initial firm size structure. The average R&D-intensive firms were already very large before the establishment of the Internal Market, so incentives

Table 5.9 Development in average firm size in manufacturing

	Million ecu[a]		Percentage change
	1985	1992	
Germany[b]	7.4	8.6	15.4
France	4.9	5.3	7.7
Italy	3.3	3.8[c]	15.5
UK	4.8	4.7	−0.2
EUR4	5.2	5.7	11.1

[a] Gross value added in 1990 prices.
[b] West Germany only.
[c] 1991 data.
Source: EU Commission (1996): 123.

Table 5.10 Average firm size and Internal Market sensitivity

Industry classes[a]	Percentage change of value added per firm in 1990 prices			
	Germany	Italy	France	UK
Sensitive sectors	15.5	12.3	2.8	3.0
Non-sensitive sectors	19.5	16.5	13.4	−4.0
All manufacturing sectors	15.4	15.5	7.7	−0.2

[a] Classified by Buigues *et al.* (1990).
Source: EU Commission (1996): 124.

to further increase firm size may be modest for those industries (EU Commission (1996), EAG (1997)).

The evidence presented above does not point to a general trend in average firm size since the mid-1980s. However, it is still likely that the establishment of the Internal Market and the globalization process have caused a significant intra-firm restructuring in the EU. Chapter 7 shows that there has been a surge in mergers and acquisitions and foreign direct investment since the mid-1980s, and this development may reflect that European companies concentrate on core competences as a strategic response to increased competition.

5.7 Market concentration

INDUSTRIAL restructuring may also have taken place at the meso-economic level due to a change in market concentration. Market concentration indicates the size of activities of the firms in the market, i.e. the size distribution of firms. The market concept is related both to specific goods and to geographical entity. Empirical studies of market concentration are often based on crude measures of concentration. The inverse of the number of firms is the most simple measure of market concentration as differences in firm size are totally disregarded. Concentration ratio of a given number of the largest firms is another very simple measure, for example concentration ratio 4 (CR4) measures the cumulated share of sales of the four largest firms in the market relative to total sales.

Empirical evidence

Empirical evidence of industrial concentration trends is presented in EU Commission (1996). Concentration is measured by calculating *concentration ratio 4* (CR4) on a 3-digit level of the NACE nomenclature of industries, i.e. the share of sales of the four largest firms in the market relative to total sales. Concentration in manufacturing is measured at the EU level and for four member states (Belgium, Germany, France, and the UK) for 1985 and 1992, and the results presented in Table 5.11.

At the EU level, industries have in general become increasingly concentrated in the examined period. This is contrary to concentration at the national level where, for three of the four countries, a small decrease in concentration has taken place. What would seem to be a paradox is explained by the increasing importance of multi-nationals. When calculating concentration ratios at the national level, subsidiaries are registered as independent firms, whereas in order to measure concentration at the EU level, the parent company and its subsidiaries are counted as only one unit. The strong increase in mergers and acquisitions since the mid-1980s (see Chapter 7) has therefore contributed to an increase in concentration at the EU level without necessarily affecting concentration at the member state level.

Concentration and competition

Industrial concentration, both at the EU and member state level, plays a role in the *mark-up* of unit costs to market prices. The Internal Market intensifies competition and pushes price–cost margins down as focus shifts from concentration at the

Table 5.11 Concentration in manufacturing at EU and member state level		
	Concentration ratio (CR4)	
	1985	1992
Belgium	54.5	52.8
Germany	34.0	35.9
France	34.4	34.3
UK	42.8	41.9
EU	20.5 [a]	22.8 [b]

[a] 1987.
[b] 1993.

Source: EU Commission (1996): 120 and 121.

national market to the EU. To some extent, the national markets are still segmented, as barriers to trade have not been completely removed, and concentration on the national market is thus still relevant. The external trade policy of the EU is also an important factor for the mark-up, as imports from third-party countries may reduce the price relative to unit costs.

The net effect of the Internal Market on the degree of competition in manufacturing has been assessed empirically in an *econometric model* by the EU Commission (1996) and London Economics (1996). The model is based on the traditional *structure–conduct–performance paradigm* in industrial economics (see e.g. Tirole (1988)) stressing the positive relation between concentration and price–cost margins. It is assessed that the price–cost margin in manufacturing in the EU without the Internal Market would have increased on average by 0.25 percentage points per year from 1980 to the end of the estimation period in 1992. However, the competitive pressure caused by the Internal Market at least temporarily suspended this long-run mark-up trend, as illustrated in Figure 5.5. The model predicts an Internal Market effect on average mark-up of −0.5 percentage points (15.5 per cent instead of 16.0 per cent). In spite of the significant increase in mergers and acquisitions, the manufacturing industry has suffered a loss of market power because of the Internal Market.

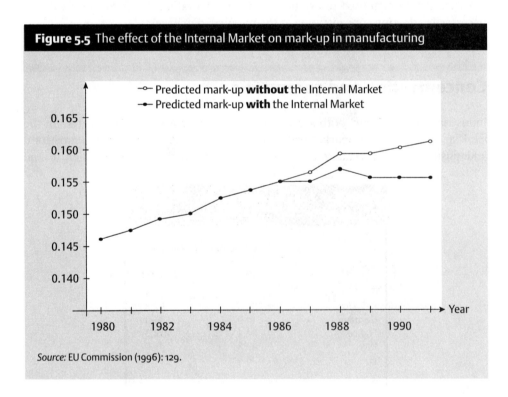

Figure 5.5 The effect of the Internal Market on mark-up in manufacturing

Source: EU Commission (1996): 129.

The competition policy of the EU

Whereas the Internal Market creates more competition in general, the aim of the EU competition policy is to prevent the misuse of market power of individual companies. The legal framework of the EU competition policy is given in the Amsterdam Treaty, especially in Articles 81 and 82. The main principle of these Articles is that collusive agreements between large companies, or misuse of market power by dominant companies on the Internal Market, is illegal when trade between member states will be affected. The EU competition policy is thus only related to cases of market misuse across borders between member states. Market misuse in individual countries, with no effect on other countries, is a matter of the competition policy at the national level. The Commission monitors competition on the various markets and takes action if the provisions appear to be violated. If so, the case may be brought to the European Court, and such cases make up a significant part of the activities of the Court. Although it is difficult to prove, the EU competition policy has probably disciplined European businesses significantly on markets dominated by a few firms.

5.8 State aid and tax harmonization

EUROPEAN business development also depends on the EU policies on state aid and taxation. State aid and member state differences on taxation may both cause distortions of trade and factor movements and so undermine the beneficial effects of the Internal Market on welfare. The concept of state aid includes all forms of preferential treatment received by individual firms or groups of firms from the public sector. This preferential treatment may be direct, e.g. in the form of subsidies consisting of direct payments from the public sector to e.g. companies producing a certain type of goods, or indirect, such as the public sector purchasing certain services with a home bias, hence distorting the usual market competition.

Within the EU cooperation, state aid is generally prohibited if it influences trade between the member states (Amsterdam Treaty, Article 87). This prohibition of state aid was introduced in the Treaty of Rome in 1957 and was therefore already in force when the customs union was established in the EU. There are, however, exceptions allowing state aid in certain cases, including a number of cases where it is desirable to further particular objectives, such as regional support with a view to furthering growth in poor regions. In such cases, the state aid supplements the structural funds supplied by the central EU budget to the poor regions (see Chapter 4). It is also possible to provide state aid to particular industries, typically shipbuilding and steel, where world market competition is particularly strong. Finally, firms in all industries may receive state aid for R&D projects, environmental and energy-saving projects, and as a measure to improve conditions for small and medium-sized enterprises (see Vanhalewyn (1999) for a more detailed description).

The above-mentioned exceptions from the rule prohibiting state aid by no means constitute a *carte blanche* for the member states to award state aid as they see fit. Their policies in this area are monitored by the Commission, which has the authority to intervene if it estimates that there is a case of abuse. The Commission has the possibility to enforce the rules by bringing the case to the European Court, and if its claim is sustained, the member state in violation of the rules can be fined.

The WTO also has rules limiting the possibilities of awarding state aid. Sanctions are, however, less extensive than under the aegis of the EU, as the WTO does not have the possibility to impose fines but only to impose countervailing duties on imports from countries attempting to create unfair competition through state aid (see e.g. Messerlin (1999) for a comparative analysis of the rules for state aid in the EU and the WTO).

Table 5.12 illustrates the volume of state aid in the member states in the years 1992–4, 1994–6, and 1996–8. Figures include all sectors of the economy with the exception of agriculture. As described in Section 5.3, the agricultural sector receives extensive support through the CAP, and for this reason, it is not included in Table 5.12.

In the years 1996–8, state aid constituted around 1.1 per cent of GDP for the non-agricultural sectors of the EU as a whole, which means that overall state aid for the non-agricultural sectors was almost of the same magnitude as the total EU budget. The share of state aid of GDP is relatively large in Germany, Italy, and Portugal. As far as Germany is concerned, the considerable state aid is to some extent related to the new 'länder' arising from reunification. Over time, state aid has decreased in most member countries, but on closer inspection, it appears that the so-called *ad hoc* state aid, given to individual firms experiencing difficulties, has increased, and this form of state aid is particularly worrying in view of the free competition inside the EU (Vanhalewyn (1999)).

Whereas state aid is subjected to common EU regulation, competence in the area of taxation has by and large been referred to the individual member states, with the proviso that customs and duties may not be used as a means of protectionism, e.g. by imposing higher duties on foreign goods than on similar, domestic goods. In order to avoid such effects, a set of minimum rates, to be imposed by the member states, have been established for a number of consumption goods (such as alcohol, tobacco, and mineral oils). Individual member states are also obliged to levy a minimum of 15 per cent value added tax (VAT) on general consumption, but in special areas, such as food, books, and newspapers, the member states are allowed to levy VAT at a lower rate.

Another problem related to the competence of the member states in the area of taxation arises in connection with the allocation of resources. It is obvious that differences in taxation levels can influence the allocation of so-called mobile sources of tax revenue within the EU, i.e. sources of tax revenue which can change location at no large cost or loss of utility. This is primarily financial capital, but real investment, and in the long run the locality of real capital, is also concerned, whereas labour, as described in Chapter 3, is by and large immobile due to cultural and linguistic barriers. Tax on capital gains provides an incentive to place capital in the member

Table 5.12 State aid in the EU, per cent of GDP

	Yearly average, per cent of GDP [a]		
	1992–4	1994–6	1996–8
Belgium	1.5	1.3	1.2
Denmark	0.9	1.0	0.9
Germany	2.3	2.0	1.5
Greece	1.3	1.4	1.2
Spain	1.1	1.1	1.0
France	1.2	1.1	1.1
Ireland	1.0	0.9	1.0
Italy	2.2	1.8	1.6
Luxembourg	2.1	1.0	0.5
The Netherlands	0.6	0.7	0.6
Austria	–	0.7	0.7
Portugal	0.8	1.4	1.6
Finland	–	0.5	0.5
Sweden	–	1.0	0.8
UK	0.3	0.5	0.5
EUR15	1.5	1.3	1.1

[a] 1992–4 in 1995 prices, 1994–6 and 1996–8 in 1997 prices.

Note: State aid to the agricultural sector has been omitted, and GDP figures have been adjusted correspondingly by substracting the value added for the agricultural sector.

Sources: EU Commission (2000): table 24. EU Commission (1998*b*): table 18.

country with the lowest level of taxation. It follows that this gives individual member countries an incentive to increase the tax base by lowering their corporate taxation compared to the other member countries. Without special regulations harmonizing tax rates, there will be a risk of tax competition between member states, and it is not surprising that corporate tax rates have fallen noticeably in almost all member countries in recent years (Eijffinger and D. Haan (2000)). The problem that this creates is not a distortion in the allocation between sectors, but a distortion in the allocation of capital in general, i.e. an overall distortion in competitiveness as a result of differences in the way in which member countries deal with corporate income. The price that the member states pay for their autonomy in this area is a relatively low revenue on corporate taxation, resulting either in lower public expenditure or harder taxation of other sources of tax revenue, such as labour income.

5.9 Concluding remarks

A wide range of industrial restructuring has taken place in the EU in the last two decades. The relative importance of the agricultural sector has declined significantly, although to some extent the CAP has delayed the migration of labour from that sector. Turning to developments in manufacturing, the industry has reacted to changes in business conditions by restructuring. Evidence seems to point to intra-industry and intra-firm specialization rather than inter-industry specialization.

It may be argued that the strategic response at firm level to a more competitive environment of an open economy is to improve the firm's core competence through deliberate efforts towards a more focused behaviour, where the firm chooses a narrow range of activities (see e.g. Skinner (1974a, b) and Caves (1989)). The success of such a strategy relies on quick market access, and mergers and acquisitions of firms with similar competences appear to be an attractive shortcut to realize this aim, as the firm gets access to a larger sales network on the international market. Through mergers and acquisitions with other firms operating in the same core activities, the firm may add to its tacit knowledge of core competence, improve its chances to capture market shares, and strengthen its market power by eliminating competitors.

This specialization has been induced by the Internal Market, the competition policy, and the disciplining rules for state aid, and has made firms operating in the EU more cost efficient. In the end, this will also benefit the European consumers, as keen competition in the Internal Market will ensure that at least part of the cost efficiency gains will be transferred into lower market prices.

Further reading

Methods and analysis of industrial economics in general are given in R. Stead, P. Curwen, and K. Lawler (1996), *Industrial Economics: Theory, Applications and Policy*, McGraw-Hill, New York. Industrial economics related to the EU is presented in D. Jacobson and B. Andréosso-O'Callaghan (1996), *Industrial Economics and Organization: A European Perspective*, McGraw-Hill, New York. A short survey of important contributors to the empirical literature on the effects of trade liberalization on competition is found in the EU Commission (1996), 'Economic Evaluation of the Internal Market', *European Economy, Reports and Studies*, 4. More specifically, A. Jacquemin and A. Sapir (1991), 'Competition and Imports in the European Market', ch. 5 in L. A. Winters and A. Venables (eds.), *European Integration: Trade and Industry*, Cambridge University Press, Cambridge, analyse the disciplinary role of intra- and extra-EU imports for mark-up, and find that only extra-EU imports seem to influence the mark-up significantly. An in-depth analysis of the industrial policy, including agriculture and the CAP, is given in J. Pelkmans (1997), *European Integration Methods and Analysis*, Longman, Harlow.

References

Buigues, P., F. Ilzkovitz, and J.-F. Lebrun (1990), 'The impact of the Internal Market by Industrial Sector: the Challenge for the Member States', in EU Commission, *European Economy Social Europe*, special edn.

Caves, R. E. (1989), 'International Differences in Industrial Organizations' in R. Schmalensee and R. D. Wilting (eds.), *Handbook of Industrial Organization*, ii, North-Holland, Amsterdam.

Davies, S., B., Lyons, *et al.* (1996), *Industrial Organization in the European Union Structure, Strategy and Competitive Mechanism*, Clarendon Press, Oxford.

EAG (1997), 'Economies of Scale', in European Commission, *The Single Market Review*, subseries V: vol. 4.

Eijffinger, C. W., and J. De Haan (2000), *European Monetary and Fiscal Policy*, OUP, Oxford.

Eurostat (1996), *National Accounts ESA, Detailed by Branch, 1970–1994*.

—— (1998), *Statistics in Focus, Agriculture, Forestry and Fisheries*, 6.

—— (1999), *National Accounts ESA, Detailed tables by branch, 1970–1997*.

—— (2000), *Eurostat årbog, Europa statistisk set, Tiårsoversigt, 1988–1998*.

EU Commission (1993), 'Social Europe Market services and European integration', *European Economy Reports and Studies*, 3.

—— (1995), *European Economy*, 59.

—— (1996), 'Economic Evaluation of the Internal Market', *European Economy Reports and Studies*, 4.

—— (1998a), *European Economy*, 66.

—— (1998b), *Sixth Survey on State Aid in the European Union in the Manufacturing and Certain Other Sectors*, COM (98) 417 final.

—— (1999), *European Economy*, 69

—— (2000), *Eighth Survey on State Aid in the European Union*, COM (2000) 205 final.

Krugman, P. (1991), *Geography and Trade*, MIT Press, Cambridge, Mass.

Leibenstein, H. (1966), 'Allocative efficiency vs. X-efficiency', *American Economic Review*, 56: 392–415.

London Economics (1996), *Single Market Review 1996: Competition Issues*, European Commission.

Messerlin, P. A. (1999), 'External aspects of State Aids', ch. 7, in EU Commission, *European Economy Reports and Studies*, 3.

OECD (1997a), *Economic Studies*, 28, 1997/1.

—— (1997b), *Science, Technology and Industry Scoreboard of Indicators 1997*.

—— (1999), *The OECD Stan Database for Industrial Analysis, 1978–1997*.

OECD (2000), *National Accounts of OECD Countries, Main Aggregates, i, 1988–1998*.

Pratten, C. (1988), 'A survey of the Economies of Scale' in *Studies on the Economics of Integration*, in European Commission, *Research on the 'costs of non-Europe': Basic findings*, ii, Office for Official Publications of the EC, Luxembourg.

Skinner, W. (1974*a*), 'The Focused Factory', *Harvard Business Review*, May–June: 113–21.

—— (1974*b*), 'The Decline, Fall and Renewal of Manufacturing Plants', *Industrial Engineering*, October: 32–8.

Sutton, J. (1991), *Sunk Costs and Market Structure: Price Competition, Advertising and the Evolution of Concentration*, MIT Press, Cambridge, Mass.

Tirole, J. (1988), *The Theory of Industrial Organization*, MIT Press, Cambridge, Mass.

Vanhalewyn, E. (1999), 'Trends and Patterns in State Aid', ch. 2, in EU Commission, *European Economy Reports and Studies*, 3.

Chapter 6
Trade: The Workhorse of Integration

Jan Guldager Jørgensen, Teit Lüthje, and Philipp J. H. Schröder

6.1 Introduction

IF there is one point on which economists will agree, it is that international trade is beneficial. According to economic theory, countries can increase their own economic welfare by trading with each other. Free trade creates an opportunity for each country to produce exactly those goods which they do best. This is the theory of *comparative advantage*. Through international trade, the division of labour and specialization which exists at the national level will be transferred to the international level. Whereas free trade therefore ought to be the rule, up to the present, economic history has recorded widespread use of tariffs and other protectionist measures.

The EU is — among other things — an arrangement to promote free trade in Europe. There are several other examples of groups of countries promoting free trade, such as the North American Free Trade Agreement (NAFTA) between Canada, the USA, and Mexico, or the Association of South East Asian Nations (ASEAN). At the global level, the creation of the General Agreement on Tariffs and Trade (GATT), later transformed into the World Trade Organization (WTO), has helped foster trade liberalization. However, the European Union is by all means the most comprehensive free-trade experiment since it embraces not only free trade in goods and services but also free mobility of capital and labour within its borders. It was the concept of free trade and the expected subsequent gains which were among the main motives behind the foundation of the European Union.

The overall objective of this chapter is to identify whether or not European integration has benefited the participating countries in terms of increased trade, increased specialization, and/or increased competitiveness. By now, intra-EU trade by far exceeds extra-EU trade in volume, but it should be borne in mind that this development is partly due to the steady growth in the number of members of the Union. By dividing overall trade into trade in services and trade in goods, the surprising observation is made that the share of trade in services of total trade is much smaller at the intra-EU level than at the extra-EU level. It follows that integration must have had the largest impact on trade in goods. Furthermore, the share of intra-industry trade — i.e. trade in similar products, such as wine traded between Italy and France — is on the rise, and it can therefore be concluded that the European development appears to be in line with the global development. However, looking at the level of specialization of individual member countries in certain export industries, it seems that, if anything, forty years of integration have resulted in less specialization. Finally, Europe's competitiveness has improved moderately in recent years and as a result, the EU trade balance (goods only) was upgraded during the mid-1990s.

This chapter will address themes of trade and economic integration as follows: Section 6.2 recapitulates some of the essential points of trade theory and also looks at developments in tariff levels resulting from trade liberalization. Section 6.3 will sketch the position of EU trade within the world economy. Section 6.4 highlights the developments in intra- versus extra-EU trade and examines the role of trade creation versus trade diversion with the aim of identifying which of the two have been dominating. Section 6.5 divides intra-EU trade into its various components and analyses whether or not integration in the EU has led to export specialization. This analysis will form the basis of a discussion of intra- versus inter-industry trade in Section 6.6, which establishes that intra-industry trade accounts for an ever increasing share of total EU trade. Finally, Section 6.7 analyses developments in European competitiveness and identifies and examines the EU's comparative advantages. Section 6.8 concludes the chapter.

6.2 Why free trade?

A**LTHOUGH** international trade is beneficial for those nations engaging in it, trade distortions such as tariffs, quotas, or technical barriers, which are harmful in an economic sense, often have been, and still are, widely used. Below, the main arguments in favour of free trade will be examined, followed by a look at the struggle between protectionism and trade liberalization — from a theoretical point of view as well as based on past European experience. But first a quick comment on what international trade actually is. When we speak of trade, we usually think of goods being shipped across borders. By now, there is much more to it than that. Also services, such as insurance and financial services, can be imported and exported, and even tourist holidays abroad fall into this category. Note that this chapter will deal with both goods and services. Note also that data may only be available for one or the other, or only as the sum of the two, so when examining tables and figures, the reader should check what the information at hand actually covers.

Gains from trade

Trade theory has identified two basic forces behind international trade: differences between countries, and economies of scale in production. In real life, it is not possible to distinguish sharply between these two factors, and the trade pattern of any specific country has to be explained by a mixture of the two. However, in order to understand the underlying theory, it is useful practice to analyse the motives separately.

Neoclassical trade theory bases its explanation of trade patterns on the differences between countries and on the assumption of perfect competition. It was David Ricardo who introduced the fundamental concept of neoclassical trade theory: *comparative advantage* in the production of certain goods. The word 'comparative' indicates that the cost advantage of producing one type of goods is measured relative to the cost of producing other types of goods, i.e. focus is on opportunity costs. Ricardo demonstrated that although a country does not have an absolute advantage in the production of any goods vis-à-vis another country, gains can still be made from international trade. What matters is that a country will specialize in the production of goods in the field in which it holds a comparative advantage, i.e. where the country's opportunity costs of producing the goods are lower than the opportunity costs of its trading partners. This specialization means that the countries involved will gain from the trade, as each country will now concentrate on producing the goods that they produce relatively best, i.e. where they can generate most output per input in relative terms. Consequently, trade will increase the consumption possibilities of consumers in all countries concerned.

The most influential neoclassical trade theory model expanding on Ricardo's point is the *Heckscher-Ohlin theory*, also known as the factor-proportions model of international trade. According to this theory, the differences between countries, and hence the source of international trade, lie in their different endowments of inputs. The comparative advantage of a country is determined by the endowment of resources and the technology of production. In other words, a country has a comparative advantage in producing the type of goods which relies most intensively on the locally abundant factors of production. Consequently, countries with a relative abundance of labour should produce and export more traditional, labour-intensive goods, whereas countries with a relative abundance of capital should produce and export more advanced, capital-intensive goods. This will result in *inter-industry* trade, i.e. one-flow trade consisting of either export or import within one product category only. An example of inter-industry trade could be Sweden exporting mobile phones to Portugal in exchange for shoes. The trade pattern is thus determined by the comparative advantages of the two countries, and both countries will experience overall gains from trade. However, it is crucial to mention that the effects on the respective incomes of the owners of the factors of production will be diametrically opposite.

Owners of the abundant factors of production gain from trade, whereas owners of the scarce factors of production lose as factor prices change. Inter-industry trade therefore changes the distribution of income between different socio-economic groups within a country.

According to *new trade theory*, on the other hand, trade can take place even if the endowments of inputs of countries are completely identical. In other words, this branch of theory does not build on the concept of comparative advantage. Instead, new trade theory takes imperfect competition into account and assumes that the driving forces behind international trade are *product differentiation* and *increasing returns to scale*. Product differentiation arises because consumers display preferences for alternative product varieties, which means that consumers will be better off when the selection of differentiated products increases. This is motivated by the desire of the individual consumer to partly have consumption variety and partly to acquire the particular product which comes closest to matching their desired product characteristics. Because of increasing returns to scale, countries will specialize in the production of a limited range of goods, and as international trade creates a market which is larger than the markets of the individual countries, it is possible to exploit economies of scale to a larger degree. Trade will now consist of importing those product varieties that are not produced domestically, and exporting those that are. This gives rise to *intra-industry trade*, i.e. two-way trade within the same product category. A typical example is the trade in cars between France and Germany. Note that in contrast to inter-industry trade, there are no changes in the distribution of income between the owners of the factors of production in a situation with intra-industry trade. Intra- versus inter-industry trade in general, and the European performance in particular, will be examined in Section 6.6.

Overall, it can be concluded that trade theory makes a strong case for international trade, but there are certain distributive consequences at the national level which may give rise to opposition. These will be examined in more detail below.

Cause and effect of protectionism

Even though free trade is beneficial for the nations engaging in it, economic history shows that, to the present, protectionism has been the rule rather than the exception. One of the main reasons for the emergence of protectionism can be found in the distributive consequences of trade. The national policy process makes it possible for various groups or industries, which may be hurt by certain imports, to lobby for the introduction of a protective tariff, even if, from a macroeconomic perspective, their country would benefit from such imports. There are other motives for protectionism. Firstly, traditional trade theory neglects dynamic considerations. Where the production activities include an element of learning by doing, a country may obtain a comparative advantage in producing a certain product if the specific industry is protected from foreign competition in the early stages. This is the *infant industry* argument. Secondly, moderate protectionism, where imports are limited but not disallowed, may improve the importing country's terms of trade—but only if the importing country is large, as a large country can influence the prices of the goods it imports via its demand. Thirdly, protectionism may be introduced as an attempt to solve long-term structural problems using short-term measures, e.g. in order to save jobs and avoid unemployment, or in order to curb a galloping trade deficit.

How do different trade barriers work, and what are the expected effects of removing them? Let us analyse the effect of imposing a tariff—the oldest form of trade policy instrument—at the theoretical level. A *tariff* is a tax levied when goods are imported into a country, and it will thus increase the price of the imported goods by a certain amount. There will be both costs and benefits connected to the increase in the price of the goods, both for the country imposing the tariff and for the different socio-economic groups in that country. First of all, consumers will demand less of the imported goods as they now have to pay a higher price. This will lead to a loss of consumer surplus. Domestic producers, on the other hand, will gain, as they will sell more at a higher price, because the price of the foreign goods is increased by the tariff. The government will also gain by collecting the revenue, which amounts to the tariff rate times the imported quantity. Typically, however, there will be an overall efficiency loss, because the higher price will distort the incentives of the consumers and producers leading to the so-called deadweight loss, or distortion loss, of a tariff.

Numerous other trade policy instruments exist. Examples of other *visible trade barriers* are export subsidies, which are payments to firms selling goods and services abroad, and import quotas, which are quantitative restrictions on the import of certain goods. The net welfare impact of such measures can be derived in a similar fashion as for tariffs. More subtle and less visible trade barriers are voluntary export restraints, in which the foreign producer limits the quantity supplied on a voluntary basis in order to avoid a possible future tariff. However, *invisible trade barriers* can also be found. One of the more obvious is the inclination of public authorities to prefer domestically produced goods and choosing domestic suppliers for public construction works, such as the building of bridges, highways, etc. Other invisible trade barriers or trade distortions are production subsidies to domestic producers, or technical regulations such as certification systems and safety standards. Although the primary policy goal of such technical barriers might concern e.g. public health and safety, and as such be unrelated to trade policy, they still have a clear impact on trade. Finally, there is a whole area of reactive trade policy measures, such as countervailing or anti-dumping duties, where a country imposes a tariff in reaction to an alleged producer subsidy abroad or a suspicion of dumping. As the imposing country receives no tariff revenue from most non-tariff-type trade policies, the welfare balance is obviously even less favourable. In addition, it is much harder to quantify non-tariff barriers or invisible barriers, and hence the picture of the true level of protectionism is blurred.

Trade liberalization, i.e. the removal of protectionist measures, can be regional or global depending on whether it is restricted to a group of countries or worldwide. Regional liberalization is thus discriminatory in the sense that some countries are not included in the trade agreement. Another dimension of trade liberalization is the scope of the cooperation. Looking at regional liberalization, the most simple form would be to establish a *free trade area* between a number of countries. The countries joining the free trade area abolish all visible trade barriers between them, but each member country has the exclusive right to decide what trade barriers it will impose on countries outside the free trade area. The next step would be to create a *customs union*. A customs union is a free trade area with a common external tariff, i.e. all member countries impose the same tariffs on countries outside the customs union. If, in addition to the requirements of the customs union, the group of countries also abolishes all invisible trade barriers internally, they will develop a *single market* for commodities. Finally, if restrictions on the mobility of factors of production are eliminated, a *common market* is established. Hence, a common market secures the free movement between member states of both labour and capital (such as foreign direct investment, e.g. the establishment of businesses, and financial investment).

The drive for free trade has had top priority also at the global level, yet in terms of effect, quite naturally, global trade liberalization has by no means been as far-reaching as in the intra-EU context. After a frustrated attempt of establishing an international trade organization after the Second World War, global trade liberalization was initiated through a system of tariffs agreements between nation states. This system was the General Agreement on Tariffs and Trade (GATT) initiated by twenty-three industrialized nations in 1948 and focusing solely on industrial products. In 1995, the agreement was converted into the World Trade Organization (WTO), counting more than 130 countries as members. The WTO still bears the features of an agreement rather than an organization, which implies that decision-making is based on the willingness of the participating countries to implement and enforce the WTO decisions. Hence, consensus politics rule. Still, despite this disadvantage, the WTO has initiated several major breakthroughs in liberalization, most recently addressing areas like tariffs on agricultural products, liberalization of trade in services, and, even more importantly, promoting widespread *tariffication*. Tariffication is a process whereby non-tariff barriers, such as quotas, are converted into tariff equivalents, i.e. the quota is abolished and replaced by a tariff. This process makes the true level of protectionism more transparent and creates a solid base for further negotiations.

Europe's removal of trade barriers

Turning to the case of the EU, the question is how far European trade liberalization has actually progressed? In principle, this issue should be examined both at member state level and vis-à-vis the rest of the world, but the history of trade liberalization in the framework of the EU has basically already been outlined by the history of integration in Chapter 1 and will therefore only be briefly touched upon here. With the creation of the EEC in 1958, the member countries began to gradually remove all internal customs duties, and by 1968, this process had been completed and the EEC had become a fully-fledged customs union with the revenue of the common external tariffs flowing into the community budget. Provisions for the free mobility of not only labour and capital but also goods and services had been included already in the first treaties, so in principle, there were no restrictions on trade. Nevertheless, a substantial number of non-tariff barriers remained, and the practice of implementing different standards and requirements—such as purity laws for beer sold in Germany or packaging requirements for margarine sold in Belgium—was as harmful to free trade as any tariff. Even worse, it was more difficult to identify such protectionist measures than tariffs. The aim of the Single European Act of 1986 was therefore precisely to tackle such non-tariff barriers, and its subsequent implementation further accelerated the free trade idea of the internal market. By the mid-1990s, when a subset of members implemented the Schengen Agreement on the abolition of border controls, the Single Market had become a reality. The conclusion is that the EU today is the most extensive economic cooperation project among sovereign nation states.

In addition, the EU has trade agreements with different groupings of countries. The most liberal access is granted to the former members of EFTA (European Free Trade Agreement). EFTA was established in 1959 by Austria, Denmark, Norway, Portugal, Sweden, Switzerland, and the UK, and later also Finland and Iceland joined. The EU and EFTA entered a free trade agreement covering all industrial goods originating in the member countries in 1984. From 1993, the free trade cooperation between the remaining EFTA countries, excluding Switzerland, was strengthened by the establishment of the *European Economic Area* (EEA) which included full access to the markets of the member countries for most goods except agricultural and fish products. As yet, the Central and East European countries have not obtained full free trade status, but they have embarked on a gradual liberalization of trade with the EU. Other agreements include various developing countries which are parties to the Lomé Convention which gives almost unlimited access to the EU. Trade liberalization in the EU therefore extends beyond the Single Market of the fifteen EU members.

Turning to the external tariff level of the EU, the development is examined and contrasted to the tariff levels of other major economies below. Table 6.1 illustrates external tariff levels in percentages. It measures effective tariff levels as approximations of production-weighted averages and is thus based on the composition of production of the importing countries. This measure is applied in order to avoid a notorious problem which arises when the effective tariff level is estimated based on actual trade flows, namely that the quantities demanded react to the tariff level. For example, if a country imposes a prohibitively high tariff on a product, then the product will not be imported at all, and as a result, the effective tariff level—weighted by actual flows—will be zero. Using production-weighted tariff levels resolves this problem. The table shows that, by this measure, the EU has been the most protectionist of the three economies in recent years. For all three economies, the average tariff on food products is above the aggregate average for all products (including food products), but the EU clearly imposes the highest tariff on food products and hence takes a rather protectionist stance on this industry. In order to put the observations in Table 6.1 into perspective, it is important to realize that the average US tariff rate after the Second World War was around 20 per cent and falling rapidly as the GATT efforts progressed during the 1950s (Krugman and Obstfeld (2000, 234)). What is surprising about Table 6.1 is that the average tariff appears to have been rising in recent years at the same time as efforts at liberalization have increased. This is due to the tariffication, which has been promoted in the latest WTO (GATT) rounds, which

Table 6.1 Average external tariff levels[a] of major economies, per cent

	Food, beverages and tobacco			For all products		
	1988	1993	1996	1988	1993	1996
USA	7.6[b]	8.2	15.9	4.4[b]	4.7	5.2
Japan	15.6	17.5	18.9	4.2	3.6	3.4
EUR15	27.4	27.1	32.5	8.2	8.4	7.7

[a] Average tariff levels are estimated by using production weights based on the composition of value added of the destination countries.
[b] 1989 value.
Sources: OECD (1996): tables 1 and 2. OECD (1999): table 7.1.

means that quantitative restrictions are turned into tariff equivalents. This also explains the sudden rise in tariffs on food products in the USA.

Obviously, it is hard to monitor the removal of less visible trade barriers. And it is even more problematic to assess their actual impact on trade. For example, the mere threat of carrying out an anti-dumping investigation may induce the foreign producer to raise prices, even if the investigation never materializes. As a matter of fact, the 1990s saw a rise in the number of anti-dumping actions initiated by the EU from 81 actions in 1993 to 117 in 1998, whereas the OECD countries in total cut the number of actions from 536 in 1993 to 314 in 1998 (OECD (1999, table 7.3)). These numbers suggest a relative increase in European trade protection. Anti-dumping actions are usually concentrated on products such as base metals, plastics, chemicals, machinery, and electrical equipment, and are typically directed at the 'Asian Tigers'.

Apart from these measures of trade liberalization and protectionism, it should also be realized that the EU, as a whole, is an active member of the WTO and as such has an important role to play in global trade liberalization. Institutionally, the EU has one seat in the WTO. Each of the fifteen EU members still have their national seats in the WTO, but in actual negotiations, the fifteen members are in fact represented by the EU. However, having only one seat at the negotiation table does not mean that the EU has lessened its influence. On the contrary, the total weight carried by the EU in negotiations might well be larger that the sum of its parts. Overall, negotiating trade policy vis-à-vis third-party countries is clearly the one area where the supranational role of the EU is most pronounced.

Even though the EU is generally perceived to be in favour of free trade, the latest WTO negotiation rounds, and in particular the issue of free trade in agricultural products, has painted a mixed picture of the EU's stance. Recent cases include the European ban on hormone-fed beef and genetically modified organisms. Both issues are motivated by public health considerations, but might also be conceived as technical barriers to trade.

Having reviewed the basic motives and effects of international trade and protectionism, let us now turn to the actual trade flows and patterns observed. The next section will open by examining the role of the EU in world trade and then make a comparison with the USA and Japan.

6.3 EU trade in a global perspective

IN 1980, total exports of goods of the EUR15 — i.e. intra- as well as extra-EU exports — amounted to more than 519bn. ecu, or 39.4 per cent of total world exports (including intra-EU exports). In 1998, total exports of the EUR15 had risen to more than 1.966bn. ecu, which made up a world share of 39.7 per cent (see Eurostat (1999, tables 1A and 5B)). For comparison, the same source states that the share of world exports of the USA and Japan in 1998 totalled 12.3 and 7.1 per cent, respectively. The export share of the EU remained constant in the period, and the EU was the largest exporter in the world both in 1980 and in 1998. However, one should be careful making such a comparison. The EU figures include both intra- and extra-EU exports, whereas the figures for e.g. the USA do not include trade between the different states of the USA. The EU figures are therefore, in a way, overestimated. The solution to this problem is to look at extra-EU trade only. The share of total world exports for the EU, the USA, and Japan is shown in Table 6.2.

Within the Triad, the EU had the largest share of world exports in the period examined, whereas Japan had the lowest. In other words, the EU is still the largest exporter in the world when measured, more correctly, in extra-EU exports only. However, whereas the shares of world exports of the EU and the USA decreased in the period, the share of Japan increased and in fact more than doubled from 1960 to 1998.

Table 6.2 shows the development in the EU share of world exports for EUR15, i.e. the current fifteen member states. A more correct measure should take into account the fact that the number of member countries has increased from six to fifteen over the past forty years. How does such a widening of the EU alter the statistics for the EU share of total world trade? Assuming that all actual trade flows stay constant,

Table 6.2 Share of world exports[a], per cent					
	1960	1970	1980	1990	1998
EUR15[b]	29.2	25.6	21.4	20.9	19.6
USA	24.4	20.4	15.6	16.5	16.3
Japan	4.6	9.0	9.2	12.1	9.5

[a] Total world exports excluding intra-EUR15 exports.
[b] Extra-EUR15 exports only.
Source: Eurostat (1999): table 1A.

two effects on the share of the EU (as a trade block) of total world trade can be identified. Firstly, trade between new and existing EU members will be reclassified from extra- to intra-EU trade. This will reduce extra-EU trade and total world trade by the same amount, i.e. the EU share of total world trade will fall. Secondly, trade of new members with non-EU countries will now be included in the total EU share, and this will increase the EU share of total world trade. For countries which have strong trade links with the EU, the first effect will dominate. Since potential members usually have strong trade links with the EU, there will be an inbuilt bias for a reduced share of the EU in world trade, i.e. extra-EU trade will fall with each enlargement.

Looking at a different aspect of the EU's role in total world trade, let us now consider the importance of this trade for the EU economy as a whole, i.e. how large a share of GDP stems from international trade. To do this, it is useful to consider the degree of openness. *Openness* can be expressed as the sum of imports and exports divided by two times GDP. For the countries in the Triad, the degree of openness with respect to trade in goods and services, measured as an average for the years 1986–96, is: EUR15 (extra-EU trade only) 10.0 per cent, the USA 11.1 per cent, and Japan 9.1 per cent (EU Commission (1997, table 2, 25)). To offer a comparison of these large economies with a small one, the degree of openness for Belgium in 1996 was as high as 69.3 per cent (EU Commission (1999, Annexe: tables 36 and 40)). This is fully in line with the preconception that smaller economies are more open to trade.

Figure 6.1 illustrates the development in openness of EUR15 in more detail, from the strict perspective of trade in goods, revealing a small overall increase in EU foreign trade in goods measured as a percentage of GDP. The years of the oil crises, 1973 and 1979, show a sharp increase in the share of imports of GDP and a worsening of the trade balance brought about by the relatively inelastic demand for oil which caused a rise in the expenditure on imports due to the rise in oil prices. Almost the entire period features a trade deficit (goods only) for the EU as a whole, and the EU trade balance only becomes positive during the mid-1990s.

If the figures for trade in services and unilateral transfers, such as international aid and net interest payments, are added to the above figures, we arrive at the current account. Net interest payments (which are in fact earnings from a European perspective) have counterbalanced the European trade deficit in particular, with the result that the current account has been hovering around zero for the past forty years. The background to this is that, today, the majority of European countries act as lenders to the developing countries. Having experienced deficits on the balance of goods and services and increased foreign debts as a consequence of the rapid industrial development in the 1960s, the European countries became more competitive as the capital stock was expanded. This development led to an improvement of the balance of goods and services and thus a reduction in the debt. At the end of the 1990s, the accumulated surplus on the balance of goods and services had changed the foreign debt into outstanding claims enabling the net interest payments to finance the current deficit on the trade balance.

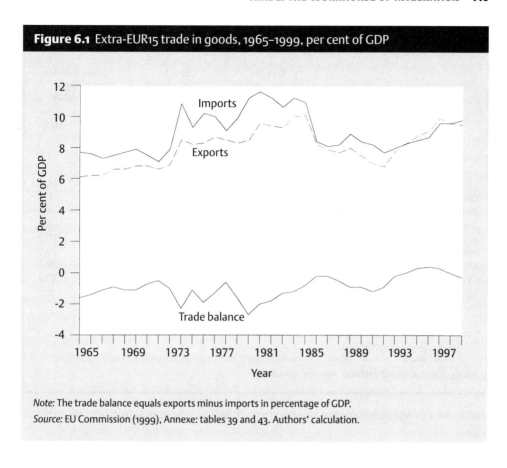

Figure 6.1 Extra-EUR15 trade in goods, 1965–1999, per cent of GDP

Note: The trade balance equals exports minus imports in percentage of GDP.
Source: EU Commission (1999), Annexe: tables 39 and 43. Authors' calculation.

The geographical trade pattern

Although the EU covers a large part of Europe, the rest of Europe remains its most important market. (Table 6.3 illustrates the geographic distribution of extra-EU exports and imports.) In 1998, this market thus absorbed a little more than 32 per cent of total EUR15 exports. Several factors are at work. Firstly, as many of those European countries which are not members of the EU are members of EFTA, they form a free trade area with the EU which—according to theory—should stimulate trade. Secondly, most of the Central and Eastern European countries enjoy so-called association status, which grants them priority in the trade with the EU. Thirdly, the Central and Eastern European countries are in the process of restructuring, and they import a large part of their new capital stock from the EU (these last two issues will be dealt with in more detail in Chapter 9). Last, but not least, proximity, and hence reduced transport costs, is a decisive factor for the observed volume of trade between the EU and other European non-EU countries. Another important market for the EU is the USA which purchased almost 22 per cent of total EUR15 exports in 1998. This market is partly characterized by a high degree of purchasing power,

Table 6.3 Geographical structure of EUR15 trade in goods, per cent

	Exports (per cent of total exports)		Imports (per cent of total imports)		Trade balance (per cent of total trade)[a]	
	1980	1998	1980	1998	1980	1998
USA	12.9	21.9	17.3	21.3	−24.4	3.0
Japan	2.3	4.3	5.2	9.2	−47.3	−35.2
Central and Eastern European countries	6.9	13.5	4.5	10.1	10.8	15.7
Other European countries	22.1	18.8	17.1	17.1	2.4	6.3
Africa	18.5	8.0	16.5	7.4	−4.4	4.9
North America excl. USA	2.6	2.1	4.2	1.8	−34.5	8.1
South and Central America	7.8	7.5	7.6	5.5	−9.4	16.7
Middle East[b]	12.7	6.8	21.9	3.7	−36.0	30.0
Other Asian countries excl. Japan	7.8	13.9	8.5	21.8	−14.5	−20.7
Oceania	2.1	2.2	1.7	1.5	0.2	20.1
Total[c]	95.7	99.0	104.5	99.4	−	−

[a] Total trade equals imports + exports of each region.
[b] Including Near and Middle East.
[c] The total should in principle be 100 and the deviation is due to notorious problems with trade data.

Source: Eurostat (1999): table 2B. Authors' calculation.

partly by a pronounced degree of economic stability, which is significant in terms of sales.

The share of Asia, including Japan, of total extra-EU exports has increased from 10.1 per cent in 1980 to a total of 18.2 per cent in 1998, and consequently, Asia forms an increasingly important market for the products of the EU. This is partly due to an increase in the importance of the Japanese market, but particularly due to an increase in the importance of the markets of the 'Other Asian countries'. This category includes all the so-called 'Asian Tigers' which absorb an increasing share of extra-EU exports. A similar development is observed for the Central and Eastern European countries, albeit for very different reasons. The share of imports from the EU of these countries has almost doubled from 1980 to 1998. The development trend has been the opposite for Africa and the Middle East as these two groups of countries consume a continuously smaller share of total EU exports. In 1980, exports to Africa and the Middle East amounted to more than 31 per cent of total EU exports, while this share had been reduced by more than half in 1998. Finally, also the share of EU exports to North America, excluding the USA, and South and Central America has been decreasing, although the development has been less clear and pronounced than in the case of Africa and the Middle East. However, it should be borne in mind that a falling share might well be associated with an absolute increase as the overall EU trade volume with the rest of the world has been increasing over the time period observed.

As it appears from Table 6.3, also in terms of imports the remaining European countries outside the EU form the most important market for the EUR15. From making up almost 22 per cent in 1980, the share increased to more than 27 per cent in 1998. Similarly, the importance of the USA as an exporter of goods to the EU is quite large. Most pronounced is the growth in the share of imports from the Asian countries, as this share more than doubled from almost 14 per cent in 1980 to 31 per cent in 1998. This pattern fits nicely with the economic boom experienced in the Asian region in that period.

Turning to the trade balance figures presented in Table 6.3, note that these figures are expressed in per cent of total trade of each region. Minus 47.3 per cent for Japan in 1980 does therefore not contribute a lot to the overall European deficit for that period, as Japan only accounted for around 4 per cent of total trade. The most significant change can be observed in the trade balance with the Middle East. While this region accounted for much of the European fuel imports in 1980, by 1998, Europe had refocused on other suppliers and own production of energy. Finally, note the significant and growing trade surplus with the Central and Eastern European countries indicating an increase in demand for products from the EU. As mentioned before, much of this demand is associated with the import of capital goods needed for the transformation and build-up of the Central and Eastern European economies.

6.4 Trade creation vs. trade diversion

So far, only the development in extra-EU trade, i.e. trade between the EU and the rest of the world, has been considered. But how does extra-EU trade development relate to intra-EU trade development, and does an increase in one decrease the other? The creation of a customs union implies that the internal customs barriers between individual countries are abolished and replaced by a common external customs tariff towards third-party countries. But does this constitute a move towards more free trade? Viner (1950) analysed the economic effects of forming a customs union and demonstrated that international trade may be affected both positively and negatively. The abolishment of internal customs barriers may give rise to a *trade creation* effect. High-cost domestic production may be replaced by low-cost production from another member state of the customs union through trade. However, there could also be a *trade diversion* effect. This effect is due to the discrimination against third-party countries through the common external tariff. If the common external tariff leads to a change in trade patterns so that low-cost production from third-party countries is replaced by higher-cost production from another member of the customs union, it is a case of trade diversion. Thus, the trade diversion effect has a welfare-reducing impact for the members of the customs union. Furthermore, third-party countries will usually expect that the trade creation and trade diversion effects will reduce their export opportunities to the member countries of the customs union.

What, then, has happened in the case of Europe in terms of trade creation and

Figure 6.2 Intra- and extra-EUR15 trade in goods, 1965–1999, per cent

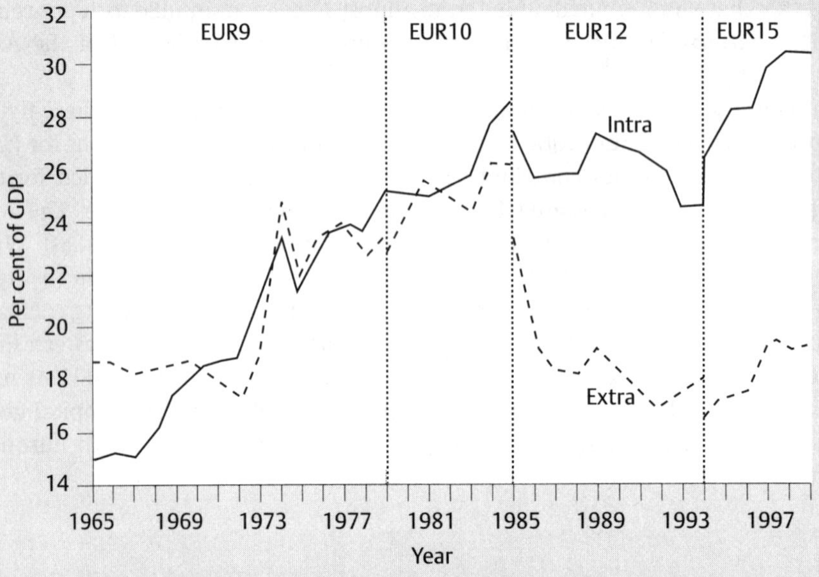

Note: Trade = exports + imports. EUR9 from 1965 to 1979, EUR10 from 1979 to 1985, EUR12 from 1985 to 1994, EUR15 from 1994 to 1999.

Sources: EU Commission (1980), Annexe: tables 23, 24, 27, and 28. EU Commission (1986), Annexe: tables 28, 29, 32, and 33. EU Commission (1994), Annexe: tables 40, 41, 44, and 45. EU Commission (1999), Annexe: tables 38, 39, 42, and 43. Authors' calculation.

trade diversion? Figure 6.2 helps to throw some light on this question by illustrating the development in intra- and extra-EU trade as a share of GDP.

Figure 6.2 shows that although extra-EU trade has been on the rise, it has been outpaced by the growth in intra-EU trade. First and foremost, the effect discussed in Section 6.3 can be identified, namely that an expansion of the Union from six to fifteen members inherently implies a reduction in extra-EU trade. This effect can be seen from the discontinuities at the vertical lines in Figure 6.2. Furthermore, and more importantly, in the first sub-period, the intra-EU line has a steeper slope than the extra-EU line, i.e. the intra-EU trade growth rate is higher than the extra-EU trade growth rate. This is an indication of the trade creation and trade diversion effects being at work. For the period after 1980, the picture is not as clear. Although the continuous enlargement of the EU has further increased intra-EU trade, a trade diversion effect cannot be observed in that period, as the growth pattern of both curves appears to be largely identical. However, what is special about the development in recent years is the creation and implementation of the Single Market programme.

This extra dimension can be included in our analysis by examining the crucial period from the mid-1980s to the early 1990s in more detail. This will be done by looking at the effect of the gradual implementation of the Single Market programme. Table 6.4 below shows shares in apparent consumption, which indicates the composition of national demand stemming from three different sources: domestic production, imports from other EU member countries, and imports from countries outside the EU. The figures have been obtained by grouping forty different industrial sectors in accordance with the extent of non-tariff barriers in each sector.

Looking at the totals, Table 6.4 mirrors the results of Figure 6.2, namely that both intra- and extra-EU imports have been increasing at the expense of domestic supply. Hence, in the implementation period of the Single Market programme, at an aggregate level, no trade diversion can be identified. In fact, this indicates that the removal of domestic non-tariff barriers does not discriminate between EU and non-EU producers.

Turning to the grouping into low, medium, and high levels of non-tariff barriers, Sapir (1996, 465–6) concludes that the industries with the lowest level of non-tariff barriers display least adjustment in supply shares. In fact, this proves that the Internal Market has the expected effect and opens the national economies to foreign producers in those areas which have previously been protected by non-tariff barriers.

Table 6.4 Apparent consumption by intensity of non-tariff barriers, EUR12

Intensity of barriers[a]	1986	1987	1988	1989	1990	1991	1992
Share of domestic production							
Total	67.4	67.0	65.4	64.0	64.3	63.1	62.3
Low	70.6	70.3	69.6	68.9	68.3	67.4	66.5
Medium	57.7	57.2	55.5	53.5	53.9	51.1	50.4
High	79.6	79.0	78.8	77.5	77.3	75.3	74.1
Share of intra-EU imports							
Total	19.7	20.2	20.6	21.6	21.8	22.4	23.0
Low	16.4	16.6	16.6	17.0	17.7	18.1	18.6
Medium	27.0	27.1	27.5	28.8	28.7	29.6	30.1
High	12.2	12.8	12.6	13.5	13.9	14.9	16.0
Share of extra-EU imports							
Total	12.9	12.8	14.0	14.3	13.9	14.6	14.7
Low	12.9	13.1	13.8	14.0	14.0	14.6	14.9
Medium	15.3	15.7	17.1	17.8	17.4	19.3	19.6
High	8.2	8.2	8.5	8.9	8.8	9.8	9.9

[a] Sapir (1996) applies a definition of intensity of non-tariff barriers taken from P. Buigues *et al.* (1990): *The Impact of the Internal Market by Industry Sector* (Special Issue of European Economy, Commission of the European Communities, Brussels). The measure includes trade barriers such as differences in standards, administrative and technical controls, limited access to public procurement, and differences in VAT and excise duties.

Note: The table shows the share of apparent consumption for manufacturing in percentage.

Source: Sapir (1996): table 1, 465.

6.5 Trade patterns within the Union

Now let us look at trade between the members of the European Union. What is it that the Europeans are trading with each other? Section 6.4 demonstrated that intra-EU trade is much larger than extra-EU trade. While extra-EU trade measured by exports amounted to a total of 730bn. ecu in 1998, intra-EU exports that same year amounted to 1.237bn. ecu (Eurostat (1999, tables 1A and 5B)), or the equivalent of the total GDP of Belgium, Denmark, the Netherlands, Austria, Finland, and Sweden together. In the following, we will first look at developments in size and then identify what kind of products are traded within the Union. Finally, we will examine whether an increased degree of specialization in intra-EU exports can be measured, i.e. if integration has fostered specialization among the member states.

Figure 6.3 shows two different measures of intra-EU exports. As all exports are also

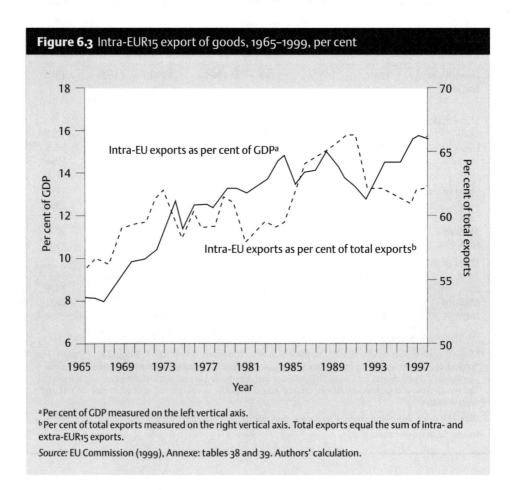

Figure 6.3 Intra-EUR15 export of goods, 1965–1999, per cent

[a] Per cent of GDP measured on the left vertical axis.
[b] Per cent of total exports measured on the right vertical axis. Total exports equal the sum of intra- and extra-EUR15 exports.

Source: EU Commission (1999), Annexe: tables 38 and 39. Authors' calculation.

imports in 'intra' terms, it is only necessary to examine one of the two flows. There is a steady increase in intra-EU exports, both as a share of GDP and as a share of total exports. The fact that intra-EUR15 exports increase more than extra-EUR15 exports is an indication of trade creation and trade diversion effects being at work. This means that the data depicted for EUR15 in Figure 6.3 make the conclusions of Section 6.4 even more clear-cut. Obviously, not all fifteen countries have been members of the EU for the entire period, but many of them have been members of EFTA. This indicates that the increase is caused not only by actual EU membership but also by EFTA membership in the first part of the period and, not least, by geographical proximity.

As it appears from Figure 6.3, 1993 was a significant year as trade between the member countries fell drastically. There is, however, a simple explanation for this. Historically, the basis of the trade statistics has been reports on trade flows prepared by local authorities, but from 1 January 1993, the customs procedures were abolished within the Internal Market. At the same time, importing and exporting firms were required to report trade with other EU countries to the national authorities. Consequently, whereas trade statistics on intra-EU trade still can be generated, the quality of the data has deteriorated. The sharp drop in 1993 therefore indicates that a certain proportion of export activities do not get documented.

Eurostat statistics on intra-EU trade by country quite naturally show that the largest EU country is also the largest exporter. The largest intra-EU exporter in 1998 was Germany, with exports to the other member countries totalling 22 per cent of total intra-EUR15 exports, followed by France and the Netherlands with a share of more than 14 per cent and almost 12 per cent, respectively. The last three major intra-EU exporters were the UK, Italy, and Belgium/Luxembourg, all accounting for an export share of around 10 per cent (cf. Eurostat (1999, table 5B)). This means that, relatively speaking, the smaller countries, like the Netherlands and Belgium/Luxembourg, are in fact most active in terms of intra-EU exports.

The composition of trade by products

Which products are the European nations trading with each other? First of all, there is the distinction between goods and services. Examples of goods are textiles, foodstuffs, or fuel, while services cover items such as insurance or transport of goods. Figure 6.4 illustrates the development in total trade (exports plus imports) in services. Developments in the extra-EU service trade is included as a benchmark.

Figure 6.4 shows a moderate growth in trade in services over the twenty-year-period. Much of this trend can be ascribed to the growth in the number and kind of service products available. Financial services in particular have experienced cross-border growth as the availability of modern means of communication has increased and regulations have been eased. A surprising result is that the level of trade in services of extra-EU trade is significantly higher than the level of intra-EU trade. The explanation can be found by looking into the background statistics. The main difference between intra- and extra-EU trade in services is found in the category

Figure 6.4 Share of services of intra- and extra-EU trade, 1979–1998, per cent

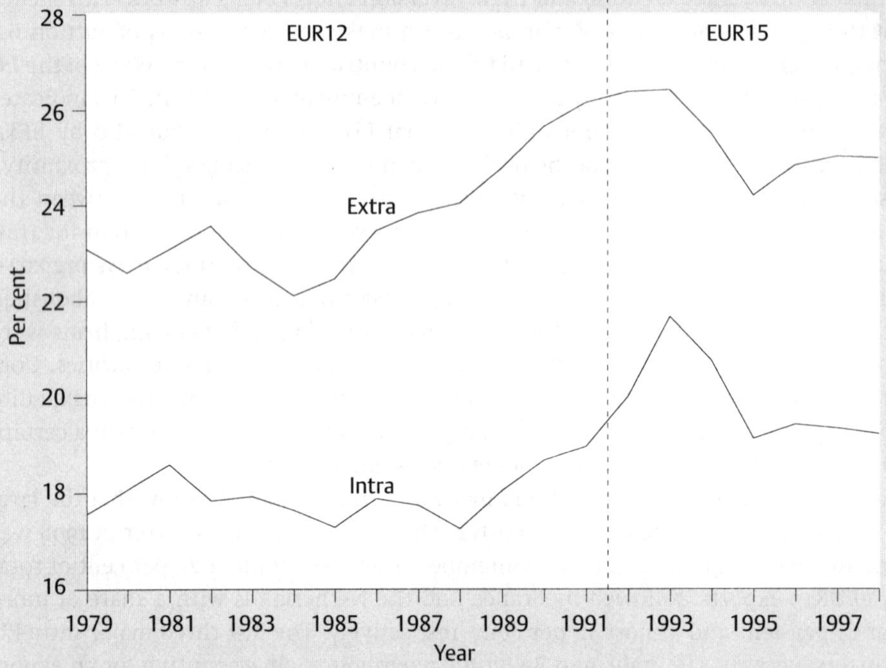

Notes: The share of services is the ratio of the sum of exports and imports of services of total trade. Total trade is the sum of imports and exports in both goods and services. Greece is not included in 1998.

Sources: Eurostat (2000): 110, 111, 116, and 117. Eurostat (1994a): 14 and 16. Eurostat (1991): 127, 128,130, and 131. Authors' calculation.

'Transport', where extra-EU trade in services is much higher than intra-EU trade. The reason is the distance parameter. As it is much more expensive to ship goods to e.g. the USA and Japan than between the EU member states, the transport service connected with extra-EU trade in goods is much more expensive than the transport service related to intra-EU trade in goods.

Trade in services is frequently subjected to non-tariff barriers in the form of regulations or other obstacles, and it can therefore develop more freely within the Union than outside, where worldwide trade liberalization in services only recently has been put on the agenda in connection with the so-called Uruguay Round of the WTO completed in 1994. In this respect, it should be expected that the closer integration and unification of regulations and requirements (i.e. ensuring truly free trade in services) found at the EU level would generate a more swift increase in the share of intra-EU trade in services. However, this is not the development depicted in Figure 6.4, as the curves indicating intra- and extra-EU trade shares develop almost identically. Yet, it cannot be concluded that the relatively close integration of the service sector in the EU has not had a higher impact on intra-EU trade than on extra-EU trade in services, because at the same time as liberalization of trade in services has taken place, liberalization of trade in goods has also proceeded, inside the EU as well as worldwide. In particular, the integration of trade in goods has advanced further in the EU than at the global level and, as illustrated in Figure 6.3, intra-EU trade in goods has increased much more than extra-EU trade in goods. This offers one explanation of why the share of intra-EU trade in services has not increased more than the share of extra-EU trade in services.

In what follows, the trade in goods, which constitutes the main bulk of intra-EU trade with a share of more than 80 per cent of total trade, will be split into its main parts. The distribution of total intra-EUR15 exports on product groups is illustrated in Figure 6.5.

The classification in Figure 6.5 is exhaustive for all classified goods, which means that all goods traded within the EU are included in the figure except those not classified into categories, which accounted for 5.7 per cent of total exports in 1998. What are the products behind these classification categories? Whereas some of these categories are self-explanatory, several others may require further explanation. For example, the category 'Other manufactures' includes such widely different products as animal oils, paper, and leather and wood manufactures, whereas the category

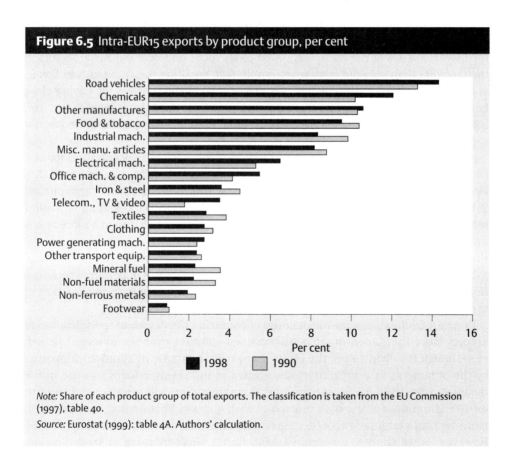

Figure 6.5 Intra-EUR15 exports by product group, per cent

Note: Share of each product group of total exports. The classification is taken from the EU Commission (1997), table 40.

Source: Eurostat (1999): table 4A. Authors' calculation.

'Miscellaneous manufactured articles' contains sanitation and furniture, as well as professional and scientific material.

While looking at the absolute levels, note that almost half of the trade in goods is composed of the top four categories 'Road vehicles', 'Chemicals', 'Other manufactures', and 'Food and tobacco'. Turning to the development from 1990 to 1998, certain growth areas can be identified, namely 'Office machines and computers', 'Electrical machines', 'Telecommunications, TV and video', and, finally, 'Chemicals'. The development in the first three categories fits nicely with the observed trends in the world economy where electronics and communication products make up the high-growth sectors, or the so-called new industries. Within the EU, these are the exact products which get traded. What, in turn, are the product groups which have been losing ground in relative terms? Areas in decline are 'Industrial machines' and 'Textiles', which could be called the traditional, or old, industries. Hence, the intra-EU trade pattern mirrors global development trends and shows a clear renewal in focus.

Has integration led to more specialization in trade?

One last item concerning intra-EU trade is the question of whether or not European integration has led to a larger degree of specialization among the member states. Do the member states of the European Union today focus on fewer industrial sectors in their exports than they did forty years ago? In fact, recalling the arguments in favour of trade in Section 6.2, specialization is one of the central motives for having close European cooperation, moving from isolated autarky towards interdependence. Yet, contrary to what is foreseen in neoclassical trade theory, such specialization has not occurred.

In order to measure specialization, the Herfindahl index of concentration for several export sectors, or rather industrial groups, is calculated for trade in goods. The available level of disaggregation for such long time-periods covers 'agriculture', 'crude materials', 'energy', 'chemicals', 'machinery and transport equipment', 'other manufacturing products', and 'other unclassified products'. It is thus at a more aggregate level than Figure 6.5. The Herfindahl index is given by $H = \sum(s_i)^2$, where s_i is the share of a certain product group, i, of the total exports of a country, thus s_i is between 0 and 1. The value of H is also between 0 and 1, where 1 denotes maximum specialization. Comparing individual years, it can be measured if a country's composition of exports has become more or less concentrated.

Table 6.5 discloses that for the majority of countries, the degree of specialization in exports has either fallen or, at best, remained constant over the observed period, even though the countries of the EU have engaged in intense integration. Supported by the arguments of comparative advantage and increasing returns to scale in the theory section, the *a priori* expectation is that integration will generate an incentive for specialization, yet the data contradict such a claim. This finding is in line with more detailed examinations of the degree of specialization carried out by Sapir (1996). However, other studies, e.g. Amiti (1999), find a weak increase in specialization.

What, then, is the explanation of the stark cases of reduced specialization observed for Belgium, Denmark, Greece, and Ireland? Looking at the data behind the index estimation, one export sector dominated in all four countries in the early years, in particular in Denmark, Greece, and Ireland, where more than 60 per cent of exports in 1960 were in agriculture and food. What has happened is that, in the decades since 1960, all three countries have experienced substantial growth in alternative export sectors. In the cases of Denmark and Ireland, a complete reorientation of their economies is observed, hence the falling degree of specialization.

The analysis in Table 6.5 nevertheless poses a number of problems. First of all, the picture presented is only a snapshot of specialization taken at five different points in time and therefore not representative of the complete trend. It is even more problematic that the calculation of specialization is based on only seven product groups, hence, if, in line with new trade theory, specialization occurs in the form of different product variants, such specialization would not be identified in Table 6.5. In fact, such a form of specialization would result in increasing intra-industry trade, the topic of the next section.

To sum up, the analysis of intra-EU trade carried out in the present section has demonstrated that growth in intra-EU trade has outpaced growth in extra-EU trade. Yet, when it comes to trade in services, intra-EU trade is less developed. The explanation of this is twofold: firstly, the bulk of trade in services is made up by transport of goods which is less expensive (and consequently makes up a smaller share) for countries in geographic proximity; secondly, in the early years of integration, focus was on the liberalization of trade in goods, leaving trade in services within the EU to simply

Table 6.5 Country specialization[a] in intra-EU exports, 1960–1998

	1960	1970	1980	1990	1998
Belgium/Luxembourg	0.40	0.34	0.25	0.23	0.25
Denmark	0.57	0.31	0.25	0.21	0.22
Germany	0.27	0.31	0.27	0.33	0.31
Greece	0.52	0.32	0.30	0.34	0.34
Spain	0.34[b]	0.24	0.26	0.30	0.31
France	0.24	0.24	0.23	0.26	0.29
Ireland	0.42	0.31	0.24	0.23	0.27
Italy	0.26	0.31	0.34	0.36	0.35
The Netherlands	0.21	0.19	0.18	0.16	0.18
Austria	—	—	—	0.37	0.33
Portugal	0.25	0.28	0.31	0.39	0.37
Finland	—	—	—	0.36	0.35
Sweden	—	—	—	0.31	0.27
UK	0.23	0.28	0.20	0.23	0.30

[a] Specialization is measured by the Herfindahl index of concentration for seven export product groups according to the SITC classification. A value of 1 indicates maximum concentration/specialization.
[b] 1961.

Sources: Eurostat (1994*b*): tables 4 and 7. Eurostat (1999): table 5D. Authors' calculation.

develop in line with the general level of global liberalization in that area. Looking at the composition of goods traded within the EU, traditional industries are losing importance while new industries, such as telecommunications, experience significant growth in their relative share of intra-EU trade. Finally, at a fairly aggregate level, there is no evidence that integration has led to higher specialization in trade among the EU members.

6.6 Measuring the share of intra-industry trade in Europe

THE neoclassical trade theory, which is founded on the theory of comparative advantage, exclusively features inter-industry trade. From this point of view, it is puzzling why Germany will import cars (or 'road vehicles' in the statistics above) from France when, at the same time, France imports cars from Germany. As mentioned in Section 6.2, new trade theory has resolved this puzzle. Table 6.6 gives a summary of the classification into inter- and intra-industry trade.

However, in real life, it is not a question of either pure inter-industry trade or pure intra-industry trade but rather a mixture of these two forms of trade. This means that both inter-industry trade, based on differences in the factor proportions of individual countries, and intra-industry trade, based on product differentiation, occur at the same time. In order to get an impression of the factors regulating international trade, it is important to identify the distribution of international trade in these two forms of trade. This can be done by using the so-called Grubel and Lloyd index (Grubel and Lloyd (1975)), which takes its point of departure in the definition of intra-industry trade, i.e. in the export value which corresponds exactly to the import value of the same product category. As a consequence, the excess export or import is a measure of

Table 6.6 Key differences between intra- and inter-industry trade		
	Inter-industry trade	Intra-industry trade
International trade with products from . . .	different industries	the same industries
The underlying theory is . . .	neoclassical trade theory	new trade theory
The production function features . . .	constant returns to scale	increasing returns to scale
Consumer preferences are . . .	homogeneous	heterogeneous
The trade gains stem from . . .	the exploitation of comparative advantages in production	a wide range of product varieties and increasing returns to scale

inter-industry trade. The share of aggregate intra-industry trade in total trade can thus be formulated as follows:

$$\bar{B} = \frac{\sum_i (X_i + M_i) - \sum_i |X_i - M_i|}{\sum_i (X_i + M_i)}$$

X_i and M_i indicate the value of the export and import of product category i, respectively, $|X_i - M_i|$ indicates net trade of product category i in absolute figures, $(X_i + M_i)$ indicates gross trade of product category i, and i = 1, 2, 3, . . . n, where n indicates the number of product categories at the selected aggregation level. The equation is thus a weighted average of the share of intra-industry trade of each product category. A value of 100 per cent is a measure of pure intra-industry trade, whereas a value of 0 per cent, on the other hand, is a measure of inter-industry trade.

The selected aggregation level is of no importance when the share of intra-industry trade is compared at the *same* level over time or across countries. But when comparing the index over different aggregation levels it is important to bear in mind that the *level* of intra-industry trade decreases the smaller the selected aggregation level is. It is possible to imagine extreme cases, where the definition of a product category for similarly functioning products is reduced to the colour of the product. If a product variety with one colour is exported, and a product variety with another colour is imported, it is a case of pure inter-industry trade with individual product colours. If, on the other hand, the definition of a product category is broadened to include similarly functioning products with different colours, it is a case of pure intra-industry trade. Table 6.7 illustrates the share of intra-industry trade for the EUR15 countries.

Throughout the examined period, the share of intra-industry trade has increased significantly for all EUR15 countries, particularly in the 1960s and 1980s. It appears from the analysis in DØR (1997) that at the end of the period, almost 62 per cent of foreign trade of the EUR15 countries was characterized by intra-industry trade. For several EU countries, such as Belgium, Germany, France, the Netherlands, the UK, and Austria, intra-industry trade in 1994 even made up between 69 per cent and almost 79 per cent of total foreign trade.

Country size, and thus the exploitation of economies of scale, is of importance for the intra-industry trade pattern. Thus, in general, large countries have a more varied production structure with more production variety granting intra-industry trade a relatively large importance. This connection can help explain the differences in the share of intra-industry trade between the countries. Another important factor for the share of intra-industry trade is the efficiency in production, and hence also standards of living, of the countries. In line with the discussion in Section 6.2, it can be assumed that the level of intra-industry trade is proportional to the wealth of the trade partner countries. The connection between standards of living and the share of intra-industry trade for the EUR15 countries is shown in Figure 6.6. The horizontal axis indicates GDP per capita at current market prices in PPS, and the vertical axis indicates the share of intra-industry trade, in both cases for 1994. Clearly, a positive connection between the share of intra-industry trade and GDP per capita for each country can be

Table 6.7 Share of EU intra-industry trade, 1961–1994, per cent

	1961	1970	1980	1994
Belgium	54.4	61.4	63.4	73.8
Denmark	32.1	47.8	51.0	60.9
Germany	40.0	27.9	56.2	69.0
Greece	7.9	17.6	21.0	39.2
Spain	24.6	33.3	37.9	64.1
France	53.0	65.1	63.0	76.5
Ireland	29.9	37.4	49.6	56.2
Italy	39.0	45.2	47.8	56.7
The Netherlands	55.9	59.9	59.6	72.4
Austria	38.5	54.4	61.7	71.5
Portugal	21.9	32.8	28.9	44.5
Finland	15.8[a]	27.9	36.2	47.3
Sweden	41.8	50.9	56.2	61.8
UK	34.2	49.5	73.0	78.6

[a] 1964.

Note: The index is defined in the text and is estimated at the 3-digit level of SITC, Revision 2, for sections 0–8. Trade covers both intra- and extra-EU trade. Luxembourg is not listed.

Source: DØR (1997) based on OECD, Foreign Trade Statistics.

identified. This is supported by the fact that the correlation coefficient, which is a measure of the strength of the connection between the two variables, is 0.71.

Whether foreign trade increases or reduces differences in industrial structure depends on whether there is a case of inter- or intra-industry specialization. In the case of inter-industry specialization, differences in industrial structure increase, whereas the effect on the industrial structure is less clear-cut in the case of intra-industry specialization. If, in connection with intra-industry specialization, an industry enjoys significant, external economies of scale, the industry will settle in a certain area, which leads to increased divergence. In the opposite case, there is a possibility that a certain industry will develop industrial environments in several areas if internal economies of scale or external economies of scale between firms in different industries exist.

6.7 Competitiveness and comparative advantage

So far, only the observed trade flows and integration as a possible explanatory factor have been examined. In the following, we will try to identify what actually motivates the examined trade patterns. There are two concepts at hand: competitive-

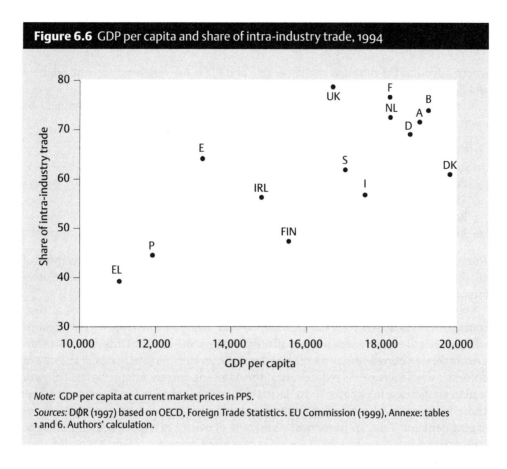

Figure 6.6 GDP per capita and share of intra-industry trade, 1994

Note: GDP per capita at current market prices in PPS.

Sources: DØR (1997) based on OECD, Foreign Trade Statistics. EU Commission (1999), Annexe: tables 1 and 6. Authors' calculation.

ness and comparative advantage. Competitiveness is a concept which covers a wide range of factors and relates to micro- as well as macroeconomic issues, such as the earning potential of firms and/or industries, total employment, and the development in the current account of the balance of payments. Below, the development in cost-competitiveness of EUR15 is analysed followed by an examination of the competitiveness of the EU, expressed in actual trade patterns. A simple measure of the comparative advantages of the EU in a number of product groups is established, and an analysis will be made of the product groups in which the EU has performed well.

Defining and measuring Europe's competitiveness

The ability to conquer market shares depends, among other things, on quantitative factors such as relative wages, relative productivity, and the nominal exchange rate. In other words, these factors make up the part of cost-competitiveness which determines the relative unit costs of production. A simple measure of the cost-competitiveness is the real exchange rate, which can be formulated as follows

$$R = e \frac{P_f}{P}$$

where e denotes the nominal exchange rate and P_f/P is the relative price, and where P and P_f are the price levels at home and abroad, respectively.

A more precise expression of the cost-competitiveness can be obtained by juxtaposing the following factors:

1. Nominal effective exchange rate
2. Real compensation per employee (non-wage costs included)
3. Price levels
4. Real productivity
5. Relative unit labour costs $(= 2 + 3 - 4)$
6. Real effective exchange rate $(= 1 + 5)$

where the nominal effective exchange rate is calculated as the weighted average of all bilateral exchange rates. In particular, the weights are based on the relative importance of each foreign country for the total trade of the home country.

The degree to which the export of individual goods is affected by changes in cost-competitiveness depends on the elasticity of both demand and supply. This explains why individual export goods are not affected to the same extent. Thus, exports measured in foreign currency may increase if domestic productivity increases, if the rate of domestic wage increases is reduced, or if the domestic currency depreciates. This will lead to an increase in exports and a decrease in prices, expressed in foreign currency, and consequently, the effect on export earnings will depend on the elasticity of export demand. Thus, in numerical terms, the elasticity of export demand must be larger than one before the export earnings in current prices increases. Naturally, such real depreciation also has an effect on imports, as import prices in real terms will rise and quantities will fall. Hence, if the purpose of a real depreciation is to tackle a trade balance deficit, a sufficient condition is that the sum of the demand elasticities for exports and imports is larger than one. This is called the Marshall–Lerner criterion.

The cost-competitiveness, and thus also the ability to conquer market shares, also depends on qualitative factors such as product quality and design, company image, marketing, financing, and the ability to execute export orders. Improvements in product technology are expressed both in improvements in the quality of existing products and in the development of new products. This means that product innovation takes place.

The development in the components of the real effective exchange rate for EUR12 in the period 1980 to 1996 is presented in Table 6.8. A minus indicates an improvement in cost-competitiveness.

Over the period, relative real productivity of the EUR12 countries as a whole has increased by more than 10 per cent, but as relative prices have increased by more than 15 per cent in the same period, relative unit labour costs have increased by almost 6 per cent. However, the fall in the nominal effective exchange rate of around 21 per cent is crucial for the real effective exchange rate falling 16.5 per cent. Whereas the competitiveness of the EU countries thus has improved over the period in

Table 6.8 Factors determining the real effective exchange rate, 1980–1996

Per cent change[a] relative to 22 industrial countries	EUR12			
	1980–7	1987–92	1992–6	1980–96
Nominal effective exchange rate	−20.3	7.1	−7.5	−21.1
Real compensation per employee	0.6	0.9	−0.3	1.3
Price levels	8.6	3.2	2.9	15.3
Real productivity	3.1	2.2	4.6	10.3
Relative unit labour costs[b]	5.9	1.9	−1.9	5.8
Real effective exchange rate[c]	−15.6	9.2	−9.3	−16.5

[a] Percentage change between the beginning and the end of the period.
[b] Relative unit labour costs in the economy as a whole.
[c] A minus indicates an improvment in cost-competitiveness.

Source: EU Commission (1997): 31.

question, it is evident from the source of Table 6.8 that the competitiveness of the USA, and of Japan in particular, has deteriorated. This is partly because competitiveness is a relative measure. The development in the USA and Japan can particularly be ascribed to an appreciation of the currencies of both countries during the 1980s.

An interesting result emerges if the development in competitiveness is compared with the trade balance of the EU in the individual periods. Recall from Figure 6.1 that the periods 1980 to 1987 and, to a lesser degree, 1988 to 1992 were associated with a trade deficit for the EU, while the period 1992 to 1996 featured an overall trade surplus. Competitiveness, as measured in Table 6.8, would be at odds with such a development. Or would it? In fact, it is not. The measures of competitiveness listed in Table 6.8 relate nicely to the observed trade deficit development, but it is important to recall that these are all growth measures, i.e. they capture a development over time, while the actual deficit is driven by the level of competitiveness (i.e. a cumulative measure), not by a change in the level. The trade surplus of the mid-1990s was thus created by the build-up in competitiveness which took place between 1992 and 1996.

Europe's revealed comparative advantage

Assessing competitiveness is one thing. How it transmits into actual trade patterns is, however, something completely different. It is therefore important to understand what it is that Europe is actually good at exporting. In other words, what is Europe's comparative advantage? As we know from the theoretical analysis in Section 6.2, a country has a comparative advantage in the production of a good if the country is relatively better at producing this good than another country. However, in order to determine the comparative advantages of a country, it is often useful to look at the actual trade figures. A simple way of measuring the comparative advantages of the EU is by looking at actual trade flows, i.e. by calculating the ratio of the export share of a product group over the import share of the same product group. This is done by measuring how much of a product group the EU exports to the rest of the world, and how much of that same product group the EU imports from the rest of the world. A ratio higher than 1 in a product group is connected with a comparative advantage. Eighteen product groups have been identified and categorized into two main groups, high-technology-intensive and low-technology-intensive products, in order to see where the EU has its strengths. A comparative advantage in high-technology-intensive product groups is desirable, assuming that the future growth sectors will be high-technology-intensive. In order to analyse the development in the comparative advantages of the EU in this field—i.e. to see whether or not the EU is advancing in high-technology-intensive product areas—the comparative advantages are calculated at two points in time: 1990 and 1998. However, before turning to the measure of comparative advantage, below is a quick introduction to the composition of extra-EU exports and imports by product groups.

Figure 6.7 shows that Europe is dependent on imports of 'Mineral fuel' (in particular oil) and 'Office machines and computers', while export best-sellers are 'Industrial machines', 'Chemicals', and 'Road vehicles'. This is good news, assuming that the high-technology-intensive sectors are the future growth sectors. Figure 6.7 also shows which product groups are the heavyweights in EU trade. Looking at exports, 'Industrial machinery' and 'Chemicals' hold the highest shares whereas 'Mineral fuel' and 'Miscellaneous manufactured articles' are product groups where the EU depends the most on imports. Having established this, we can now turn to the measure of revealed comparative advantage.

Figure 6.8 indicates that the EU had comparative advantages in most of the high-technology-intensive sectors both in 1990 and in 1998. However, the development in comparative advantage is going the wrong way for six out of nine product groups, the three exceptions being 'Office machines and computers', 'Telecommunications, TV and video', and 'Other transport equipment'. Turning to the low-technology-intensive product groups, note that in all sectors, where the EU had a comparative advantage in 1990, the development up to 1998 has been negative. Another interesting observation is that the development in comparative advantage in the 'Mineral fuel' product group is slightly positive. That development could be associated with the introduction of new, less fuel dependent technology at the same time as the UK, the Netherlands, and Denmark have increased their oil production.

There are a number of caveats in the presentation in Figure 6.8. Firstly, the measure of comparative advantage does not take the world trade volume in the respective categories into account. There could, for example, be a massive worldwide trade in telecommunication products in which Europe could be a laggard, but by importing less of such products from abroad, the simple comparative advantage measure appears to rise in Figure 6.8. Having said that, it is worth mentioning that European producers in fact perform quite well in the telecommunications industry, so for this industry, this simple measure is a good indicator of comparative advantage. However,

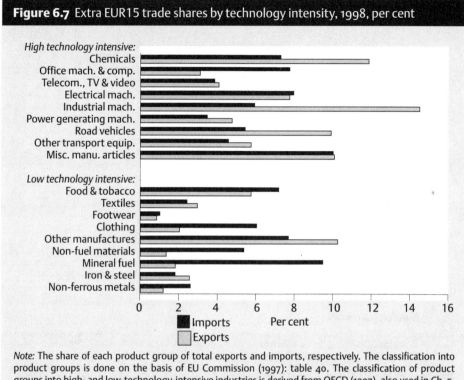

Figure 6.7 Extra EUR15 trade shares by technology intensity, 1998, per cent

Note: The share of each product group of total exports and imports, respectively. The classification into product groups is done on the basis of EU Commission (1997): table 40. The classification of product groups into high- and low-technology-intensive industries is derived from OECD (1997), also used in Ch. 5, Table 5.6.

Source: Eurostat (1999); table 3A. Authors' calculation.

a more sophisticated measure of comparative advantage, the Standard Revealed Comparative Advantage index introduced by Balassa (1965), takes the problem of world trade volume into account. The index is calculated as the ratio of the export share of a certain product of a country over the export share of the same product of total world trade. Secondly, Figure 6.8 is not normalized for the observed developments, i.e. the relative comparative 'dis'-advantage scale goes only from zero to 1, while the relative comparative advantage scale goes from 1 to infinity. This means that the length of an arrow to the right exaggerates the true development, while an arrow to the left understates it.

Overall, the two illustrations of competitiveness and comparative advantage paint a mixed, yet slightly promising picture of the EU as a trading block. There are clear improvements in competitiveness, also compared with the other two large trading areas, the USA and Japan, and the EU is experiencing export growth in several high-technology industries, industries which can be expected to set the agenda for the decade to come. Nevertheless, the true measure of sustainability is the current account, and judged by this measure—as explained in Section 6.3—Europe is doing fine.

Figure 6.8 Developments in revealed comparative advantages, EUR15, 1990s

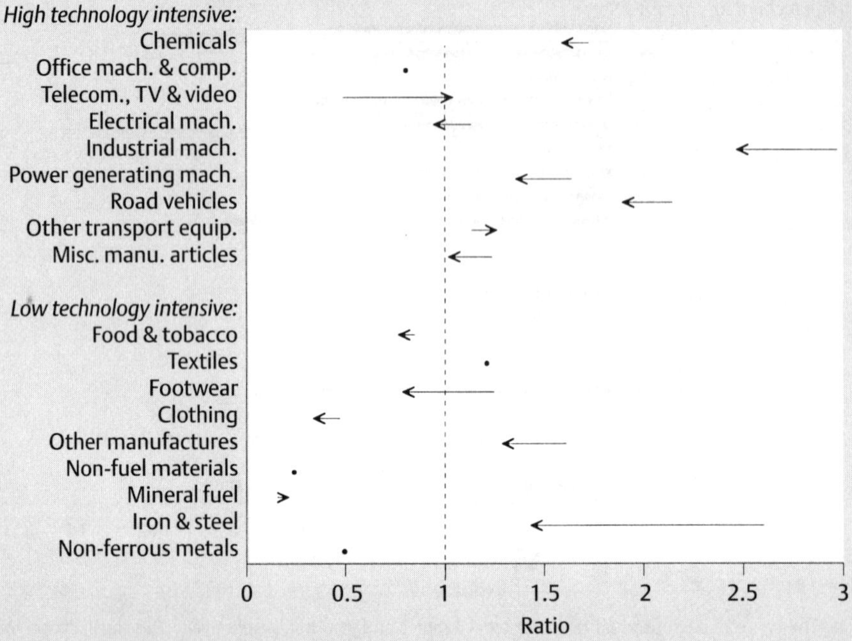

Note: Revealed comparative advantage for each sector is defined as the ratio of the sector's share of total exports to the sector's share of total imports. The arrows indicate the development in revealed comparative advantage from 1990 to 1998. The classification into product groups is done on the basis of EU Commission (1997): table 40. The classification of product groups into high- and low-technology-intensive industries is derived from OECD (1997).

Source: Eurostat (1999): table 3A. Authors' calculation.

6.8 Concluding remarks

BESIDE the overall political aim of a peaceful post-war structure for Europe, the idea of free trade has always been the key to integration. This has been manifested firstly in the initiation of a customs union and later by the implementation of the Single Market programme. One could say that free trade in Europe has been the means to an end, namely that of bringing the nations of Europe closer together.

This chapter has addressed the issue of EU trade and its interrelation with integration from several perspectives, showing that the European policy of linking integration and trade liberalization has been a success. The EU maintains its position as the largest, single trade block in the world and manifests this status through a significant degree of trade openness as well as an important—although not always altruistic—

role in global trade liberalization. This having been said, the external tariff of the EU is nevertheless higher than those of the USA and Japan. It has been demonstrated that in the early years of integration, a possible trade diversion effect may have harmed trade with countries outside the Union, but for the past twenty years, intra- and extra-EU trade have been growing at almost equal speeds. Within the EU, trade is of increasing importance, enhancing further the interdependence of the European economies, yet specialization, in the sense that each member country focuses on fewer export industries, cannot be detected. Still, growth in intra-industry trade is substantial, proving that specialization, in the new trade theory sense of the term, is in fact taking place. Finally, an analysis of the competitiveness and revealed comparative advantages of the EU has disclosed that the EU holds a sound position, where productivity gains combined with nominal depreciation have ensured price competitiveness, and where the focus of trade activity, to a large degree, is in the area of high-technology-intensive industries. All in all, trade policy is the one area where the EU comes closest to being a federal state and has been highly successful in creating internal liberalization.

Consider once more the type of specialization found in Europe: the individual EU countries have not specialized in different industries; instead, each industry has engaged in specialization. This means that the volume of intra-industry trade is growing. While growing intra-industry trade can be expected to have little or no impact on the factors of production it can be expected that specialization in the neoclassical sense gives rise to—potentially very large—adjustment costs for the factors of production because this means that in each country, certain industries will close while others will grow. It thus appears that, so far, European integration in the area of trade has been soft in terms of the adjustment required of the factors of production. By this token, it is doubtful whether this pattern of trade specialization will apply for the future Eastern enlargement, or if trade will result in a neoclassical type of specialization where factors of production have to go through major adjustments.

Further reading

Any textbook on international economics will cover micro- and macroeconomic aspects of trade theory. A standard reference is P. R. Krugman and M. Obstfeld (2000), *International Economics — Theory and Policy*, 5th edn., Addison-Wesley, Harlow. J. D. Hansen and J. U.-M. Nielsen (1997), *An Economic Analysis of the EU*, 2nd edn., McGraw-Hill, New York, focuses on theories analysing the impact of economic integration on trade. A more descriptive approach to issues of international trade, with a host of information also on institutional matters, is provided by T. A. Pugel and P. H. Lindert (2000), *International Economics*, 11th edn., McGraw-Hill, New York. An empirical study on the impact of the Internal Market on trade is found in EU Commission (1996), 'Economic Evaluation of the Internal Market', *European Economy Reports and Studies*, 4.

References

Amiti, M. (1999), 'Specialization Patterns in Europe', *Weltwirtschaftliches Archiv*, 135: 573–93.

Balassa, B. (1965), 'Trade liberalization and "Revealed" Comparative Advantages', *Manchester School of Economics and Social Studies*, 33: 99–123.

DØR (1997), *Dansk Økonomi Forår 1997*, Det Økonomiske Råd, Copenhagen.

EU Commission (1980), *European Economy*, 7.

—— (1986), *European Economy*, 29.

—— (1994), *European Economy*, 58.

—— (1997), 'The European Union as a World Trade Partner', *European Economy Reports and Studies*, 3.

—— (1999), *European Economy*, 69.

Eurostat (1991), *International Trade in Services, EUR12—from 1979 to 1988*.

—— (1994a), *International Trade in Services, EUR12—from 1983 to 1992*.

—— (1994b), *External Trade Statistical Yearbook 1958–1993*.

—— (1999), *External and Intra-European Union Trade: Statistical Yearbook, Data 1958–1998*.

—— (2000), *International Trade in Services—EU, Annexe to the Publication EU International Transactions—1999 edn., Data 1989–1998*.

Grubel, H. G., and P. J. Lloyd (1975), *Intra-Industry Trade. The Theory and Measurement of International Trade in Differentiated Products*, Macmillan Press, Basingstoke.

Krugman, P. R., and M. Obstfeld (2000), *International Economics—Theory and Policy*, 5th edn., Addison-Wesley, Harlow.

OECD (1996), *Indicators of Tariff and Non-Tariff Trade Barriers*.

—— (1997), 'Technology and Non-Technology Determinants of Export Share Growth', *Economic Studies*, 28.

—— (1999), *OECD Economic Outlook*, 65.

Sapir, A. (1996), 'The Effects of Europe's Internal Market Program on Production and Trade: A First Assessment', *Weltwirtschaftliches Archiv*, 132: 457–75.

Viner, J. (1950), *The Customs Union Issue*, Stevens, New York.

Chapter 7
Foreign Direct Investment: Flows and Motives

Jan Guldager Jørgensen

7.1 Introduction

IN neoclassical international trade theory, goods and factor movements are substitutes. This connection was emphasized by Mundell (1957). Goods movements contribute to equalizing prices of goods, thus limiting factor price differences and reducing factor movements. Factor movements contribute to equalizing factor prices, thus limiting differences in prices of goods with the result that goods movements across borders to some extent will dry up.

The Single Market ensures free movement of goods, persons, services, and capital. Based on Mundell's perception, a fall in either goods or factor movements should therefore be expected following the formation of the Single Market. The actual development has proven to be more complex. Since the Single Market was established, intra-EU trade has become more extensive (see Chapter 6), and at the same time, capital movements, in the form of direct investments, have increased rapidly. This will be demonstrated in this chapter, and the reasons behind the development will be identified. Labour mobility, on the other hand, is low and the establishment of the Internal Market has not changed this significantly, as was demonstrated in Chapter 3. Regarding trade, intra-industry trade is of large and increasing importance, consisting to a large extent of two-way flows of similar goods. The same is true for capital movements with the existence of two-way flows of direct investments between member states. On the face of it, it does not make sense that two different firms from two different countries engaging in the production of exactly the same good should invest in product facilities in each other's countries. However, the reason is that capital, in the form of direct investments, consists of *heterogeneous capital goods*, which are connected to the specific know-how of the investing firm. This chapter will examine these issues in depth.

Section 7.2 opens with a definition of multinational companies and describes different types of foreign direct investment. The section also discusses the rationale behind the existence of multinationals and the importance of integration for multinational companies as presented in theoretical literature. Section 7.3 looks at foreign direct investment in a global context with special emphasis on the EU, whereas Section 7.4 makes a closer analysis of foreign direct investment flows related to the EU in the period in which the Internal Market was created. Within the EU, there are large differences between different sectors in terms of attracting foreign direct investment, and this is the focus of Section 7.5. Finally, the extent of two-way flows between member states will be illustrated in Section 7.6, and the findings of the chapter will be summarized in Section 7.7.

7.2 The effects of integration on foreign direct investment

THIS section will examine the theories associated with the effects of integration on foreign direct investment. The effects expected *a priori* are by no means clear-cut. Let us start by defining some terms. A multinational company is defined as a company that owns and controls value-adding activities in more than one country. The way in which the multinational company establishes ownership of value-adding activities in other countries is through *Foreign Direct Investment* (FDI).

Foreign investment is investment made by a firm in another firm in another country and can be divided into *direct* foreign investment and *portfolio* investment. Investment is direct if the investor has a permanent interest in the foreign company and achieves full or partial control of the company through the investment. This can be in the form of acquisition of, or merger with, an existing firm, purchase of shares in an existing firm, or the establishment of completely new firms and manufacturing plants. The latter form of FDI is referred to as greenfield investment. Finally, in connection with the restructuring of Central and Eastern Europe, a new type of FDI has arisen, brownfield investment, which is a hybrid between acquisitions and greenfield investment. The multinational company takes over an existing firm and utilizes e.g. its knowledge of the market while at the same time replacing the entire capital stock by introducing new technology.

What is the distinction between portfolio and direct investment? If an investor owns more than 10 per cent of the voting shares, it constitutes FDI (cf. OECD definition of 1996). Note that the terms 'firm' and 'company' should be interpreted broadly as they cover both private and public firms, organizations, cooperatives, etc., and that the 10 per cent limit to some extent is arbitrary but generally accepted as a dividing line. If, on the other hand, the foreign investment amounts to a share purchase of less than 10 per cent of the shares in a firm, by definition, this constitutes portfolio investment. Portfolio investment also includes deposits in banks and financial investment in government or private securities. This chapter will only focus on FDI.

The Internal Market has an influence on whether or not it is advantageous for a firm to pursue foreign direct investment. This is because the rationale for establishing a multinational company changes *pari passu* with integration. The most holistic and frequently used theory for the establishment of multinational companies is Dunning's eclectic paradigm—the so-called OLI model (see e.g. Dunning (1993)). Below, the OLI model will be described, and possible effects of the Internal Market on the internationalization of firms through the establishment of subsidiaries will be discussed.

The OLI model

When a firm decides on a strategy on how to supply a foreign market, one option may be to establish subsidiaries. In order for the firm to choose this strategy, however, the OLI model defines three basic prerequisites which must be in place. Firstly, the firm must have *owner-specific advantages* (O), i.e. advantages which that firm alone possesses and which can be used freely by the firm if it starts production in different locations. Owner-specific advantages typically consist of tacit knowledge of advanced production technologies, innovation, R&D, a trade mark, or a reputation for good quality. Secondly, the firm must choose to avail of the owner-specific advantages for its production in several different countries. In other words, there must be *localization advantages* (L) connected with having production in several places rather than servicing the markets through exports from one production location. As localization advantages are connected with a certain location, they are external for the firm. Traditional localization advantages relate to the relative factor endowments, and thus the factor payments, of a region or a country, such as low factor returns on labour (i.e. low wages). Other examples are market size, infrastructure, trade barriers, tax policies, political climate, including political incentives for FDI, and psychological barriers, e.g. in the form of language and culture. Thirdly, there must be an incentive for the firm to control the production in various production locations itself rather than to transfer the owner-specific advantages to local independent firms e.g. through a licence. In other words, there must be *internalization advantages* (I). The firm's decision to control the production itself can be a consequence of a malfunctioning market, e.g. for semi-manufactured goods. Other reasons can be the wish to reduce transaction and negotiation costs as well as the moral hazard and adverse selection costs connected with a licensee, i.e. to avoid problems caused by asymmetric information. Finally, a more prosaic and immediate reason for a firm to become internationalized through the setting up of a subsidiary can be the existence of taxes and duties.

Through the existence of a subsidiary, the firm may manipulate the internal transfer price and thus reduce the payment of taxes and duties.

Integration and FDI

When a firm chooses to establish a subsidiary, internal as well as external conditions are taken into account. The firm is part of a specific environment and must conform to the political and economic rules in force at any given time. An integration process places the firm in a new environment and consequently forces it to reconsider the internationalization of its activities as the integration process affects the different factors of the OLI model and hence the basis on which multinational companies make decisions. Obviously, the integration process changes the firm's localization advantages, as the Internal Market reduces the internal trade barriers between member countries. Thus, for firms already operating in the EU, the creation of the Internal Market weakened the argument for establishing a subsidiary elsewhere in the EU in order to reduce trade costs. The Internal Market, on the other hand, does not influence direct trade costs of firms outside the EU that wish to supply the EU market, and consequently, the argument for reducing trade costs carries the same weight for these firms also after the establishment of the Internal Market.

This fact was pointed out already in the 1960s by Kindleberger (1966), who was the first to analyse the effects of a customs union on foreign direct investment flows. Parallel to trade theory concepts such as trade creation and trade diversion, introduced by Viner (1950) in connection with the establishment of a customs union (see Chapter 6), Kindleberger developed a similar concept for capital. *Investment creation* is the strategic response of multinational companies to trade diversion. This concept covers capital flows from firms outside the customs union who establish subsidiaries inside the union to avoid its outside tariff wall, known as the *jump-the-tariff-wall* argument. *Investment diversion*, on the other hand, is the strategic response to trade creation. Investment diversion represents capital flows caused by the reorganization of subsidiaries inside the customs union. Because the internal trade barriers are eliminated and the mobility of goods inside the union is increased as a consequence, it may be advantageous for a firm to exploit economies of scale in the production by reducing the number of manufacturing plants inside the customs union. According to Kindleberger's theory, the formation of a customs union, with its consequent change of localization advantages, will have two effects on the foreign direct investment flows in the member countries of the customs union: partly an increase through investment creation, and partly a reorganization and, consequently, a decrease through investment diversion.

However, not only localization advantages, but also other factors relating to integration may influence the volume of foreign investment. These include *inter alia* the internal conditions of the firm. Integration may increase the gains stemming from the owner-specific advantages. Owner-specific advantages are often characterized by being knowledge-based and particularly related to sunk costs in the form of R&D, and an integrated economy with better utilization of economies of scale in a larger market can increase the R&D efforts of the firms (see Chapter 5). The integration process in itself, where markets that used to be segmented become integrated, increases the possibilities for firms to internationalize their production. The removal of barriers between countries and a general harmonization of legislation makes it easier for a multinational company to build up an efficient hierarchic structure. Harmonized legislation makes it easier for firms to take advantage of 'economics of common governance', i.e. to exploit the gains attached to coordinating several subsidiaries.

The formation of the Internal Market has had such a radical impact on the industrial environment that more factors than those mentioned above influence the internationalization of firms. The conclusion is that an integration process may influence the different OLI components in a variety of dimensions, and on this background, it is not possible to make a definitive prediction of how the volume of FDI will develop. Thus, in the light of the OLI model, the integration process may both enhance and reduce the incentive to form a multinational company. Consequently, based on the theory of the OLI model, determining the effect of the EU integration process on the establishment of multinational companies becomes an empirical question.

7.3 EU's external FDI position

TURNING to the empirical evidence on FDI and an analysis of FDI flows in relation to the EU, there are three distinctions which are of particular importance. One is geographically determined, as it is essential to differentiate between intra-EU and extra-EU flows. Intra-EU flows consist of FDI between EU member states, whereas extra-EU flows consist of FDI between countries outside the EU and the EU member states. The second distinction relates to the direction of the capital flows. A country's *inward* FDI flows—or FDI *inflows*—consist of capital flowing into the country from abroad, whereas a country's *outward* FDI flows—or FDI *outflows*—consist of capital flowing from the country to other countries. A final distinction is made between FDI flows and the FDI stock. The inward—or outward, as the case may be—FDI stock of a country equals the accumulated FDI inflows into (or outflows from) the country at a given point in time.

In 1999 there were around 60,000 multinationals worldwide with at least 500,000 foreign affiliates (UN 1999). The same source documents that, since the mid-1980s, there has been a large increase in FDI flows in the world. It is not surprising that the majority of FDI outflows is from the developed countries due to their abundance of capital. It appears, however, that the majority of inflows is also into the developed countries. There are thus extensive two-way capital flows where the firms utilize their owner-specific advantages internationally by establishing subsidiaries. However, since the beginning of the 1990s, the developing countries have obtained a larger share of the capital flows. This is in particular due to an increase in FDI inflows into these countries from the developed countries.

FDI flows

Table 7.1 shows the share of world FDI flows in 1998. Collectively, the Triad accounts for as much as 66.2 per cent of world FDI inflows and 83.7 per cent of world FDI outflows, making the Triad a net investor. The EU plays an important part, both in terms of world FDI inflows and outflows. However, the calculation of the EU share includes both intra- and extra-EU FDI flows. For example, a German firm investing in France is included in the figures for FDI inflows for the EU, but a Texas-based firm investing in California does not enter the statistics for the USA. Bearing this in mind, the result is that the EU was the source of 59.5 per cent of world FDI outflows and the recipient of 35.7 per cent of world FDI inflows. The EU thus holds an important position in the Triad by being both the largest investor and the largest recipient of FDI. Japan has a negligible share of inflows (0.5 per cent), which may be explained by its special enterprise culture, but on the other hand, Japan is an important investor with 3.7 per cent of outflows. The USA is a net recipient with a share of inflows of 30.0 per cent and a share of outflows of 20.5 per cent. In the group of 'other' countries, Asia distinguishes itself by being the largest recipient of FDI, but also by being the second largest investor after 'developed countries'. This is not surprising, taking the Asian Tigers into account. Proportional to their size, the Central and Eastern European countries also receive a relatively large share of world FDI. Chapter 9 will

Table 7.1 Share of world FDI flows (per cent), 1998

	Inflows	Outflows
EUR15[a]	35.7	59.5
USA	30.0	20.5
Japan	0.5	3.7
Other	33.8	16.3
Developed countries	5.3	7.9
Central and Eastern Europe	2.7	0.3
Africa	1.2	0.1
Latin America and the Caribbean	11.1	2.4
Asia	13.2	5.6
Rest	0.3	0.0
Total	100.0	100.0

[a] Including intra- and extra-EU FDI flows.

Source: UN (1999), Annexe: tables B.1 and B.2. Author's calculation.

make a more specific analysis of the special set of problems related to Central and Eastern Europe.

FDI stocks

Table 7.2 demonstrates that FDI stocks as a proportion of GDP for the EU have increased considerably in the period from 1980 to 1997. This increase reflects the development in both intra- and extra-EU FDI flows, which are both included in the calculation. The same is true for the USA where the FDI stock as a proportion of GDP has increased considerably. Nevertheless, the absolute level of FDI inward stock relative to GDP is still lower in the USA than in the EU. The significance of the accumulated investments in Japan in relation to GDP is very low compared to the EU and the USA. Bearing in mind that both intra- and extra-EU FDI flows are included, it appears that FDI is more important for the EU economies than for the economies of the USA and, particularly, Japan.

7.4 The Single Market and FDI

THIS section will examine the evidence of the effects of the Internal Market on FDI—does it measure up to the theoretical assumptions made in Section 7.2? The fact is that there has been a large increase in FDI flows in the EU since the early 1980s. Figure 7.1 shows intra- as well as extra-EU FDI inflows.

The numbers behind the Figure are overall, aggregate figures and include all types of FDI, e.g. greenfield and brownfield investments, mergers, and acquisitions. The period has seen a large increase in intra-capital flows at the same time as the EU has become a more attractive place of investment for non-EU countries. It is an open question, however, whether this development in FDI flows to the EU member states is

Table 7.2 FDI inward stock as proportion of GDP, per cent

	1980	1985	1990	1997
EUR15[a]	5.5	8.6	11.0	15.2
USA	3.1	4.6	7.2	8.4
Japan	0.3	0.4	0.3	0.6

[a] Including intra- and extra-EU FDI flows.

Source: UN (1999), Annexe: table B.6.

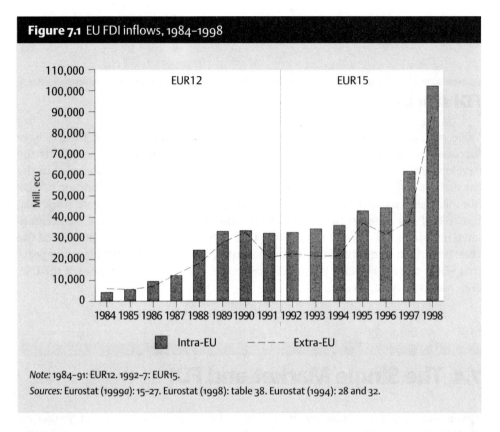

Figure 7.1 EU FDI inflows, 1984–1998

Intra-EU   Extra-EU

Note: 1984–91: EUR12. 1992–7: EUR15.

Sources: Eurostat (1999a): 15–27. Eurostat (1998): table 38. Eurostat (1994): 28 and 32.

attributable solely to the changed conditions in the EU caused by the creation of the Internal Market, or whether the development is a mere reflection of a general tendency in accordance with the worldwide globalization process. The EU Commission demonstrates that the EU has attracted a larger share of worldwide FDI in the period around the establishment of the Internal Market, as the share has increased from 28.2 per cent in the beginning of the 1980s to 44.4 per cent in 1993 (EU Commission (1998a)). This development therefore indicates that the introduction and implementation of the Single Market has had significant importance for the development in FDI flows—intra- as well as extra- in the EU.

The increase in extra-EU FDI inflows after the introduction of the Single Market may be due to the fact that the removal of non-tariff barriers, administrative simplifications, the prospect of a large and growing market, and the possibility of benefiting from economies of scale has turned the EU into an attractive place for investment. This development is entirely in line with Kindleberger's predictions on investment creation.

In terms of intra-EU FDI flows, a similar, extraordinary increase has taken place. Over the period, FDI increased from 4.3bn. ecu in 1984 to more than 100bn. ecu in 1998. The first peak was observed in 1990, when FDI flows amounted to 33.5bn. ecu. FDI flows then stabilized at that level for a couple of years only to increase again from 1994. The increase until 1990 was due to the fact that firms reacted to the new conditions by initiating a major reorganization of production. This reorganization, which could be a direct consequence of the changed external conditions caused by the establishment of the Internal Market, was time-consuming and apparently only reached maximum impact in 1990. In a long-term perspective, a fall in FDI flows must therefore be expected upon the completion of the reorganization, unless external conditions change again.

FDI often takes place in the form of cross-border mergers and acquisitions (M&As). Figure 7.2 shows the development in the number of cross-border M&As in the manufacturing industry between EU member states in the period when the Single Market was introduced and implemented. When counting the number of mergers and acquisitions, differences in the size of the operations are neglected. The figure shows that the number nearly tripled from 1986 to 1989 and that the development, to a large extent, follows the development in the value of intra-EU FDI flows (see Figure 7.1).

Measured in value of total FDI flows as well as in number of cross-border M&As, the development in intra-EU FDI flows in the period around the creation of the Internal Market does not comply with Kindleberger's predictions on investment diversion. What could be the reason? Kindleberger only takes the improved possibility of using economies of scale into account, which diminishes the advantageousness of FDI. Other conditions, on the other hand, could support reaching the opposite conclusion of Kindleberger. Special conditions in individual industrial sectors play a crucial part.

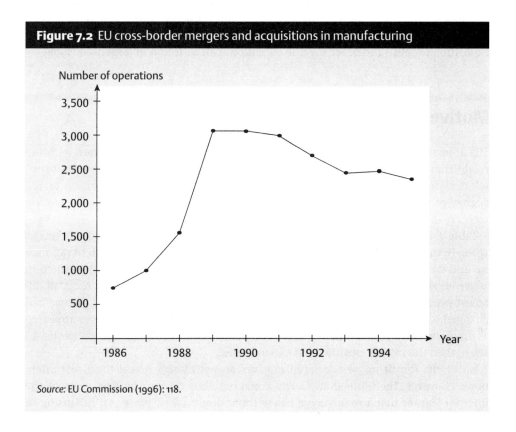

Figure 7.2 EU cross-border mergers and acquisitions in manufacturing

Source: EU Commission (1996): 118.

First, integration may lead to the establishment of subsidiaries as a consequence of the improved possibilities of utilizing differences in factor prices in the production process. If the production process can be split vertically, it may be profitable to establish subsidiaries and produce intermediate goods in the location with the lowest costs. Second, some industries are characterized by a high concentration (see Chapter 5) of a few, dominating firms, where maintaining market power is crucial. In connection with an integration process and the subsequent increase in competition between firms, it may be an advantageous strategy to re-establish market power through M&A. Third, if the strategic response at firm level to the increased competitive environment has been to improve the firm's core competence by deliberate efforts towards a more focused behaviour (see e.g. Skinner (1974a, b) and Caves (1989)), M&As can be the result. The success of such a strategy relies on quick market access, and M&As of firms with similar competence may offer the firms the necessary network for sales on the international market. Fourth, some industrial sectors experience large uncertainty about sales conditions, due to uncertainty about market conditions. By being closer to the market, via the establishment of a subsidiary, firms may reduce this uncertainty. This factor is more important in connection with an integration process, as the importance of the international market is increased due to larger sales. Fifth, transport costs may be decisive. In some industries, transport costs are substantial, and in such cases, establishing themselves in several countries may be the firms' preferred solution. Sixth, and final, the strategic element may be decisive in many sectors. In connection with an integration process, in the long term it may, for example, prove advantageous for a firm to be the first in a market. A theoretic exposition of these and other specific conditions can be found in Jørgensen (1998).

Motives for M&A

The above theoretical explanations for the increase in M&As in connection with the establishment of the Internal Market are to a large extent confirmed by the firms' self-declared motives. The Commission carries out control and supervision of the degree of competition on the markets, *inter alia* through registering large-scale mergers in the EU. This offers an insight into the reasons behind M&A.

Table 7.3 shows a marked shift in the declared motives of firms to merger in recent years. In the mid-1980s, mergers were in particular motivated by the wish to rationalize and create synergy effects, i.e. reducing costs by carrying out several production activities simultaneously. Diversification, i.e. spreading production on a range of different products and sectors, was also a frequent motive. By 1991–2, the picture had changed completely. Rationalization, synergy, and diversification no longer appeared as frequent motives. In many cases, the reasons for merging were a desire to strengthen the market position and expand sales.

Naturally, the firms' self-declared motives do not always reveal their real intentions. However, the table shows such a marked shift during the first years of the Internal Market that a real change has without doubt taken place. An expansion in

Table 7.3 Share of firms' main motives for mergers, per cent

	1985–6	1988–9	1991–2
Expansion	17.1	31.3	32.4
Diversification	17.6	7.1	2.1
Strengthening market position	10.6	42.2	44.4
Rationalization and synergies	46.5	14.4	16.2
R&D	2.4	0.0	0.0
Other	5.9	4.9	5.0
Total	100.0	100.0	100.0

Source: EU Commission (1994): table 1.

the breadth of production is replaced by an expansion in the depth, where the firms concentrate their efforts on what they produce best. This change in company strategy seems universal.

FDI in member states

Table 7.4 shows FDI flows in member states. The first part of the table shows the distribution of intra-EU FDI inflows between member states. It should be noticed that 1987 only includes EUR12, whereas 1992 and 1998 cover EUR15. One should therefore be careful when comparing 1987 with the two other years. Technically, when the number of countries increases, the share of a country will decrease even though the relative importance of the country remains unchanged.

In 1998, the five largest recipients—Germany, the Netherlands, Finland, Sweden, and the UK—have a share of no less than 72 per cent of total investment. For Germany, the share has increased from 12.4 per cent in 1987 to 16.6 per cent in 1998, but with an exceptionally larger share of 24.7 per cent in 1992. A decisive explanation for this development is the reunification and the entire reconstruction of the former East Germany. Many foreign firms—both in industry and service—have been involved in this reconstruction and these firms may have chosen to establish subsidiaries. The share of the Netherlands displays large variations between the three periods, which indicates that very specific conditions have determined FDI inflows to the Netherlands in individual years. The same volatility in FDI flows holds true for Finland and Sweden. The table shows an enormous increase from 1992 to 1998. However, the source to the table documents that the shares of Finland and Sweden were only around 2.2 per cent in 1997. This points again to the volatility of FDI flows, where specific conditions are important in determining the FDI inflows in a period. Ireland, which is a small member state, has experienced an incredible increase from 0.5 per cent in 1987 to 3.4 per cent in 1998. This increase is even more remarkable when it is

Table 7.4 Intra-EU FDI inflows, 1987, 1992, 1998

	Per cent of total intra-EU FDI inflows			Per cent of GDP of member states		
	1987[a]	1992	1998	1987[a]	1992	1998
Belgium/Luxembourg	11.8	15.7	8.3	1.1	2.8	3.6
Denmark	1.4	2.5	0.4	0.2	0.7	0.3
Germany	12.4	24.7	16.6	0.2	0.5	0.9
Greece	0.0	0.0	0.5	0.0	0.0	0.5
Spain	1.3	0.9	1.5	0.1	0.1	0.3
France	26.0	23.3	8.3	0.4	0.7	0.7
Ireland	0.5	1.1	3.4	0.2	0.8	4.6
Italy	5.3	10.1	4.6	0.1	0.3	0.4
The Netherlands	11.7	4.9	12.6	0.7	0.6	3.7
Austria	n.a.	1.2	0.5	n.a.	0.3	0.3
Portugal	0.0	1.1	0.5	0.0	0.5	0.5
Finland	n.a.	2.5	12.8	n.a.	1.0	11.4
Sweden	n.a.	0.5	10.9	n.a.	0.1	5.3
UK	27.7	11.5	19.0	0.6	0.5	1.5
Total	100.0	100.0	100.0	–	–	–

[a] EUR12.

Sources: Eurostat (1998): table 38. Eurostat (1999a): 14, 15, 26, and 27. EU Commission (1999), Annexe: table 5. Author's calculation.

taken into consideration that Austria, Finland, and Sweden have been included in the set of data. An important explanation for this large increase is that Ireland officially—and successfully—has led an active policy to attract foreign firms. The share of France in 1998 only amounts to a little less than one-third of that in 1987, and is now at the same level as that of the small member states of Belgium/Luxembourg. The share of the UK has also decreased, but with a share of 19.0 per cent in 1998, the UK is still the largest recipient of investment. Its popularity is often ascribed to its cultural, geographic, linguistic, and structural position. One thing that the small member states, and especially Ireland, Finland, and Sweden, have in common, is that their positions as places of investment have been strengthened. But in general, the core member states (Belgium/Luxembourg, Germany, France, Italy, and the Netherlands) and the UK represent the all-important part of FDI inflows. EU Commission (1998b) thus adduces that many firms position themselves with a subsidiary close to or directly in the large market 'in the middle' of the EU rather than in the areas in the periphery of the EU where factor costs may be lower. This distribution of FDI between member states confirms the importance of *agglomeration advantages*, i.e. the fact that it can be advantageous for firms in the same industry to be present in the same geographic area.

Measured as a proportion of GDP of individual member states, intra-EU FDI flows fluctuate a lot (see second part of Table 7.4). In 1998, FDI flows constituted a larger share of GDP of all member states than in 1987. The largest shares, however, are found in Belgium/Luxemburg, Ireland, the Netherlands, Finland, and Sweden, which, using international trade as a measure, are all characterized by being very open economies. These countries are thus also the most open with respect to capital flows in the form of multinational companies. The very high shares for e.g. Finland and Sweden in 1998 again illustrate that FDI flows are highly unstable from year to year. The large economies of Germany, Spain, France, and Italy have significantly lower shares. On the other hand, the UK, which is also a large member state, distinguishes itself by having a share of 1.5 per cent, which is due to its popularity as a place of investment.

In summary, it has been established that intra- as well as extra-EU FDI inflows have increased significantly in the period around the establishment of the Single Market. Similarly, worldwide FDI flows have increased in the same period. But as the EU share of worldwide FDI flows has increased at the same time, it can be deduced that the creation of the Internal Market has had a positive effect on the increased establishment of subsidiaries. Turning to the member state level, we found especially that the small member states of Ireland, Finland, and Sweden, but also the large member state of Germany, have increased their shares of total intra-EU FDI flows in the period from 1987 to 1998. However, the core member states and the UK still accounted for 69.4 per cent of total EU intra FDI flows in 1998.

7.5 **The sectoral dimension**

FDI also has a sectoral dimension. The share of FDI distributed on main sectors is shown in Figure 7.3, and as can be seen, throughout the period from 1992 to 1998 the majority of FDI was in the service sector. Before 1992, Eurostat used a different grouping of agriculture and industry in particular, but overall, the pattern is the same as shown in Figure 7.3 — services received the largest share of FDI in the period 1984 to 1991 as well (Eurostat 1994).

In 1998, the share of the service sector was 76.7 per cent, corresponding to more than 76bn. ecu, while the share of industry was 23.8 per cent, corresponding to more than 23bn. ecu. The share of the primary sector is negligible, and from 1996, a small disinvestment in the sector can even be observed. In other words, the agricultural sector is of no importance with respect to FDI. The figure thus reflects the dominance which the service sector has had in general in developed economies (see Chapter 5). It should also be remembered that service is generally less tradable than manufactured products, which is why FDI may be the only way to supply a foreign market.

Table 7.5 shows the development in the distribution of intra-EU FDI between selected industrial sectors in manufacturing. In general, it is noticeable that there are

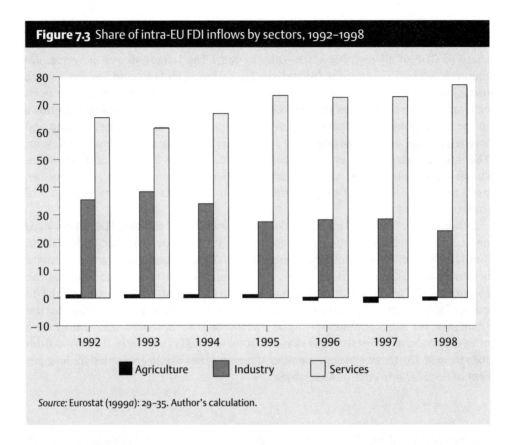

Figure 7.3 Share of intra-EU FDI inflows by sectors, 1992–1998

Agriculture   Industry   Services

Source: Eurostat (1999*a*): 29–35. Author's calculation.

both large differences between individual industries and large shifts in the share of FDI between various industries.[1] Note also that the development in a given sector in the period from 1984 to 1992 can be attributed to other factors than just the establishment of the Single Market. Structural changes in the investment pattern can be induced by e.g. the technological development, introduction of new products, and the opening of the Central and Eastern European economies.

On the face of it, it is surprising that the largest increase in FDI flows throughout the period has been in the less technology-intensive sectors. The largest shifts have been towards food products, transport equipment, and other industries, whereas the relative importance of chemicals in terms of FDI has declined drastically. In the literature it is pointed out that multinationals play a large part in know-how intensive sectors. These sectors are often technology-intensive and are characterized by a high level of R&D relative to sales, a large share of professional and technical workers in their workforce, new and/or technically complex products, and high levels of product

[1] In the main sector of services, 'Finance, banking and insurance' and 'Business services' have received a markedly larger share of total intra-EU FDI flows in the period 1984 to 1992 and at the same time, they are also the sub-sectors which enjoy the largest absolute FDI shares in 1992 (Dunning (1997)).This development may be due to the establishment of the Internal Market as well as to the deregulation and liberalization which has taken place in the service sector in general.

Table 7.5 Share of intra-EU FDI in manufacturing, 1984–1992, per cent

	1984–6	1987–9	1990–2
Technology-intensive	*73.0*	*47.0*	*50.6*
Chemicals	30.8	28.4	9.9
Non-electrical machinery	15.7	3.2	10.1
Electrical and electronic	18.4	13.3	15.3
Transport equipment	8.1	2.1	15.3
Less technology-intensive	*26.9*	*43.0*	*49.5*
Food products	9.6	22.7	27.2
Metal and metal products	0.7	6.4	3.5
Other industries	16.5	23.9	18.8
Total manufacturing	*100.0*	*100.0*	*100.0*
Ecu (billions)	*1.33*	*6.67*	*9.02*

Note: Annual average.

Source: EU Commission (1996): table 15, 91.

differentiation and advertising (see Caves (1982) and Markusen (1995)). A possible reason for less technology-intensive industries to have a relatively large share of FDI after 1987 may be that the Internal Market has stimulated market and resource seeking FDI (cost saving through relocation of parts of the production process). The effect of such a restructuring may be a temporary increase in FDI flows into less technology-intensive industries. If this assumption is correct, a larger share of FDI must be expected to be directed towards high-technology-intensive industries in the future.

7.6 The neoclassical paradigm

IN neoclassical theory, the rate of return on production factors is related to their marginal productivity. Capital is assumed to be homogeneous and knowledge is a free benefit equally available for all. This means that, according to the neoclassical theory, capital will move in one direction—that is where the return on capital is the highest. Based on this theory, FDI flows should be expected to be one-way—from the richest member states to the poorest. This, however, is not the case. There are significant two-way flows between the member states, rich as well as poor. In the following, this will be examined based on a more detailed analysis of FDI flows for one individual country. France has been chosen as the example as it is one of the core members of the EU. Table 7.6 shows the geographic distribution of the inward and outward FDI flows between France and the other member states in 1998.

The table demonstrates that there are significant *two-way flows* between France and

Table 7.6 Intra-EU FDI flows of France, mill. ecu, 1998

	FDI outflow	FDI inflow	Net outflow[a]	Gross flows[b]
Belgium/Luxembourg	3,969	3,602	367	7,571
Denmark	142	100	42	242
Germany	2,177	8,262	−6,085	10,439
Greece	−806	5	−811	811
Spain	876	167	709	1,043
Ireland	459	215	244	674
Italy	1,062	−79	1,141	1,141
The Netherlands	3,474	2,108	1,366	5,582
Austria	560	76	484	636
Portugal	154	139	15	293
Finland	39	242	−203	281
Sweden	80	213	−133	293
UK	3,460	4,909	−1,449	8,369
Total	15,647	19,959	−4,312	35,606

[a] FDI outflows − FDI inflows.
[b] | FDI outflows |+| FDI inflows |.

Note: In columns 1 and 2, '−' indicates disinvestment whereas in column 3, '−' indicates that France is a net recipient of FDI.

Source: Eurostat (1999a): 148–9. Author's calculation.

all the other member states. At the same time, the table shows that FDI inflows and outflows are particularly extensive between France and its closest neighbours, Belgium/Luxembourg, Germany, the Netherlands, and the UK. The prosperity level in these countries does not differ significantly from that in France and thus the capital flows cannot be explained by differences in the endowment of capital. Notice particularly the FDI flows between France and Belgium/Luxembourg. French firms invested 3,969m. ecu in Belgium/Luxembourg, while firms from Belgium/Luxembourg invested 3,602m. ecu in France. This leaves a net outflow from France of a modest 367m. ecu. But in reality, gross flows between the countries totalled 7,571m. ecu. This significant interrelation between the capital markets in France and Belgium/Luxembourg, as well as the other close and relatively wealthy neighbouring countries, underlines the importance, not only of geographic proximity but also of close cultural and linguistic links.

A more detailed picture of FDI net outflows from France appears from Figure 7.4. The second axis indicates net FDI outflows per capita, whereas the first axis indicates GDP per capita. The individual positions of the member states are indicated in the figure.

The predictions of the neoclassical theory using France, which is a rich country, as the basis is indicated by the declining line. The poorer a country is, the smaller is the capital/labour ratio, and the higher is the rate of return on capital. This means that the theory predicts large net outflows from France to poorer member states and

Figure 7.4 FDI net outflows from France to other member states, 1998

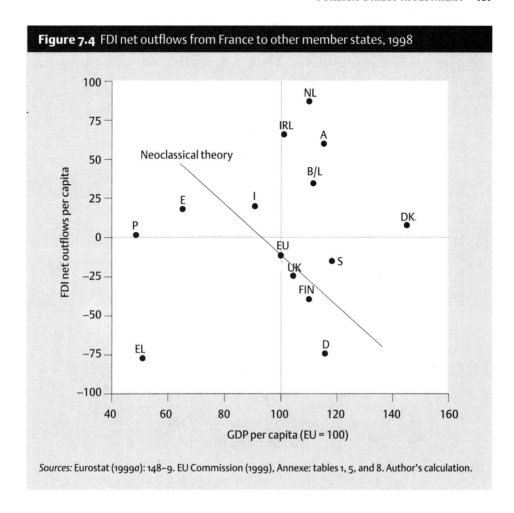

Sources: Eurostat (1999a): 148–9. EU Commission (1999), Annexe: tables 1, 5, and 8. Author's calculation.

negative net outflows from France to richer member states. This is not the picture observed in the figure. The largest FDI net outflows from France are to the Netherlands, which is at the same prosperity level as France, whereas the largest negative FDI net outflows from France are related to Greece. This is to a large extent due to the fact that some French multinationals withdrew from Greece in 1998 (disinvestment). Greece might be an outlier, but even if Greece is excluded, the figure does not support the neoclassical theory. Based on the figure, it is therefore not possible to make a general conclusion on net FDI outflows from France to the other member states—be it the rich or the poor.

'New Trade Theory' predicts large trade flows between similar countries. Recent FDI theories have also argued that the level of FDI flows will be higher between similar countries (Markusen and Venables (1998), Markusen (1995)). How does this prediction fit with the FDI flows to and from France?

Figure 7.5 gives an illustration of GDP per capita in member states compared with gross FDI flows per capita from France to other member states. The figure only

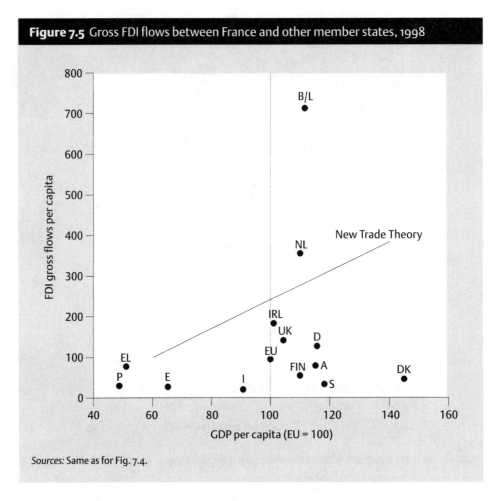

Figure 7.5 Gross FDI flows between France and other member states, 1998

Sources: Same as for Fig. 7.4.

supports this line of thought to a certain extent. Gross FDI flows between France and the poor member states (GDP per capita index < 100) are small. Regarding the rich member states (GDP per capita index > 100), gross FDI flows are large between France and especially Belgium/Luxembourg and the Netherlands, whereas the gross flows between France and the other rich member states of Denmark, Austria, Finland, and Sweden are small and at the same level as the poor member states. Gross flows between France and the remainder of the rich member states (Germany, Ireland, and the UK) take a middle position.

The correlation between trade and FDI flows is depicted in Figure 7.6. The figure relates gross trade flows per capita to gross FDI flows per capita from France to other member states. Gross trade flows per capita equals imports + exports between France and another member state relative to the population of the member state in question. In general, the figure shows a clear correlation between FDI and trade. The positive relation is particularly visible for the member states of Belgium/Luxembourg, the Netherlands, and Ireland, which are all characterized by having extensive relations with France, both in terms of trade and FDI. A possible explanation of the correlation

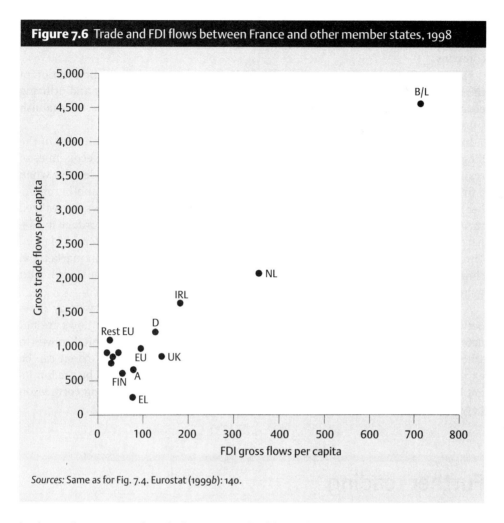

Figure 7.6 Trade and FDI flows between France and other member states, 1998

Sources: Same as for Fig. 7.4. Eurostat (1999b): 140.

is that a large part of trade is composed of intra-firm trade, e.g. trade between a subsidiary and its parent company.

7.7 **Concluding remarks**

MULTINATIONAL companies play an increasing part in the world economy. The EU takes the lead by being the largest investor and main recipient of FDI. In the period around the establishment of the Single Market, its position seems to have been strengthened, as the EU obtained a larger share of worldwide FDI. This indicates that the Internal Market has had a positive effect on the development of FDI flows in the EU. Thus, the establishment of the Internal Market—which, in the OLI framework, mainly is a change in the localization advantages—made it more advantageous for firms to utilize their owner-specific advantages in a multinational company.

FDI flows from non-EU countries into the EU have increased since the creation of the Internal Market. The prospect of entering a large, uniform market and utilizing economies of scale in the production has encouraged non-EU firms to establish subsidiaries in the EU.

Intra-EU FDI flows have also increased significantly since the establishment of the Single Market, even despite the improved possibility of implementing economies of scale in the production. Thus other, often industry-specific, factors are decisive when a firm from one EU member state chooses to establish a subsidiary in another member state. One explanation is that a very large share of intra-EU FDI flows are realized through cross-border M&A. Particularly M&A can be an advantageous strategy in connection with an integration process such as the formation of the Internal Market. Through M&A, firms can both maintain market power in the common market and concentrate on core competences, which may be a necessity when faced with increased competition.

A conspicuous feature of FDI flows in the EU are the significant two-way flows between EU member states. At the same time, it appears that net FDI flows are not determined by the predictions of the neoclassical theory, i.e. that capital moves to where the return is the highest, and that gross FDI flows to a certain extent can be explained by the reasoning of 'New Trade Theory'—that FDI flows will be predominant between similar countries. Finally, it appears that there is a strong correlation between FDI flows and trade between EU member states.

Further reading

A descriptive analysis of FDI in relation to the EU can be found in Eurostat (2000), *European Union Direct Investment Analytical Aspect, Data 1988–1998*, just as the UN (1998), *World Investment Report* describes the development in worldwide FDI. On a theoretical level, a systematic overview of the correlation between integration and FDI is offered in G. N. Yannopoulus (1992), 'Multinational Corporations and the Single European Market' in J. Cantwell (ed.), *Multinational Investment in Modern Europe — Strategic Interaction in the Integrated Community*, Edward Elgar, Aldershot.

References

Caves, R. E. (1982), *Multinational Enterprises and Economic Analysis*, Cambridge University Press, Cambridge.

—— (1989), 'International Differences in Industrial Organizations', in R. Schmalensee and R. D. Wilting (eds.), *Handbook of Industrial Organization*, ii, North-Holland, Amsterdam.

Dunning, J. H. (1993), *Multinational Enterprises and the Global Economy*, Addison-Wesley, Wokingham.

—— (1997), 'The European Internal Market Programme and Inbound Foreign Direct Investment', *Journal of Common Market Studies*, 35(1).

EU Commission (1994), *European Economy*, 57.

—— (1996), 'Economic Evaluation of the Internal Market', *European Economy Reports and Studies*, 4.

—— (1998a), *European Economy Supplement A*, 7, July.

—— (1998b), *Single Market Review, Subseries IV: Impact on Trade and Investment, 1: Foreign Direct Investment*.

—— (1999), *European Economy*, 69.

Eurostat (1994), *Direct Investment in the European Community 1984–91*.

—— (1998), *European Union Direct Investment Yearbook 1997*.

—— (1999a), *European Union Direct Investment Data 1988–1998*.

—— (1999b), *External and Intra-European Union Trade: Statistical Yearbook Data 1958–1998*.

Jørgensen, J. G. (1998), 'Regional Integration og multinationale virksomheder—En økonomisk analyse af vilkårene for multinationale virksomheder i et integrationsmiljø', *Afhandling fra Det Samfundsvidenskabelige Fakultet*, Odense University.

Kindleberger, C. P. (1966), 'European Integration and The International Corporation', *Columbia Journal of World Business*, 1(1).

Markusen, J. R. (1995), 'The Boundaries of Multinational Enterprises and the Theory of International Trade', *Journal of Economic Perspective*, 9(2).

—— and A. J. Venables (1998), 'Multinational Firms and the New Trade Theory', *Journal of International Economics*, 46(2).

Mundell, R. A. (1957), 'International Trade and Factor Mobility', *American Economic Review*, 47(2).

OECD (1996), *OECD Benchmark Definition of Foreign Direct Investment*, 3rd edn.

Skinner, W. (1974a), 'The Focused Factory', *Harvard Business Review*, May–June, 113–21.

—— (1974b), 'The Decline, Fall and Renewal of Manufacturing Plants', *Industrial Engineering*, 6(10): 32–8.

UN (1999), *World Investment Report 1999, Foreign Direct Investment and the Challenge of Development*, UN.

Viner, J. (1950), *The Customs Union Issue*, Stevens, New York.

Chapter 8

Monetary Integration: Old Issues — New Solutions

Jørgen Drud Hansen and Finn Olesen

8.1 Introduction

WHILE the formation of the Single Market was a process lasting several years, the introduction of the common currency, the *euro*, took place at a specific point in time. As at 1 January 1999, eleven EU member states established a common currency by fixing their exchange rates irrevocably to the euro. The euro will only take a physical form, and the national currencies be phased out, a couple of years into the new millennium, but with a specified, fixed exchange rate between the euro and the currencies of the eleven countries, from an economic-political point of view, the common currency is already a reality.

Even if participation in the common currency begins at a fixed point in time, the preparation of the introduction of the euro started already in the early 1990s. Individual countries thus had to adapt their economic policies with a view to qualifying for membership of the euro through fulfilment of a series of *convergence criteria*. The background for this procedure was the desirability of adjusting the economies to the common currency and in so doing, rendering as much credibility to the project as possible. Only those countries which, in the years leading up to the introduction of the euro, had experienced a high degree of exchange rate stability within the European currency cooperation under the *European Monetary System*, EMS, could join the monetary union. A concurrent requirement was that the countries should have sound public finances and a certain homogeneity with respect to inflation and interest rates. The EU Commission's enthusiastic eulogy of the effects of the EMU project is expressed in the preface of a report containing the Commission's evaluation of the economic development of individual EU countries in terms of fulfilling the convergence criteria:

The introduction of the euro confirms the advent of a genuine culture of stability in Europe that is essential to the establishment of a stable, sound and efficiently managed economic framework. (EU Commission (1998a: 7))

This optimistic expectation of the effects of a common currency is, however, controversial. Stability is a Janus head consisting of both nominal stability, e.g. low and stable price inflation, and real stability, e.g. high and stable employment. It is not given that these two forms of stability will occur at the same time, and it is certainly not given that a possible increase in price stability in the euro area will be followed by increased stability in employment.

The purpose of this chapter is to illustrate this problem in more detail. Section 8.2 gives a retrospective overview of the many attempts at monetary integration in the EU. Section 8.3 discusses whether the EU member countries, or a section of them, can constitute a so-called *optimum currency area* within which the economic benefits of establishing a formalized economic and monetary union generally exceed the costs. An important feature of the *Economic and Monetary Union*, EMU, is the requirement that those countries wishing to participate in the common currency must qualify themselves by meeting the convergence criteria. These criteria are analysed in Section 8.4, whereas Section 8.5 illustrates the perspectives for the monetary policy in the euro area. Given that the overall objective is price stability, the section discusses how this objective is specified and how the *European Central Bank* (ECB) operationalizes it in its monetary policy strategy. Section 8.6 describes the role of fiscal policy in the EMU, and puts focus on the so-called *Stability and Growth Pact*. The chapter concludes with a summary and offers some prospects for the future.

8.2 A brief history of monetary integration

SEEN in a historic perspective, from the very beginning, European integration has been aimed at developing close economic and monetary cooperation between the member states of the Community (Ungerer (1997)). The first concrete plans of such a formalized cooperation appeared as early as 1969.

Later on, in 1971, the need for a closer cooperation resulted in the Werner plan, based upon which the Council of Ministers adopted a resolution which had as its declared political goal the eventual establishment of an economic and monetary union. Based on this resolution, a system of joint fluctuation, subsequently dubbed the 'snake in the tunnel', was established in 1972. It included the original six EC countries as well as the UK, Ireland, Denmark, Sweden, and Norway. It was determined that the maximum mutual exchange rate fluctuations of the currencies of these countries could be ± 2.25 per cent. However, as the international economy was also marked by continuous financial instability at the beginning of the 1970s, the snake in the tunnel soon turned out to be rather problematic. The UK was thus forced to leave the cooperation, and later also France, Italy, and Sweden withdrew from the snake in the tunnel arrangement.

In 1973, the European Community was enlarged by the UK, Ireland, and Denmark. Inspired by this, towards the end of the year, the European Council decided that the economic policies of individual member states should be coordinated. Although several other resolutions with the same aim followed, in reality they were all at a rather informal level.

It was not until the end of the decade that the monetary cooperation between the countries was reinforced in a concrete way. At a French–German initiative, the snake in the tunnel arrangement was changed into the European Monetary System (EMS) in 1979. However, the UK chose to stay outside the fixed exchange rate cooperation of the Community, just as Norway used this opportunity to leave the snake in the tunnel and thus also the EMS.

In the new system, the old, so-called parity grid of ± 2.25 per cent was maintained, committing all the participating countries to ensure that their currencies would only fluctuate within this band. At the same time, as opposed to the previous snake in the tunnel arrangement, the new exchange rate cooperation was supported by clear commitments by the participating countries to make interventions. These commitments were formulated in such a way that both the central bank with a strong currency and the central bank with a weak currency, facing a pressure to devalue, were equally obliged to actively intervene during a currency crisis. The intervention should be made in a cooperation between the central banks, in which the central bank with the strong currency, which later increasingly proved to be the German mark, was obliged to intervene in favour of the central bank with the weak currency.

Although, in principle, the ultimate goal of the cooperation continued to be a formalized economic and monetary union, at the beginning of the 1980s, the political will to realize this goal seemed to be missing. Again based on a French–German initiative, in 1988 it was decided to have a committee prepare a new report which should make a concrete proposal for the gradual implementation of an economic and monetary union. The result was the Delors Report which outlined a three-stage development plan for the establishment of a full-blown economic and monetary union. The first stage, which contained very little in terms of concrete commitment, became effective as from 1 July 1990. Later that same year, an intergovernmental conference was held with the purpose of detailing the activities and timetables of the second and third stages, which should constitute the final transition to economic and monetary union. These efforts led to the adoption of the Maastricht Treaty on European Union, which was ratified in 1992.

In connection with the ratification of this Treaty, several countries chose to hold a referendum on the issue. Surprisingly, the outcome was considerably less resolved than expected. Denmark, for instance, voted against the Maastricht Treaty in June 1992, and later only a marginal majority of French voters confirmed the accession to the Treaty. As a natural consequence of this rather hesitant support to the future common currency among the populations of many European countries, the currencies of several member states came under increasing pressure as from the summer of 1992. After a number of futile attempts at maintaining the exchange rate cooperation in an unaltered form, *inter alia* through determined efforts at rejecting speculative attacks on key currencies, the cooperation in effect broke down at the beginning of August 1993, when the parity grid was expanded to ± 15 per cent.

At the same time, the member states confirmed their continued willingness to implement the EMU according to the provisions of the Treaty. The Treaty thus came into force on 1 November 1993, and it was agreed to start the second stage as from 1 January 1994. In this stage, the *European Monetary Institute* (EMI)—the forerunner of the European Central Bank—was established. Similarly, certain common directives for the finance policies of individual countries came into force. Monetary financing of public sector deficits was thus no longer allowed, just as a procedure to prevent disproportionately large public budget deficits was initiated. This meant that the Commission should monitor the development of the public budgets of the member states. If the deficit of a member state continued to total more than 3 per cent of GDP, if deemed necessary, the Commission could request that member country to reduce its deficit. However, in the second stage, the Commission had no other sanctions than to publicize its request if it turned out that the member country in question did not comply with it.

At the end of 1996, based on reports from the EMI as well as from the Commission, the European Council formally decided that the third stage would be implemented starting on 1 January 1999, which also marked the introduction of the euro. Initially, the national currencies continue to be the only physical currencies in circulation, but their conversion to euro is based on irrevocably fixed exchange rates, and they will be phased out and replaced by euro coins and notes from the year 2002.

Both before and after the drafting of the Maastricht Treaty, the attitude to the expediency of the EMU arrangement has been ambivalent. Among economists, there have been arguments both for and against the perception that the different regions of the European Union are sufficiently homogeneous in an economic sense to constitute an optimum currency area. Similarly, opinions differ on the appropriateness of the specific framework of the EMU. This applies both to the convergence criteria, which individual member states have to meet before entering the EMU, and to the institutional framework covering the monetary and fiscal policy of the EMU. These controversies will be discussed in more detail below.

8.3 Costs and benefits of the EMU

THIS section will analyse some of the most important benefits and potential costs of the EMU. By way of introduction, the possible conflict between the pursuit of improved microeconomic efficiency versus the desirability of macroeconomic stability is touched upon. This is followed by a discussion as to what extent the European countries historically have performed fairly similarly. This will be reinforced by an illustration of the development in unemployment. The section will be concluded by a more detailed analysis of whether or not the EMU can be characterized as a sufficiently large optimum currency area.

Microeconomic efficiency vs. macroeconomic stability

The monetary union will give the member countries several obvious benefits. First, firms and consumers will be rid of foreign exchange transaction costs, as mutual payments will be carried out in the common currency, euro. The cost saving arising from this is assessed to around 0.3 to 0.4 per cent of GDP for the EMU countries (see the EU Commission (1990)). Secondly, exchange rate uncertainty concerning payment obligations between member countries will disappear. Trade and capital movements are often curbed by exchange rate uncertainty, and this is demonstrated, for example, by the fact that firms often assume costs of hedging against potential adverse exchange rate fluctuations by buying futures. It is, however, difficult to estimate the importance of eliminating this exchange rate uncertainty in monetary terms. Thirdly, a common currency will ensure larger price transparency and, as a consequence, competition will increase in individual markets. The consequence of this will be a reduction in the differences in prices of the same product between countries. Finally, a common currency will exclude competitive devaluations and the consequent sudden changes in the mutual competitiveness of individual countries. These benefits will thus also contribute to a general strengthening of the Internal Market.

The most important cost of the common currency is the loss of major economic policy instruments, which the participating countries will experience. With a common currency, individual countries lose the possibility of re- or devaluing, and similarly there will only be one common monetary policy for the entire euro area. This may give rise to situations where individual member countries have different preferences for the common monetary and exchange rate policy. This may in turn lead to larger instability in employment in individual member countries. The problem arises in the case of so-called country-specific asymmetric shocks, where production and employment develop differently in different countries. In such situations it is desirable for individual countries to pursue their own independent economic policies. If the instruments are not available, the countries will not be able to influence the economic development, and the asymmetric influences will remain uncorrected.

The invalidation of the monetary and exchange rate policy within the national economic policy already arises in a fixed exchange rate regime with free movement of capital. Obviously, in such a regime, the use of exchange rate instruments at the national level is made impossible. If there is mutual trust that the exchange rate parities agreed upon are observed, the mobility of capital will lead to identical interest rates, and there will also be a *de facto* common monetary policy. The 1980s and early 1990s saw long spells of trust in the fixed exchange rates between the countries participating in the EMS, and consequently, the exchange rate differences between these countries were limited.[1] However, in a fixed exchange rate regime, it is an open question how the common monetary and exchange rate policy is determined. In principle, it can either be a joint decision by the participating countries, or one of the countries can take the lead. In the EMS, the latter became the case. Germany played a dominating role in the monetary policy implemented in the entire fixed exchange rate area and as a consequence, the monetary policy was to a large extent determined by internal factors in the German economy. The role of the other countries in the EMS was thus reduced to accepting German monetary policy.

The European experiences of asymmetry

The problem about a group of countries committing themselves to a common monetary and exchange rate policy through agreements on fixed exchange rates, or through the establishment of an actual currency union, is thus that there is a risk of a conflict of interests between the countries on economic policy. The conflict of interests can manifest itself in differences in opinion between the countries about the desired development, employment, inflation, investments, and balance of payments. In the following, this problem is illustrated through the development in unemployment.

Figure 8.1 compares the development of unemployment in Denmark, France, Finland, and the UK with the development of unemployment in Germany, the largest economy in the euro area, in the period 1987–94. In the early 1990s, Denmark, France, Germany, and the UK all participated in the fixed exchange rate cooperation of the EMS, and similarly, Finland aimed at maintaining fixed exchange rates with the EMS countries.

In Figure 8.1, average unemployment as a percentage of the labour force in individual years is indicated by U_i, where i = F (France), FIN (Finland), UK (United Kingdom), DK (Denmark), and D (West Germany). The figure also shows the average unemployment rate for the entire period 1987–94, $\overline{U}_i$. The combinations of unemployment in areas I and III show *symmetric situations* in the sense that the unemployment rate in one country is below and in the other country above the average unemployment rate for the entire period, as opposed to areas II and IV, which show *asymmetric situations*. It is particularly when the economies move into asymmetric situations that the need for an independent monetary and exchange rate policy arises.

In the beginning of the period, i.e. until September 1993, the fixed exchange rate cooperation was based on a parity grid of ± 2.25 per cent, after which the parity grid was increased to ± 15 per cent. However, both France and Denmark chose to shadow

---

[1] When differences still occurred within the EMS, it was due to the fact that the system allowed restricted exchange rate fluctuations within the agreed parity grids. Furthermore, there may have been market expectations of changes in the central parities. If the market expects that the currency for country B depreciates against country A, the interest rate in country B will be higher than in country A. This correlation is illustrated in more detail in Appendix 8A (see relation (A4)).

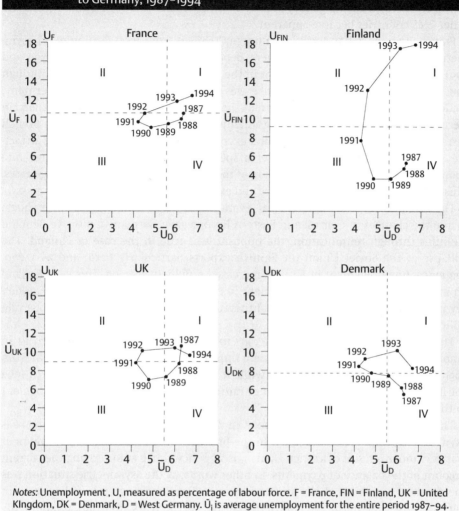

Figure 8.1 Unemployment rates in France, Finland, the UK, and Denmark relative to Germany, 1987–1994

Notes: Unemployment , U, measured as percentage of labour force. F = France, FIN = Finland, UK = United KIngdom, DK = Denmark, D = West Germany. $\bar{U}_i$ is average unemployment for the entire period 1987–94.

Source: EU Commission (1997), Annexe: table 3. Authors' calculation.

the German mark. In the period until November 1992, Finland exercised a fixed exchange rate policy which, in practice, meant a fixed exchange rate vis-à-vis the other EMS countries. After November 1993, the Finnish Central Bank let the currency float. With relatively free mobility of capital there was just limited room for manoeuvre to carry out an independent monetary and exchange rate policy in the period up to the autumn of 1993.

Unemployment in Germany was decreasing in the period 1988–91, in particular due to the increasing demand created by reunification. However, at the same time, the inflationary pressure was on the increase. As a consequence, the German Central

Bank tightened the monetary policy with the result that unemployment increased significantly in the years after 1991. As this tightening of the monetary policy was felt in the entire fixed exchange rate area, the risk of tension between Germany and the other EMS countries became apparent.

France experienced an increase in unemployment from 1990 leading to an asymmetric development in unemployment between France and Germany in 1990 and 1991, but from 1991, the development in the two countries was symmetric, although the level of unemployment in France was significantly higher than in Germany. Undoubtedly, reducing unemployment had higher priority in France than in Germany. Given these differences in unemployment levels and priorities, a French distancing from German monetary and exchange rate policy seemed like an attractive resort. This evaluation gave rise to speculative attacks on the exchange rate cooperation which led to the expansion of the parity grid of the fixed exchange rates. This partly freed the French monetary and exchange rate policy from the German.

The scenario for Finland is a clear example of a significant asymmetric shock. While the changes in Central and Eastern Europe gave Germany a positive demand stimulus through reunification, the opposite was true in the case of Finland. The collapse of the Soviet Union hit Finnish exports particularly hard, and as a consequence, unemployment in Finland increased rapidly from 1990. This gave Finland an urgent need for a rapid improvement in competitiveness and a less strict monetary policy. In November 1993, Finland therefore abandoned the fixed exchange rate policy.

The development in the UK from 1987 to 1992 followed the same pattern as in France, i.e. in the first years, employment improved in the UK and Germany, but from 1990, unemployment rose in the UK while it fell in Germany. Hence, already in 1992 the British pound left the fixed exchange rate cooperation after which unemployment in the UK stabilized.

The development in unemployment in Denmark over the years 1987–92 was asymmetric compared to Germany. In the first part of the period, this development was very much a result of a strict, Danish fiscal policy aimed at improving the current account of the balance of payments. In other words, as the asymmetric situation was the result of a political choice in Denmark, the fixed exchange rate policy was not felt as a constraint. In the last part of the period, i.e. the years after 1991, undoubtedly also Denmark had a wish for a less strict monetary policy, albeit this wish was subordinated to the fixed exchange rate policy vis-à-vis the German currency.

The experiences from the fixed exchange rate cooperation at the end of the 1980s and early 1990s indicate that conflicting interests about the common monetary policy are likely to arise. In case of vigorous asymmetric shocks, for instance like the one hitting Finland around 1990, it may be expedient to allow the currency to depreciate in order to obtain a rapid improvement in competitiveness. Several European countries have thus experienced the lack of instruments under a fixed exchange rate system as an actual problem.

Drawing this conclusion it should be borne in mind, however, that for a number of European countries in the early 1990s, the course of developments described above was a result of a dramatic change in political systems in Europe. This gave rise to a uniquely exceptional situation related especially to the reunification of East and West Germany as well as radical changes in the trade flows between a number of countries. Such situations may also arise in future, but in a historical perspective they are rare. Besides this, the above analysis is simplified in various ways. Even though Germany is the largest economy, the choice of Germany as a reference country for asymmetric developments is arbitrary, and for obvious reasons, Germany was strongly influenced by the political events of the 1990s. Similarly, using average unemployment as a measure of an equilibrium unemployment rate is a simplification.

Various cases of asymmetric shocks, illustrated by the development in unemployment, are described above. There are, however, also benefits of participating in a monetary union, and when selecting the form of exchange rate regime, weighing the benefits against the costs is therefore of significant importance. It is exactly this set of problems which is systematized by the theory on optimum currency areas.

EMU and the criteria for an optimum currency area

The theory on optimum currency areas consists of a series of criteria used to assess the expediency of a country abandoning its own currency in favour of a common currency. The concept of the optimum currency area was originally formulated by Mundell (1961), but several others have subsequently contributed to the further development of this theory; see Tavlas (1993) for a survey of old as well as more recent contributions.

The most important criteria may be grouped under the following six headings: (1) *Policy preferences*, (2) *Industrial structure*, (3) *Openness of the economy*, (4) *Mobility of labour*, (5) *Wage and price flexibility*, and (6) *Fiscal integration*.

1. *Policy preferences*: It is important that the countries entering a monetary union have similar goals or preferences for the economic policy. In other words, in order to obtain identical economic situations in individual countries with respect to unemployment, inflation, and balance of payments, there must be a uniform perception of the preferable future economic development. If this precondition is not present, even symmetric shocks will provoke desires to implement different economic policies, and cooperation on a policy instrument, in the form of a common currency, may thus feel rather constraining. For example, the speculative pressure on the French currency in 1993, which led to the expansion of the parity grid of the EMS, was to a certain extent underpinned by a widely held opinion that reducing unemployment was a higher priority in France than in Germany.

2. *Industrial structure*: The risk of asymmetric shocks, as first pointed out by Kenen (1969), depends in particular on the differences in industrial structures between countries. If the industrial structures are very different between the countries wishing to form a monetary union, changes in the composition in demand will influence the countries differently, with asymmetric shocks as a consequence.

The main sectors and industrial structures of the member states are described in

Chapter 5. Regarding the overall distribution on main sectors, agriculture is still relatively important in Greece, Portugal, and Ireland, although this difference from the other member states is diminishing rapidly. Chapter 5 also illustrates differences in industrial structures in manufacturing (see the calculated indices of manufacturing divergence in Table 5.8).

It is, however, difficult to estimate the significance of the measured differences in industrial structures because the classification of industries influences the indices of divergence. Add to this that the risk of country-specific asymmetric shocks not only depends on differences in industrial structure, but also on the probability of *industry-specific asymmetric shocks*, i.e. differences in the development in activities in individual industries in the entire monetary union. Finally, the development in activities in individual countries is influenced by the development in total market shares in individual industries in each country. In areas where the mobility of goods is high, the development in market shares is determined, among other things, by the development in salaries. If, however, the mobility of goods is low, local demand is important for the development in activities in individual areas.

It is probably not the differences in industrial structures between the EU countries which will be the largest source of country-specific asymmetric shocks in the EMU. By now, agriculture only makes up a modest share in all EU countries, and it is therefore unlikely that differences in the share of activities in agriculture will contribute to significant country-specific asymmetric shocks (internally in individual countries, however, there are large regional variances in the share of activities of agriculture, and the risk of regional asymmetric shocks is therefore larger). The differences in industrial structures in manufacturing are probably also so limited that future industry-specific asymmetric shocks will only to a limited degree be transformed into actual country-specific asymmetric shocks.

The most significant reason that country-specific asymmetric shocks become a problem is the limited mobility of goods and services. Despite the establishment of the Internal Market, the relationship between firms and their customers is characterized by stickiness, and therefore it takes time for the firms to change their outlets. It was exactly this situation which hit the Finnish economy so hard. It was not immediately possible to create a compensating demand for Finnish exports when the Soviet Union collapsed, and this negative asymmetric shock had a very negative impact on Finnish employment. Although the Single Market contributes to increasing the mobility of goods and services, that similar situations may arise in future cannot be ruled out.

3. *Openness of the economy:* The openness of the economy reflects the degree of integration of the goods market measured, for example, by the value of exports and imports of an individual country relative to its gross domestic product (GDP). If the goods markets are highly integrated through trade, the benefits of a common currency, in the form of exchange transaction costs saved, reduced exchange rate uncertainty, and increased price transparency, are relatively large. The effect of asymmetric shocks on the economic development will furthermore be dampened by the trade between the countries since changes in activity in one country automatically will make the aggregate demand in other countries move in the same direction

via export and import. If the countries are closely connected to each other through export and import, there will be significant *aggregate demand spill-overs*. Even if the countries are hit by asymmetric shocks, this will only to a limited degree lead to an asymmetric development in unemployment. The costs of a common currency will consequently be lower and, at the same time, the benefits in the form of exchange transaction costs saved and reduced exchange rate uncertainty will be higher.

For very open economies, it is problematic to use the exchange rate instrument in the economic policy in the case of asymmetric shocks. This view was emphasized by McKinnon (1963), who pointed out the risk of inflation if attempts are made at stimulating employment through depreciation, because prices on imports will increase immediately. In an open economy, where imports are relatively large, higher prices on imports will have a significant effect on the total price level, and this may evoke demands for salary increases which will only further enhance the inflationary process.

Openness also plays a role in the choice of policy instruments aimed at influencing the current accounts on the balance of payments. If there is a political wish to remove a deficit on the current accounts, in very open economies it is expedient to implement a contractionary fiscal policy, as this will have a significant effect on the current accounts because of the high marginal propensity to import. This was exactly the strategy followed by Denmark in the late 1980s (see the discussion related to Figure 8.1). In tightly closed economies, on the other hand, it is inexpedient to influence the current accounts through the fiscal policy due to the effect on employment. Here, a change in exchange rates will influence the current accounts more selectively, i.e. without having a strong impact on employment.

If the core of EMU countries in terms of trade consists of Germany, France, Italy, and Spain, with the exception of Greece, the small EU countries are closely connected to this group of core countries. Judging from the demand spill-overs and the inflation problem, as well as the benefits of the common currency, this group of countries will thus have a larger interest in establishing a common currency. Similarly, Chapter 6 demonstrates that intra-EU trade, measured as a share of GDP, has increased during the past forty years. This development in openness between the EU countries increases their interest in a common currency.

4. *Mobility of labour:* The mobility of labour, as first suggested by Ingram (1959) and Mundell (1961), may contribute to an *automatic stabilization* in a monetary union which is hit by asymmetric shocks. Where mobility of labour is easy, unemployed persons will migrate from the country with failing demand to the country with increasing demand. This will ameliorate the effects of the asymmetric shock on the rate of unemployment and, as a consequence, the need for an independent monetary and exchange rate policy will be reduced.

However, as pointed out in Chapter 3, since the mobility of labour between member states is very low, there is no doubt that it will not be possible to solve the stabilization problem through migration between the countries in the euro area. It might also be argued that extensive migration in the EU, as a reaction to asymmetric shocks, will conflict with other goals of EU cooperation which do not concern employment, for example the breakdown of cultural differences due to extensive migration. Maintaining differences in culture is indeed an independent goal, cf. Article 128 of the Amsterdam Treaty.

5. *Wage and price flexibility:* If labour does not migrate, wage flexibility may dampen the effect of asymmetric shocks. This has previously been pointed out by Friedman (1953), among others. By reducing the nominal wages in a monetary union, countries, in which employment has been negatively effected by asymmetric shocks, may strengthen their competitiveness vis-à-vis their union partners and thus stabilize their own employment. The absence of an independent monetary and exchange rate policy in the euro area therefore increases the need for flexible and well-functioning labour markets. Labour market flexibility in the EU is described in Chapter 3, and the main conclusion is that the labour markets in several EU countries are relatively inflexible compared to the USA. It is possible, however, that the establishment of the monetary union will increase labour market flexibility in the long run. If this happens, wage flexibility will have an even larger stabilizing effect on the economic development than now.

6. *Fiscal integration:* Considering the pros and cons of establishing a monetary union, Kenen (1969), among others, has pointed out the importance of fiscal policy integration. If a strong element of *federal fiscal policy* is established, under which the monetary union as an institution collects taxes and defrays expenditures, the effects of the asymmetric shocks are dampened. For those countries experiencing a negative effect on activities from asymmetric shocks, the federal tax payments to the union are reduced at the same time as the federal transfers increase, i.e. net payments to the union will fall. The opposite is true for those countries experiencing a positive effect on activities from asymmetric shocks, as their net payments to the union will increase. Federal fiscal policy will thus add an *element of solidarity* to the monetary union, according to which demand is redistributed from countries experiencing an increase in activities to countries experiencing a decrease in activities.

In the EMU, however, this element is extremely small. Thus, EU expenditures only total around 1.25 per cent of GDP of the entire union. In comparison, public expenditure at the federal level in the USA totals around 20 per cent of GDP (US Census Bureau (1999): table 5.42). To this should be added that both expenditure and income of the EU budget is relatively insensitive to the business cycle and that the Union Treaty requires a balanced budget (Article 199 of the Amsterdam Treaty). There are no plans to make significant changes to these factors in the coming years. The long-term perspectives for the EU budget were determined by the Council of Ministers at the end of 1998 when it was decided that up to the year 2005, the budget should continue to amount to only around 1.25 per cent of total GDP of the EU. These narrow budgetary limits will of course restrict the capacity to implement a federal fiscal policy.

Within the EU cooperation there is thus a patent dilemma between the wish to retain an autonomous fiscal policy at the national level and the desire to give fiscal policy a more active role in the efforts to overcome the effects of asymmetric shocks. In an attempt to solve this dilemma, Italianer and Vanheukelen (1993) have outlined a proposal for an efficient, automatic stabilization mechanism at the federal level which will not put a significant strain on the budget. According to their proposal, the mechanism will be released if a country within the euro area is hit by an asymmetric shock, which means that the unemployment rate of that country will increase by more than the Union average. In such clear cases of asymmetric shocks, an automatic transfer of resources from the federal budget to the country in question must take place. However, the transfer will be restricted to the period where the asymmetric shock occurs, and this is exactly why the strain on the budget is limited. The suggested stabilization mechanism will thus not eliminate the need for a flexible labour market in case of prolonged unemployment.

The effects mentioned above are general for all member countries of the monetary union. However, the formation of the EMU has some additional effects which will only have an immediate influence on certain member states. The Amsterdam Treaty (Art. 105) stipulates that the common central bank, the European Central Bank, will be independent of governments and public institutions in general. The primary objective of the monetary policy will be to secure price stability. On paper, the position of the European Central Bank is therefore similar to that of the German Central Bank, which has obtained a high degree of credibility in terms of maintaining price stability. By transferring the institutional design of the German Central Bank to its European counterpart, the idea is that the credibility of the low-inflation policy led by the German Central Bank will be transferred to the European Central Bank in a similar fashion. Accordingly, the inflationary expectations of those countries which traditionally have had a high inflation will be removed without the costs traditionally attached to such a move, i.e. without an extended period of high unemployment. Particularly the southern European member states, Spain, Italy, and Portugal, will benefit from their participation in the EMU in this respect.

In summary, the eleven countries participating in the euro will reap microeconomic efficiency gains, but at the same time, they will also be exposed to the risk of macroeconomic instability. The theory of the optimum currency area lists some structural characteristics which are of importance to strike a balance between the costs and benefits of a common currency. Reviewing the structural characteristics of the initial eleven countries reveals a mixed picture of this balance.

There is a risk that asymmetric shocks will arise also in future and that they will lead to asymmetric developments in activity. In such cases, in an EU context, only the wage and price flexibility can be expected to automatically contribute to a macroeconomic stabilization of the economic development of the member countries. The economic-political possibilities of stabilizing economic activities in cases of asymmetric shocks are tied to the national fiscal policy, but in certain cases, the possibility of availing of this policy is limited by the obligation of the EMU member countries of maintaining sound public finances (see Section 8.6).

8.4 EMU and the convergence criteria

ESTABLISHING an EMU with eleven member countries has been a long, continuous process, as described in Section 8.2. While Denmark, Sweden, and the UK all chose not to enter the Union from 1 January 1999, Greece was unable to meet the convergence criteria for membership at the time.

The Maastricht Treaty of 1992 laid down five convergence criteria. In May 1998, on the basis of each country's economic performance in 1997, it was determined which countries met the defined criteria. Three of these five criteria all focus on *monetary* convergence, as they relate to price and exchange rate stability as well as convergence of long-term interest rates. The remaining two criteria focus more on *real* convergence, as they relate to the public finances.

More specifically, participation in the common currency is conditional upon the fulfilment of the following convergence criteria: (1) *Price stability*, (2) *Exchange rate stability*, (3) *Convergence of long-term interest rates*, (4) *Low public deficit*, and (5) *Low public debt*.

1. *Price stability:* A country's rate of inflation may not exceed the average inflation rate of the three best performing member states by more than 1½ percentage points.

2. *Exchange rate stability:* The member state must have demonstrated exchange rate stability under the exchange rate mechanism (ERM) of the European Monetary System (EMS) for at least two years, without having devalued its currency against the currencies of any other member state.

3. *Convergence of long-term interest rates:* The long-term interest rate may not exceed the average long-term interest rate of the three best inflation performing member states by more than 2 percentage points.

These monetary criteria will help identify whether individual countries at present, or in future, need to avail themselves of the exchange rate instrument in their economic policy as a result of the monetary development. If the inflation rate in one country exceeds the inflation rate in the other member countries of the monetary union, that country will lose competitiveness and a devaluation may become necessary. The criterion on exchange rate stability reveals if a country actually has made use of this instrument within the last two years. The criterion of long-term interest rate convergence tests the initial competitiveness of each country. If, due to poor competitiveness, a country has a structural problem in the form of unemployment and a deficit on the current accounts, this will often be reflected in a high, long-term interest rate, as the risk of devaluation will be calculated into the interest rate level.

4. *Low public deficit:* The member state must avoid excessive government deficits, defined as 3 per cent of GDP.

5. *Low public debt:* The public debt of the member state must not exceed 60 per cent of GDP.

These last two criteria are garnished with exceptions opening up for a flexible interpretation. It is, for instance, possible to disregard the maximum 3 per cent public deficit criterion if the ratio is close to 3 per cent or if the excess public deficit is 'exceptional and temporary'. Furthermore, being in excess of the 60 per cent debt ratio does not automatically preclude a country from membership if the ratio is 'sufficiently diminishing and approaching the reference value at a satisfactory pace' (Amsterdam Treaty, Article 104c). The aim of these criteria is to ensure that the public deficit does not lead to an uncontrollable increase in the public debt, which will erode the basis of the monetary union in the long run.

There is an intrinsic relation between public deficit, real growth, inflation rate, and public debt. If the public deficit and the real growth rate both make up 3 per cent of GDP and, at the same time, the inflation rate is 2 per cent p.a., in the long run, the public debt burden will stabilize at exactly 60 per cent of GDP. As an example, let us assume that in a given year, the data for a member country are: a GDP of 100bn. euro, a public debt totalling 60bn. euro, a public deficit of exactly 3 per cent of GDP, a real growth rate also of 3 per cent p.a., and an inflation rate of 2 per cent p.a. In one year, the public debt will increase by 3bn. euro to 63bn. euro, while GDP in current prices will increase to 105bn. euro, i.e. the debt burden will remain at 60 per cent of GDP. Experience shows that long-term real growth in GDP of several member states only amounts to 2–3 per cent p.a. The aim of the European Central Bank is to reduce inflation to less than 2 per cent p.a. If the central bank succeeds with this policy, growth in GDP in current prices will thus be less than 5 per cent p.a., and as a consequence, the long-term debt, which reflects a public deficit of 3 per cent of GDP, will exceed 60 per cent of GDP.

Who qualifies for membership of the euro?

Table 8.1 illustrates the economic development of individual member states in 1997, which determined their future membership of the EMU. The table shows that the EU countries converge fairly well in terms of monetary homogeneity (inflation and long-term interest rate). Greece, Sweden, and the UK did not participate in the fixed exchange rate cooperation of the EMS, and therefore they did not fulfil the convergence criterion in this area. Concerning the criteria relating to the public finances, the debt criterion in particular causes problems for most EU countries, and even those countries which joined the EMU in its third phase did not completely live up to the 60 per cent debt restriction in 1997. Only Spain, France, Luxembourg, and Finland were capable of fully complying with this convergence criterion. However, the participation of the other countries was also secured as it was estimated that the debt rate of these countries *was diminishing at a satisfactory pace*, in other words, the flexible interpretation was adopted.

Table 8.1 Member state performance in relation to Maastricht, 1997

	Exchange rates (ERM participation)	Rate of inflation	Long-term interest rate	Public deficit[d] (% of GDP)	Public debt (% of GDP)
Belgium	✓	1.4	5.7	2.1	122
Denmark	✓	1.9	6.2	−0.7	65
Germany	✓	1.4	5.6	2.7	61
Greece	✓[a]	5.2	9.8	4.0	109
Spain	✓	1.8	6.3	2.6	69
France	✓	1.2	5.5	3.0	58
Ireland	✓	1.2	6.2	−0.9	66
Italy	✓	1.8	6.7	2.7	122
Luxembourg	✓[b]	1.4	5.6	−1.7	7
The Netherlands	✓	1.8	5.5	1.4	72
Austria	✓	1.1	5.6	2.5	66
Portugal	✓	1.8	6.2	2.5	62
Finland	✓[c]	1.3	5.9	0.9	56
Sweden	÷	1.9	6.5	0.8	77
UK	÷	1.8	7.0	1.9	53
Reference value	—	2.7	7.8	3.0	60

[a] Since March 1998.
[b] Since November 1996.
[c] Since October 1996.
[d] Minus indicates a surplus.

Source: EU Commission (1998*a*): table 1.1.

A critical view of the convergence criteria

The rationale behind the convergence criteria is, however, not obvious, as pointed out by several (see e.g. De Grauwe (2000) for critical remarks). First, the criteria are retrospective, although it seems more relevant to make an evaluation of a potential member country's future economic performance. Whether a monetary union will experience problems with competitiveness caused by inflation depends on the differences in inflation rates after the establishment of the monetary union, not before. Secondly, the reference values for public deficit and public debt are arbitrary (Pasinetti (1998)), and for several countries, meeting these criteria has been a painful process creating further unemployment (Wyplosz (1997)). Finally, and perhaps most fundamentally, the convergence criteria are not related to the criteria for an optimum currency area as defined in economic theory.

The Maastricht Treaty does not contain convergence criteria relating to the development in unemployment or real growth in GDP of the member states, let alone industrial structures, mobility of labour, or fiscal integration. Omitting employment and growth from the convergence criteria may seem surprising, especially bearing in mind, as demonstrated in some of the previous chapters, that the integration process in a number of areas—the European labour markets, for instance—has not yet been completed satisfactorily.

A possible explanation of this paradox may be found in the economic reasoning which is characteristic of the Treaty. The economic theory behind the convergence criteria of the EMU is based on an assumption of full equilibrium in the long run as it is expressed in the neoclassical paradigm. Behind the goal of transforming the individual member states into a common, efficient, and well functioning economic and monetary union, it is thus possible to detect the perfect competition model, which forms the basis of analysis so characteristic of the provisions on macroeconomic policy of the Maastricht Treaty. If the market mechanism is well-functioning, as assumed in the model on perfect competition, there is no actual need to formulate some real economic convergence criteria, such as a target for the annual growth rate of GDP or an acceptable unemployment rate, as the market mechanism automatically ensures the realization of these goals. Provided the wage and price formation is sufficiently flexible, the economies will always be close to realizing full employment.[2]

Such flexibility is, however, not characteristic of the EU countries. Consequently, most member states experience a significant level of unemployment, and there are important differences in economic growth between individual member states. In concrete terms, real growth in GDP in 1997 varied between 1.5 per cent—in Italy—up to as much as 10.0 per cent in Ireland, whereas the average growth rate of the EU was 2.7 per cent. Similarly, unemployment was lowest in Luxembourg and Austria—3.7 and 4.4 per cent, respectively—and highest in Finland and, in particular, Spain with unemployment rates of 14.0 and 20.9 per cent, respectively. The average unemployment rate in the EU in 1997 was 10.7 per cent. It therefore seems justified to also make the desirability of a satisfactory real economic convergence between the member countries explicit. Unless such a convergence is established, the EMU will prove inexpedient in the long run, and its viability will be threatened.

Whereas from an economic point of view, the rationale behind the convergence criteria is weak, the criteria may be based on political considerations. Traditionally, several Southern European countries have had high inflation, and by posing demands of low inflation, low interest rates, and exchange rate stability, Germany and the other low-inflation countries have wanted to test the willingness of some of the future EMU member countries to impose monetary stability.

---

[2] Appendix 8.A formally illustrates the theoretical connection between the three monetary convergence criteria.

8.5 The new framework of monetary policy

A LTHOUGH the fixed exchange rate system of the EMS had some of the features of an actual monetary union, the introduction of the euro changed the macro-economic policy environment of the EU considerably. This applies to both the monetary and the fiscal policies.

Responsibility for the monetary policy has been transferred to the European Central Bank[3] with a view to standardizing the monetary policy in the entire euro area. In contrast to the EMS cooperation, it is no longer possible to realign the central parities of the fixed exchange rate cooperation or to avail of a limited exchange rate flexibility within the established target zones.

An independent and conservative central bank in Europe

The European Central Bank as an institution is completely independent of the national governments and the other EU institutions, and the board of directors of the ECB is prohibited from taking orders from other institutions. The ECB must organize its monetary policy in strict accordance with the guidelines laid down for its activities. The primary objective of the monetary policy is to maintain price stability. This objective is accentuated in the Amsterdam Treaty, e.g. in Article 4, which prescribes that the EU must establish:[4]

a single monetary policy and exchange rate policy the primary objective of both shall be to maintain price stability and without prejudice to this objective, to support the general economic policies in the Community, in accordance with the principles of an open market economy with free competition.

Price stability is only one economic policy preference of the governments. Employment plays an equally important role. But the primary obligation of the ECB is to ensure price stability. The EMU project builds on the idea of establishing an independent and 'conservative' central bank. In this context, 'conservative' should be taken to indicate that the central bank puts higher emphasis on price stability than the governments and society in general. The independence of the ECB is secured through stipulations giving it full control of the monetary supply. Furthermore, the

[3] More precisely, a *European System of Central Banks* (ESCB) has been established consisting of the ECB and all central banks of the EU, whether or not they are participating in the common currency. However, the ECB is solely responsible for the monetary policy of the euro area. The Governing Council of the ECB consists of members of the participating countries only.

[4] See also Articles 98 and 105 in the Amsterdam Treaty, which both specify the objective of price stability. Furthermore, Article 105 contains the provision on the activities of the ECB.

governments and EC institutions in general are prohibited from taking up loans with the ECB, as it does not offer any credit facilities to public authorities. In short, the ECB operates under perfectly free market conditions. Finally, the ECB cannot be obliged to intervene in the currency markets if this conflicts with the objective of price stability.

This institutional framework of the monetary policy constitutes one of the controversial areas of the EMU project. Admittedly, price stability offers some clear benefits. Markets become more transparent, which increases competition, and at stable prices, the financial markets function more efficiently, as inflation creates insecurity about saving and investment decisions. Also, a clear and credible accentuation of the ECB's objective of price stability will create widespread expectations of monetary stability, and the inflationary expectations will not become an independent source of wage and price increases. According to traditional economic theory, there are no direct, long-term costs of pursuing an economic policy with the aim of ensuring price stability (Dornbusch *et al.* (1998)). Thus, in the long run, there is no connection between average inflation and average unemployment (in line with the dynamic Phillips curve theory). In the long run, production is determined by the production capacity which in turn depends on the labour force, education, capital supply, and technological and organizational know-how, among other things.

The heaviest criticism of making the ECB independent and strongly conservative is that the adaptation to full exploitation of the production capacity of the economy can be a lengthy process. Because of imperfect competition on the industrial and labour markets, the price and wage rigidities prevent a rapid adaptation to full employment. A strict, conservative central bank will react immediately with a contractionary monetary policy in response to inflationary shocks, and in cases of price and wage rigidities, the consequence will be a heavy fall in economic activity. A strict, conservative central bank may thus cause larger instability in the economic activity, i.e. price stability is achieved through larger output instability. In itself, such output instability is inexpedient. To this should be added that long-term unemployment may disqualify the labour force and lead to slower technological development. Employment instability may therefore have negative consequences on the long-term development in standards of living. These considerations may create a wish for a soft central bank, which will also take employment rates into consideration when determining the monetary policy. In this controversy, as in the discussion of the convergence criteria, a determining factor is whether there is significant confidence that economic imbalances will be corrected swiftly by the market forces.

The Harmonized Index of Consumer Prices

Price stability as an objective of the monetary policy is more precisely related to the development in consumer prices measured in the *Harmonized Index of Consumer Prices* (HICP). For a more detailed introduction of this index, see the EU Commission (1998*a*: 74) and ECB (1999*b*: 31). The index, which exclusively registers consumer prices, is computed on a monthly basis by Eurostat for all EU member countries. The index is harmonized in the sense that the computation of the price level of individual countries is made on the same basis, i.e. it is possible to make an immediate comparison of the measured price developments in individual countries. The ECB target variable is HICP for the entire euro area calculated as a weighted average of HICP for the individual euro countries. The weights of the national price indices are based on private consumption in individual countries as a percentage of total private consumption in the entire euro area (see Table 8.2). Below, we will look into how, concretely, the ECB seeks to meet the objective of price stability.

The monetary policy strategy of the ECB

The monetary policy strategy of the ECB rests on three main elements, which are presented in more detail in ECB (1999a):

■ A quantitative definition of the primary objective . . . price stability
■ The "two pillars" of the strategy used to achieve this objective:
  (a) a . . . reference value for the growth of a broad monetary aggregate
  (b) a broadly based assessment of the outlook for future price developments and the risks to price stability in the euro area as a whole. (ECB (1999a: 45–6))

■ The quantitative formulation of the objective of price stability prescribes that the yearly price increase measured in HICP for the euro area must be less than 2 per cent (ECB (1999a)). At the same time, the ECB establishes that its aim is to meet this objective in the medium term only. A price increase of more than 2 per cent will thus not automatically elicit a more contractionary monetary policy if it is a temporary phenomenon provoked, for example, by a strong increase in prices of

Table 8.2 Relative size of the euro-11 countries, 1997, per cent.		
	GDP	Private consumption
Belgium/Luxembourg	3.9	3.9
Germany	33.2	35.1
Spain	8.4	8.4
France	22.2	21.4
Ireland	1.2	1.0
Italy	18.2	18.1
Luxembourg	0.3	0.2
The Netherlands	5.8	5.5
Austria	3.3	3.0
Portugal	1.6	1.7
Finland	1.9	1.6
euro-11	100.0	100.0

Source: EU Commission (1998b): tables 5 and 13.

imported goods. Similarly, the ECB points out that a fall in prices is incompatible with the monetary policy strategy. These clarifications contribute to making the monetary policy strategy transparent and accountable to the public, and the ultimate objective of this is to keep inflationary expectations down.

For 1999 and 2000, the ECB has determined a reference value for the annual growth rate of the money supply of 4½ per cent. The money supply is defined as M3, i.e. broad money comprising not only notes, coins, and sight deposits, but also time deposits and short bonds. For a more detailed definition of M3 (see ECB (1999a: table 2.4)). The yearly growth rate of M3 is determined on the basis of a three-month moving average growth rate of M3, thus ensuring that short-term liquidity fluctuations do not lead to adjustments of the monetary policy.

The reference value for the growth rate of the money supply is determined by the primary objective that inflation must be below 2 per cent, (see ECB (1999a: 46)). The correlation between price level and money supply is determined by the quantity theory of money. To be specific, the inflation rate equals the growth rate of the money supply plus the growth rate of the velocity minus the long-term growth rate of production (see Appendix 8A, relation 7). The ECB estimates that the long-term real growth of production totals 2–2½ per cent p.a. and also estimates that the velocity of M3 decreases by around ½–1 per cent p.a. A growth rate of the money supply of 4½ per cent p.a. consequently implies a long-term growth rate of the price level of around 1–2 per cent p.a.

The reference value for the growth rate of M3 is a target for the development in the money supply in the medium term. There will thus not be an automatic adjustment of the monetary policy if the growth rate of M3 deviates from the reference value. This follows from the 'second pillar' of the ECB's monetary policy strategy where the ECB indicates that it intends to base its estimate of whether or not the objective of price stability is threatened on a broad assessment. The conditions that will be taken into consideration include developments in wages, fiscal policy indicators, exchange rates, as well as price and cost developments in general. These broad formulations of the monetary policy strategy of the ECB add a certain flexibility to the explicitly quantitative objectives for price, the development and growth in the money supply. The ECB has to implement a monetary policy for the entire euro area, in the nature of things without specific, prior experience of the effects of the monetary policy on the group of countries belonging to the monetary union. Presumably, it is this fact which has resulted in a monetary policy strategy which clearly formulates the overall objective of price stability, but where the guidelines on how to reach the goal are specified more broadly.

From a German angle to a euro-11 angle

Although the ECB leads a monetary policy based on the same primary objective of price stability which guided the German Central Bank when it was leading the monetary policy of the EMS, the reaction pattern of the two institutions is bound to differ. The difference is that the *policy area* of the ECB consists of all eleven euro countries, whereas the policy area of the German Central Bank is restricted to Germany. As it appears from Table 8.2, Germany only makes up around one-third of GDP or private consumption of the euro-11 area, and as a consequence, the inflationary development in Germany will only have a limited influence on the ECB's decisions concerning the monetary policy (see Dornbusch (1998)). If, for example, Germany leads an expansionary fiscal policy, and this results in inflationary tendencies in Germany, the expected reaction from the ECB, in the form of a contractionary monetary policy, will be more moderate compared to the expected reaction from the German Bundesbank during the period of the ERM. The ECB policy will therefore have a smaller impact on the positive effect of the expansionary fiscal policy on German economic activity.

Asymmetric monetary policy impacts

Although the influence of the monetary policy will move output in the same direction in all euro countries, the effect of the monetary policy will differ from country to country. These *asymmetric impacts* of the monetary policy are due to structural and institutional differences between the euro countries. The monetary policy in the euro area influences output via two main channels: changes in interest rates on the one hand; and changes in the euro exchange rate on the other. It is the effects of these two factors which may differ widely from country to country. Thus, the size of the *public debt burden* varies from country to country (see Table 8.1). An interest rate increase in particularly debt-ridden countries, such as Belgium and Italy, will increase the transfers from the public to the private sector significantly. This will contribute to maintaining the level of private consumption, which will curb the contractionary effect of the interest rate increase. Similarly, the degree of *openness* towards the rest of the world varies from country to country. Here, openness is measured as the share of trade with countries which are not members of the euro or otherwise attached to the euro through a fixed exchange rate agreement. The effect of the monetary policy on the euro exchange rate will influence activity in the sector for tradable goods for those countries which are relatively open towards countries outside the euro area, making differences in openness an additional source of asymmetry. It also varies from country to country whether the financial sector extends loans at variable or fixed interest rates. For countries where variable interest rates are dominating—such as the UK and Italy—the effect of changes in monetary policy on consumption and investment demand will be more rapid. This relation is described in more detail in Dornbusch *et al.* (1998), which also describes the importance of institutional differences in other areas, such as differences in the behaviour of private financial institutions in terms of adapting their lending rates when the central bank changes its interest rates.

There are thus several conditions which contribute to differentiating the effect of the monetary policy in the euro area. However, there is no consensus in economic literature on the importance of these differences with respect to the impact of the monetary policy on individual member countries. This set of problems is illustrated in a number of analyses based on macroeconomic models (see e.g. OECD (1999) for an overview of contributions). The results of individual analyses underline the differences in effect of monetary policy on individual countries, but none of them gives a clear picture of which countries are influenced the most by the monetary policy of the ECB.

It is possible that a number of these structural and institutional asymmetries between the euro countries will disappear over time. The monetary policy of the ECB will be independent of the specific, institutional conditions in individual euro countries. It is thus the institutional conditions rather than the monetary policy which will have to be adapted, as the need may be. Such an automatic pressure for an *institutional harmonization* of the financial markets can be expected where the differences are based on tradition only, e.g. traditions of variable vs. fixed interest rate loans. There will, however, in future also be areas where such harmonization will be difficult. This is true for instance of differences in public debt burdens where harmonization requires a long period of adaptation.

The overall theme of this section has been the importance of monetary policy in the euro area. The primary objective of the monetary policy of the ECB is price stability defined as a price increase measured in HICP of less than 2 per cent p.a. The monetary policy strategy which will help achieve this objective is flexible, as the growth in money supply is only one of several indicators which the ECB will take into consideration. With the entire euro area as its policy area, the monetary policy reaction of the ECB to a specific price development in a member country will be proportional to the relative economic importance of that country in the euro area measured by the share of private consumption. As a consequence of the remaining important institutional differences between the euro countries, the impact of the monetary policy is likely to differ from country to country.

8.6 The fiscal policy framework

WITH the establishment of an independent and conservative central bank in the EMU, and with the EMU in its third stage, more attention is paid to the member countries' possibilities of using fiscal policy instruments. How can it be ensured that the fiscal policy, as it is formulated by individual member countries, does not create tension between participating countries within the EMU? The Stability and Growth Pact, which is explained below, was created as a measure against this.

Compared with the Maastricht Treaty, the Amsterdam Treaty contains several clauses which explicitly focus on employment in the EU. For example, Article 2 points out that one of the important objectives of the Union is:

to promote economic and social progress and a high level of employment and to achieve balanced and sustainable development, in particular through the creation of an area without internal frontiers, through the strengthening of economic and social cohesion and through the establishment of economic and monetary union, ultimately including a single currency in accordance with the provisions of this Treaty.

As a consequence (see Article 125):

Member States and the Community shall, in accordance with this Title, work towards developing a coordinated strategy for employment and particularly for promoting a skilled, trained and adaptable workforce and labour markets responsive to economic change with a view to achieving the objectives defined in Article 2 of the Treaty on European Union and in Article 2 of this Treaty.

Presumably, the primary reason for these clauses is the fact that in the 1990s, the EU generally experienced a considerable level of unemployment. With the implementation of the third phase of the EMU looming on the horizon, the fear that the development in employment could be further destabilized might have grown, given that the member countries would lose the opportunity to implement independent monetary and exchange rate policies as from 1 January 1999. The fear of a disappointingly low level of employment seems particularly justified if individual economies experience asymmetric impacts of economic shocks.

The Stability and Growth Pact

As a reaction to these challenges, in 1997, the heads of state or of government of the EU member states adopted a resolution on a Stability and Growth Pact. In particular, the Pact focuses on the initiatives that can be taken if a budget deficit of a member country becomes disproportionately large. The Pact concretely defines this as a deficit larger than 3 per cent of GDP. As an example, the Pact specifies sanctions that can be imposed on a member country unless the country itself takes efficient measures to fully remove—or, as a minimum, reduce—its unsustainable budget problem.

The first sanction is in the form of a non-interest bearing deposit. If, contrary to expectations, after two years, the member country still disregards the recommendations of the EU, the deposited amount is automatically converted into an actual penalty. The size of the penalty is progressive. Where the budget deficit only marginally exceeds the 3 per cent GDP limit, a penalty of 0.2 per cent of the country's GDP is paid to the EU. If the public deficit is larger, the size of the penalty grows, in concrete terms with an additional 0.1 per cent of GDP for each percentage point in excess of the 3 per cent limit. However, regardless of the size of the deficit, the deposit or penalty cannot exceed 0.5 per cent of the country's GDP.

But the heads of state or of government also built in an escape clause, namely that the adopted sanctions will not be imposed if the disproportionately large budget deficit is due to extraordinary circumstances. According to the Pact, an extraordinary situation would undoubtedly arise if a country's GDP in real terms decreases by more than 2 per cent in the year in which the public deficit exceeds the 3 per cent limit.

The adopted sanctions must be assumed to be of such a magnitude that the member countries will have a strong incentive to adjust their fiscal policies rather than being forced to make a deposit. This tightens the fiscal policy as compared to a situation where a Pact had not been adopted.

A member country which pursues a less strict and, according to the spirit of the Pact, imprudent fiscal policy may thus be forced to make an extraordinary tightening of its policy. This will happen if the business cycle develops less favourably than expected, as an unexpected slowdown in the business cycle will have a negative effect on the government budget because of the automatic fiscal stabilizers. This is partly because revenue will decrease as a consequence of a reduction in tax payments, partly because public expenditures will increase due to a rise in government transfers to e.g. the unemployed. It may therefore become necessary for the country to implement an unwanted fiscal contraction in order to avoid the sanctions laid down by the Stability and Growth Pact.

Such unwanted fiscal contractions will often come as a surprise, at least to most economic agents. As a consequence, the consumption and investment expectations in the private sector will often be influenced negatively. In a situation with deteriorating business cycles, it is likely that the recession will be further enhanced. If this is the case, the public finances will deteriorate yet again.

An analogous effect is not found in the case of an unexpected boom. The adoption of the Stability and Growth Pact implies that in future, the automatic stabilizers in the euro countries will have an asymmetric impact on member states with weak public finances (Hansen and Jørgensen (1999)). From a purely stabilization policy point of view, this is obviously extremely inexpedient. It may therefore be rational for individual countries to aim at a public budget deficit sufficiently below the 3 per cent limit to allow the country to experience a slowdown in the business cycle—whether it materializes or not—without increasing the actual budget deficit to a level which will impose a sanction in the form of a deposit. In a transition period, however, this may lead to a recessive pressure on the economy.

According to conventional macroeconomic theory, the long-term demand side effect of fiscal policy is insignificant to the output level, and a long-term strategy to achieve balance or surplus in the public budget will thus not imply lower output in the long run. Implementing prudent fiscal policy in order to live up to the demands in the Stability and Growth Pact should therefore neither hamper the way fiscal policy stabilizes the level of output nor long-run trends of output growth. Furthermore, it will strengthen the output stabilization capacity if a federal transfer mechanism is implemented. The idea of such a mechanism is to transfer means from the federal EU budget to the budget of the member state experiencing a significant negative asymmetric shock. The problem of such a stabilization mechanism is partly the political aversion to bestow fiscal competence at the EU level, partly the risk of *moral hazard* in the member states, e.g. increased wage pressure in a member country in the expectation that the EU will suspend a safety net below the country if employment falls due to failing competitiveness.

8.7 Concluding remarks

THE launch of the euro on 1 January 1999 constituted a remarkable leap forward in the economic integration process in Europe. A common currency implies common monetary and exchange rate policies, and the macroeconomic conditions in the euro area will therefore be decisively influenced by the monetary union.

The European Central Bank has been entrusted with responsibility for the monetary policy. The ECB is independent of the political system and is primarily obliged to ensure price stability. Individual member states are free to carry out independent fiscal policies but strictly within the scope of the restrictions imposed by the Stability and Growth Pact.

The monetary policy influences the general economic development in the entire euro area, whereas fiscal policy influences the relative development between individual euro countries. It is therefore an obvious choice to use fiscal policy instruments to stabilize the economy when countries are hit by asymmetric shocks. It is a precondition, however, that public income and expenditure is planned with a view to creating a budget surplus or at least a balance in the medium term, i.e. in the course of a full business cycle. Unless this precondition is fulfilled, there is a danger that the Stability and Growth Pact will limit the possibilities of using fiscal policy instruments to stabilize output even if fiscal policy may not have an impact on activities in the long run.

The rationale behind the special design of the EMU is to influence the behaviour of governments, national institutions, and decision-makers in general to enable the monetary union to contribute to meeting EU's overall objective of an economy characterized by price stability and improvement in standards of living. The decision to create a conservative and independent central bank, which can create expectations of price stability, should be seen in this light. Similarly, the provisions of the Stability and Growth Pact are an attempt at influencing the long-term planning of the fiscal policy with a view to avoiding excessive long-term deficits in the member countries.

Although the euro countries have participated in a fixed exchange rate cooperation before, the institutional framework of the EMU is significantly different. This makes it difficult to estimate the perspectives for the EMU and to assess which further institutional measures might be introduced in order to enhance the EMU.

The EMU comprises only eleven of the fifteen EU member states. In protocols to the Maastricht Treaty, the UK and Denmark have secured the right to permanently remain outside the monetary union. The other EU countries outside the monetary union, Greece and Sweden, are obliged to enter the monetary union when it is estimated that they fulfil the convergence criteria.[5] Similarly, for a number of Central and Eastern European countries currently in accession negotiations with the EU, actual membership of the EU will impose an obligation to join the common currency

---

[5] Greece has since joined the EMU on 1 Jan. 2001.

once the convergence criteria have been met and their economies in general make it feasible for them to participate. However, as pointed out in the previous chapter, given the structural differences between the Central and Eastern European applicant countries and the current euro countries, it is plausible that the inclusion of these countries into the monetary union lies several years into the future.

This chapter has analysed the EMU project from an economic perspective. So far it is an open question if the economic benefits outweigh the economic costs. However, it should be emphasized that the development in European integration is a result of political decisions and not only based on economic considerations. By entering the EMU project, Germany does not only renounce its role as a leader in European monetary policy, it also has to submit to the common decisions of the ECB. The other euro countries, on the other hand, gain influence on the economic policy in the euro area. For Germany, the *quid pro quo* has been political support for German reunification and German Ost-politik in general.

8.A Appendix

As mentioned in Section 8.3 the rationale behind the specified convergence criteria can be justified in traditional economic theory (the neoclassical paradigm). This connection is explained in more detail below.

Let relation (A1) represent Purchasing Power Parity where P is the domestic price level while P_F is the foreign price level. E is the exchange rate (amount of domestic currency per unit of foreign currency) implying that $P_F E$ expresses foreign price level in terms of domestic currency. Thus, if PPP holds, it does not matter whether a given goods basket is purchased domestically or in a foreign country. The price of the goods basket is the same and possibilities of goods arbitrage do not exist.

$$P = P_F E. \tag{A1}$$

If the relation holds over time, a potential difference in domestic and foreign inflation rates must imply a corresponding change in the exchange rate. This is expressed in relation (A2):

$$dP/P - dP_F/P_F = dE/E. \tag{A2}$$

Similarly, Uncovered Interest Rate Parity (UIP) is represented by relation (A3), where i denotes the domestic nominal interest rate; similarly, i_F denotes the foreign nominal interest rate. As it follows from the relation, the two interest rates will be equal unless the market expects a change in the exchange rate, a change which subsequently is assumed to affect the actual exchange rate, whereby the actual and expected exchange rates equal one another.

$$i = i_F + dE/E. \tag{A3}$$

Combining PPP and UIP produces relation (A4):

$$i - i_F = dP/P - dP_F/P_F = dE/E. \tag{A4}$$

Aiming at domestic and foreign inflation rate convergence—the objective of price stability of the EMU—simultaneously requires convergence with respect to domestic and foreign interest rates. If the objective of stable prices and interest rates is met, stable exchange rates between countries will follow automatically. It thus appears from relation (A4) that the three EMU convergence criteria for monetary stability are interdependent and necessarily must be pursued simultaneously. Rewriting relation (A4) into relation (A5) demonstrates that, similarly, convergence of the real interest rates of the domestic and foreign country is ensured.

$$i - dP/P = r = r_F = i_F - dP_F/P_F. \tag{A5}$$

What remains is to determine the inflation rates of both countries. This may be done by applying the Quantity Theory of Money (QT), see relation (A6). Here, M describes the nominal money supply, V is the income velocity of money, P is the price level, and Y is the level of real output.[6]

$$MV = PY. \tag{A6}$$

Rewriting the quantity theory into its relative version produces relation (A7):

$$dM/M + dV/V = dP/P + dY/Y. \tag{A7}$$

Again, rewriting this relation under the assumption of a constant income velocity of money, it becomes evident that the inflation rate is determined by the difference in growth of the nominal money stock and the growth rate of real output:

$$dP/P = dM/M - dY/Y. \tag{A8}$$

Relation (A4) may now be transformed using relation (A8) thus creating relation (A9) which combines three pivotal economic theories: Purchasing Power Parity (PPP), Uncovered Interest Rate Parity (UIP), and the Quantity Theory of Money (QT):

$$dP/P - dP_F/P_F = i - i_F = [dM/M - dY/Y] - [dM_F/M_F - dY_F/Y_F] = dE/E. \tag{A9}$$

Assuming similar domestic and foreign real output growth rates, differences in inflation rates between the countries are solely determined by different growth rates in their nominal money stocks.

In the long run, according to classical theory, the increase in a country's money supply is therefore the determining factor of the country's inflation rate. In the short run, however, this relation may not be particularly significant. On the contrary, the inflation rate is likely to be determined by the development in costs. This especially, is where the wage formation of individual countries is of particular importance.

---

[6] Relation (A6) is formulated for the domestic country. With subscript F attached to the four variables of the relation, an analogous quantity relation for the foreign country appears.

Further reading

Monetary integration in a historical perspective can be found in H. Ungerer (1997), *A Concise History of European Monetary Integration—From EPU to EMU*, Quorum Books, Westport. D. Gros and N. Thygesen (1998), *European Monetary Integration*, Longman, Harlow, present a survey of the motives and events which led to the establishment of the EMU, and offer a thorough economic assessment of costs and benefits of monetary integration in Europe as well as an economic analysis of the institutional design of the EMU. P. De Grauwe (2000), *Economics of Monetary Union*, OUP, Oxford, focuses on the economic problems of making a monetary union in Europe as well as on the economic policy issues in the EMU. A more theoretical economic analysis of monetary integration may be found in J. D. Hansen and J. U.-M. Nielsen (1997), *An Economic Analysis of the EU*, McGraw-Hill, New York. An empirically oriented analysis of the EMU project is given in OECD (1999), *EMU: Facts, Challenges and Policies*.

References

De Grauwe, P. (2000), *Economics of Monetary Union*, 4th edn., OUP, Oxford.

Dornbusch, R., C. Favero, and F. Giavazzi (1998), 'Immediate Challenges for the European Central Bank', in D. Begg, F. von Hagen, C. Wyplosz, and K. Zimmermann (eds.), *EMU: in Prospects and Challenges for the Euro*, CEPR, CES, MSH, Blackwell, Oxford.

ECB (1999*a*), *Monthly Bulletin*, January 1999, European Central Bank.

—— (1999*b*), *Monthly Bulletin*, April 1999, European Central Bank.

EU Commission (1990), *European Economy*, 44.

—— (1997), *European Economy*, 63.

—— (1998*a*), *European Economy*, 65.

—— (1998*b*), *European Economy, Supplement A*, 314.

Friedman, M. (1953), 'The Case for Flexible Exchange Rate', in *Essays in Positive Economics*, University of Chicago Press, Chicago, 157–203.

Gros, D., and N. Thygesen (1998), *European Monetary Integration*, 2nd edn., Longman.

Hansen, J. D. and J. G. Jørgensen (1999), 'How to Play Safe in Fiscal Policy', *European Union Review*, 4(3).

—— and J. U.-M. Nielsen (1997), *An Economic Analysis of the EU*, McGraw-Hill, New York.

Ingram, J. C. (1959), 'State and Regional Payments Mechanisms', *Quarterly Journal of Economics*, 73: 619–32.

Italianer, A., and M. Vanheukelen (1993), 'Proposals for Community Stabilization Mechanisms: Some Historical Applications', in EU Commission, *European Economy Reports and Studies*, 5: 493–510.

Kenen, P. (1969), 'The Theory of Optimum Currency Areas an "Eclectic View"', in

R. A. Mundell and A. K. Swoboda (eds.), *Monetary Problems of the International Economy*, Chicago University Press, Chicago, 41-60.

McKinnon, R. I. (1963), 'Optimum Currency Areas', *American Economic Review*, 53: 717-24.

Mundell, R. A. (1961), 'A Theory of Optimum Currency Areas', *American Economic Review*, 51: 509-17.

OECD (1999), *EMU: Facts, Challenges and Policies*.

Pasinetti, L. (1998), 'The Myth (or Folly) of the 3% Deficit/GDP Maastricht "Parameter"', *Cambridge Journal of Economics*, 103-16.

Tavlas, G. S. (1993), 'The "New" Theory of Optimum Currency Areas', *The World Economy*, 6: 663-83.

Ungerer, H. (1997), *A Concise History of European Monetary Integration—From EPU to EMU*, Quorum Books, Westport, Conn.

US Census Bureau (1999), 'Statistical Abstract of the United States', *The National Data Book*, 119.

Wyplosz, C. (1997), 'EMU: Why and How It Might Happen', *Journal of Economic Perspectives*, 4: 3-22.

Chapter 9
Eastern Enlargement: The New Challenge

Philipp J. H. Schröder

9.1 Introduction

THE eastern enlargement of the European Union is an unprecedented challenge, in scope and content not unlike German reunification, forced onto the European agenda by the political realities of the early 1990s. A mere ten years ago, a union—or just close cooperation—with countries from both sides of the river Elbe was unthinkable. Today, actual membership negotiations have started and are proceeding at a rapid pace.

Eastern enlargement is fundamentally different from previous enlargements for three main reasons. First, the number of potential new members is high. Currently, there are ten active applications from Central and Eastern European (CEE) countries. Secondly, the CEE countries are all former socialist economies, or so-called *transition economies*, which means that they are in transition from a centrally planned economic system towards a market economic system. The pace and scope of transformation have been different in different countries, and the prospect of membership hinges on a successful transition. Thirdly, and in part as a consequence of the first point, the current enlargement round will increase the number and diversity of member states so much that institutional reform of the EU is inevitable. Some of the central themes of such reform are voting rules in the Council, the number and allocation of Commissioners between members, the size of the Parliament and last, but not least, a reform of the budget and the CAP.

This chapter introduces and discusses the *membership criteria* and enlargement process, and examines the applicant countries' economies utilizing many of the concepts and theories introduced in previous chapters. In particular, the applicant countries will be compared with each other and measured against the EUR15 based on an examination of their economic performance, demographics and labour markets, main sectoral structures, trade and foreign direct investment (FDI), as well as monetary arrangements. In addition to these comparisons, some transition specific issues, namely privatization and the 'degree' of being a market economy, will be addressed. All these issues are relevant for an understanding and evaluation of the enlargement process.

Who are the applicants? The ten Central and Eastern European countries, which are in active accession negotiations with the EU, are Bulgaria, Czech Republic, Estonia, Hungary, Latvia, Lithuania, Poland, Romania, Slovak Republic, and Slovenia. Apart form these ten countries, the current enlargement round includes applications from Cyprus, Malta, and Turkey. The issues relating to enlarging the EU with these three countries are very distinct from eastern enlargement. First, the economies of Cyprus, Malta, and Turkey are not in a process of transition from a centrally planned economic system towards a market economic system. Secondly, the three countries are very heterogeneous in terms of their economic development, economic problems, and relations to the EU. The problems of integrating these countries into the European Union are very different from those relating to the CEE countries and would require a separate analysis, which is outside the scope of this chapter. Their applications will therefore not be addressed further here. As to the process of eastern enlargement, in the period from 1997 to 1999, the applicants were divided into a so-called first wave and second wave, indicating the Commission's evaluation of their respective progress towards joining the EU. This distinction was discontinued in December 1999, and all ten countries are now in actual negotiations. The grouping into first and second wave will nevertheless be applied throughout this chapter, as it provides a useful classification when checking the performance of the different countries. It is repeatedly demonstrated that, for certain economic parameters, first and second wave distinction is out of line with the actual performance of individual countries, so eliminating this distinction was the right decision. Yet, it also becomes clear that the performance of the ten CEE countries varies considerably, and that actual admission into the EU will have to take place in several waves. Concerning a time frame for the first CEE country to actually join the EU, dates much earlier than 2005 must be considered unrealistic.

This chapter is structured as follows: Section 9.2 gives a brief introduction to the common features and elements of economies in transition, whereas Section 9.3 reviews the policies and politics of the enlargement process to date. Sections 9.4 through 9.8 address various economic aspects of the applicant countries, ranging from demographics to monetary issues, and compares the candidates with each other as well as with the EUR15. Finally, Section 9.9 draws the conclusions of the chapter.

9.2 Economics of transition

TRANSITION is the shift from a *centrally planned* economic system towards a *market economic* system. Within the centrally planned economic system, both prices and quantities were fixed and dictated by a central authority, and this, combined with an obscure system of incentives, made it difficult for such a system to take excess demand and supply signals into account. In all centrally planned economies, this resulted in shortages—visualized in queues—and widespread economic waste, e.g. unsaleable output, low rates of innovation, and substandard product quality. At the outset of transition, almost all productive assets were state owned and had to be privatized in order to introduce new private owners. The State-Owned Enterprises (SOEs) were tremendous in size, often employing tens of thousands of workers, and they usually assumed monopolistic positions. Furthermore, the main focus of socialist economies was on industry, leaving the service sector underdeveloped, and the development of a service sector is therefore an important element of transition. Finally, it should be remembered that—in the early years of reform—most of the transition economies had a political system in a state of flux. The overall conclusion is that, to start with, the economies of these applicant countries are fundamentally different from those of the EUR15.

Output collapse and high inflation

Two notorious macroeconomic events in all transition economies are high inflation and output collapse. This is illustrated in Table 9.1. The table shows data for the ten applicant countries, grouped into Central and Eastern Europe and the Baltic states, as well as for EUR15 and Russia. Although the three Baltic states, Estonia, Latvia, and Lithuania, were republics of the former Soviet Union, CEE will be used synonymously for all ten applicant countries in the remainder of this chapter. Note also that in this and all other tables, first- and second-wave classification is marked by lower-case roman numbers. Let us now turn to the table. If 1989 is accepted to be the year of outset of reform, a glance at the second column reveals that only four of the applicant countries have recovered from transitional recession yet. The collapse of the central plan—in effect an adverse supply shock—and the resulting political power vacuum contributed to the initial fall in GDP. Subsequent causes were the reallocation of production between sectors, and the switch in production activity and production methods within firms, which led to a temporary fall in output. The data show that the relative gap in GDP between CEE and EUR15 has been widening since 1989. In other words, the CEE economies have to catch up with a moving target, and the only country which manages to be within the range of the EUR15 cumulative growth is Poland. The data on GDP growth in 1999 show moderate growth figures for a number

Table 9.1 GDP and inflation in transition countries

	GDP (in real terms)		Inflation (year-end)	
	Growth 1999 (per cent)	Level 1999 (1989 = 100)	1992 (per cent)	1999 (per cent)
Bulgaria (ii)	2.5	68	79.4	6.2
Czech Republic (i)	−0.2	93	12.7	2.5
Hungary (i)	4.5	99	21.6	11.2
Poland (i)	4.1	122	44.3	9.8
Romania (ii)	−3.2	75	199.2	54.8
Slovak Republic (ii)	1.9	101	9.1	14.0
Slovenia (i)	3.8	108	92.9	8.0
Estonia (i)	−1.4	76	953.5	3.9
Latvia (ii)	0.1	60	959.0	3.2
Lithuania (ii)	−4.1	62	1,161.1	0.3
EUR15	2.1	119	4.6	1.4
Russia	3.2	57	2,506.1	36.8

Notes: Data on growth and level of GDP for 1999 are EBRD estimates. Inflation data for 1999 (EBRD estimates) show percentage change in retail/consumer price level at the year-end. (i) indicates first wave and (ii) second wave classification.

Sources: EBRD (2000): tables 1.1 and 1.3. EU Commission (1999): tables 10 and 25.

of countries, while Romania, Estonia, and Lithuania experience outright recession. For the transition economies to swiftly catch up, faster growth rates are required.

The early years of transition featured high inflation rates. Price liberalization and seigniorage financing of public deficits both contributed to this, but by 1999 most of the applicant countries had a good grip on inflation, even though the EUR15 average of 1.4 per cent was still out of reach.

The data presented on Russia show that the initial output collapse and the level of inflation were both more severe than in the CEE region, and in the late 1990s, growth prospects worsened due to the Russian crisis. Based on these observations, transition can be divided into three main phases: liberalization, stabilization, and structural adjustment. Figure 9.1 illustrates development over time. Starting at point *a*, which indicates the initial crisis of the centrally planned system (accompanied by low growth rates), reforms are introduced in the late 1980s and/or early 1990s, starting with price liberalization and the gradual abolishment of control mechanisms, removal of subsidies, and the general implementation of a new legal framework, including possibilities for private ownership and economic activity. As a consequence, prices are rising and output is falling further. This macroeconomic shock is counteracted in the stabilization phase—predominantly by fighting inflation. Tight control of government budget deficits and fixed or semi-fixed exchange rate regimes are the most common stabilizing devices. The final phase consists of structural adjustment and includes privatization, which, in principle, is part of liberalization

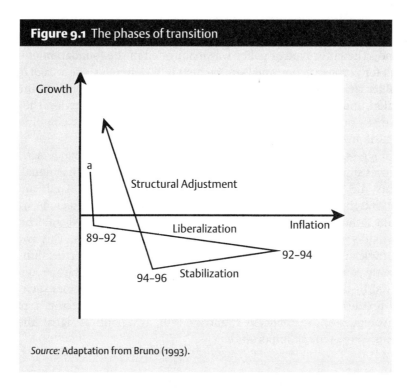

Figure 9.1 The phases of transition

Source: Adaptation from Bruno (1993).

but typically stretched over a long period of time, and restructuring. Privatization concerns the reallocation of property rights—usually to the means of production—from the state to private hands. Restructuring denotes the reorientation of firms into more efficient units, gaining competitiveness and fuelling growth.

9.3 A brief history of eastern enlargement

As mentioned in the introduction, the three central problems of eastern enlargement are the large number of potential new members, the fact that the applicants are not well-established market economies, and the pressure in the EU to reform. In 1989–90, the situation was characterized by a pronounced mismatch of high expectations in the East and the reluctance of the EU to provide. The reform countries of the East saw sudden membership, or at least Marshall aid-like transfers, as the fast lane to prosperity. The EU, on the other hand, never actually had an *Ostpolitik* and found itself faced with an issue that it was unfit to deal with. It soon became evident that the first item on the agenda of the EU in 1989–90 was not enlargement, but economic and monetary union.

The early EU policies concerning Central and Eastern Europe focused on trade and cooperation agreements (starting as early as 1989 in the case of Hungary), and technical and financial assistance (starting in 1990 for Bulgaria, Czech Republic, Hungary, and Poland). The latter type of policy was manifested in the foundation of the European Bank for Reconstruction and Development (EBRD) in 1990. The area of operation of the EBRD covers the entire Central and Eastern Europe, including the former Soviet Union, and as such is not confined to the ten applicant countries. The declared aim is to make public money available for productive investments, combined with a clear sense of promoting private entrepreneurship.

Major progress, in terms of a long-term strategy, came with the *Europe Agreements*. A few countries signed Europe Agreements as early as 1991, but the first actual, interim agreements did not come into force until 1992 (Hungary, Poland, and Czech Republic), and the last Europe Agreements came into force as late as 1998–9 (Estonia, Latvia, and Lithuania in February 1998, Slovenia in February 1999). The Europe Agreements determine the 'association' status of the applicants. This is a notion based on trade and technical and financial as well as 'political' partnership, but it is not explicitly connected to future membership. In practice, the Europe Agreements were flawed by a series of exemptions covering e.g. sensitive sectors such as steel, food and textiles, and this was particularly harmful, as these sectors represented core competences of the applicant countries. Still, as a political signal, the Europe Agreements were of major importance.

The Copenhagen Criteria

The actual breakthrough for eastern enlargement came with the European Council meeting in Copenhagen in June 1993, where the notion of 'conditional acceptance of eventual membership' was introduced. The EU acknowledged that membership was the ultimate aim of the CEE countries, and what has subsequently become known as the Copenhagen Criteria are in fact the conditions which the applicants have to fulfill before membership becomes feasible.

The Copenhagen Criteria require:

- Stable institutions guaranteeing democracy, rule of law, human and minority rights.
- Existence of a functioning market economy. Capacity to cope with the competitive pressures and market forces within the Union.
- Ability to adopt and implement the *acquis*. Adherence to the aims of political, economic, and monetary union.

The second and third criteria have clear economic dimensions and will feature throughout the remainder of this chapter. Apart from establishing the above criteria, the European Council also related enlargement to the EU's capacity to absorb new members, thereby introducing a sort of 'opt-out' clause. Finally, the European Council also stepped up requirements of market access (trade, opening up of sensitive sectors), financial assistance, and political dialogue.

It is useful to identify the economic content of the Copenhagen Criteria. The stability issue does not just have a dimension in terms of democracy, but also in terms of the 'existence of a functioning market economy', where the main condition is a stable and growing economy. In fact, this criterion could be interpreted to imply that a certain level of 'richness', i.e. compatibility with the GDP levels of existing members, is necessary. The requirement of a 'functioning market economy' is a clear indication that liberalization (abolition of planning, price controls, subsidies, etc.) and structural adjustment (privatization and restructuring) must be completed, or at least proceed satisfactorily. Membership is not an option for a half-way reformed, centrally planned economy. Next, the 'capacity to cope with competitive pressures' can be linked to the strength of the economy and the degree of trade openness. Facing international competition, the applicants should not just rely on cheap labour, tariff protection, and repeated devaluations. This criterion implicitly requires a sound current account position. Finally, the criterion of 'adherence to the aims of [. . .] economic and monetary union' relates to sound government budget policies, low and stable inflation rates, and exchange rate stability, in line with the convergence criteria outlined in Chapter 8.

The road ahead

The EU policies concerning the CEE countries, as they have been expressed from 1993 until today, should be understood as mere refinements of the Copenhagen Criteria. The pre-accession strategy was formulated in Essen, Germany, in 1994, outlining the process and defining the assistance that the EU can give to the applicant countries. By 1995, concrete legislative, administrative, and regulative targets, which the CEE countries had to achieve before starting actual membership negotiations, were defined. In fact, this amounted to detailing the Copenhagen Criteria and formed a substantial part of the *Agenda 2000* incentive of 1997 (see Chapter 1). Agenda 2000 included a detailed evaluation of the applicant countries based on all the dimensions introduced above, and it was in this process that the *first- and second-wave* countries were defined. The first-wave countries, consisting of the Czech Republic, Estonia, Hungary, Poland, and Slovenia, were allowed to start actual membership negotiations during 1998, whereas the second-wave countries, consisting of Bulgaria, Latvia, Lithuania, Romania, and Slovak Republic, were still in an extended evaluation process. From then on, the process featured an 'open-door' policy. Already in the autumn of 1998, the progress of all ten applicants was evaluated once more, an exercise which resulted in Latvia, Lithuania, and Slovak Republic being named as the best performers of the second-wave. By December 1999, after a new evaluation round, it was decided at the Helsinki summit to remove the division into first- and second-wave. Thus, actual membership negotiations were initiated with all second wave countries in early 2000, consisting to a large degree of tedious and lengthy detailing and adjustment of national legislation to EU legislation. In the process, the Commission and the applicant governments go through the *acquis*, chapter by chapter, reviewing the applicant's performance and outlining necessary changes.

Having started membership negotiations is one thing, actually becoming a member is quite another. This leads us to the topical question of the date of accession. Naturally, the applicant countries push for rapid accession, while the existing members want to buy time, both to deal with the demands of national interest groups, and to be able to solve a host of internal issues such as budget and CAP reform and voting rules. Agenda 2000 assumes a scenario of 2003, but recently, given the massive internal reforms that the EU has to go through, 2005 or 2006 have been voiced as more realistic dates. Irrespective of which the final date will be, it is no doubt driven more by political will than by economic realities. Having said that, it is also certain that actual enlargement will take place in waves, so that a group of strongly performing transition economies will not have to wait until a group of laggards have fully adjusted. Presumably, the first-wave–second-wave distinction applied in the period 1997–9 will not be the actual accession constellation of the future. In fact, one finding of this chapter is that the countries with the best economic performance—those countries that are most likely to form the group of countries to actually join in this decade—might well be composed of both first- and second-wave countries, rather than strictly first-wave countries.

One of the central political obstacles to eastern enlargement is the question of the impact on the EU budget and the related issue of financial reform. This problem focuses on the costs that the new members will impose on the budget and hence on the existing members. There are two points worth noting in this respect. First, financial reform is inevitable, and therefore independent of whether or not eastern enlargement will take place. Secondly, the inclusion of the CEE countries into the EU will mean that the area as a whole will reap substantial long-term economic benefits from integration which can easily compensate for the short-term costs of enlargement.

9.4 The economies of Central and Eastern Europe

THIS section will examine the economies of the applicant countries by comparing them to the EUR15. The areas of interest are population size, national income, composition of GDP by main sectors, and, finally, the labour market situation. Table 9.2 gives an overview of population and GDP figures in 1999. In order to make comparison possible, data must be expressed in a common currency, but simply using market exchange rates might underestimate the GDP of a CEE country, since they do not take account of the prices in the non-tradable sector. If non-tradables—typically services—are very cheap in a CEE country, then GDP converted at market exchange rates will understate domestic purchasing power. The solution is to use PPP-adjusted

GNP figures, which measure internal purchasing power, while GDP converted at market exchange rates measures a country's external purchasing power, which is relevant in terms of trade.

Table 9.2 includes the ten applicant countries, Russia, and EUR15. In order to illustrate the variation within the EUR15, Denmark and Portugal are also included separately. Starting with population size, the total CEE population amounts to 104.7 million which means that inclusion of all ten applicants would increase the population of the EU by more than 25 per cent. Compared to Russia, on the other hand, the applicant countries are all relatively small. Of the five largest countries, three, i.e. the Czech Republic, Hungary, and Poland, are in the first-wave. Total population of the first wave countries is 62.6 million, so inclusion of these countries alone would increase the population of the EU by almost 17 per cent.

Turning to GDP at market rates, note first of all that the combined GDP of all ten applicants amounts to a mere 4.3 per cent of GDP of the EUR15, so as a market for goods from the EUR15, for the time being, the region is only of limited importance. In fact, a country like Denmark, with a population of only 5.3 million, generates almost half as much GDP, namely 163.1bn. ecu. Notably, the five first-wave countries alone generate a GDP of 265.1bn. ecu, amounting to 3.3 per cent of GDP of the EUR15. This clearly indicates that those countries which were included in the first-wave are the

Table 9.2 Population and national income at market and PPP rates, 1999

	Population (million)	GDP, market rates [a]		GNP, PPP [b] per cent of EUR15
		billion euro	per cent of EUR15	
Bulgaria (ii)	8.2	11.2	0.1	0.5
Czech Republic (i)	10.3	50.7	0.6	1.6
Hungary (i)	10.1	46.2	0.6	1.4
Poland (i)	38.8	145.1	1.8	3.9
Romania (ii)	22.4	31.9	0.4	1.6
Slovak Republic (ii)	5.4	17.7	0.2	0.7
Slovenia (i)	2.0	18.5	0.2	0.4
Estonia (i)	1.4	4.6	0.1	0.1
Latvia (ii)	2.4	5.8	0.1	0.2
Lithuania (ii)	3.7	10.0	0.1	0.3
Total CEE	104.7	341.6	4.3	10.7
Russia	146.7	171.9	2.2	11.8
EUR15	375.8	7,941.1	100.0	100.0
Denmark	5.3	163.1	2.0	1.7
Portugal	9.9	104.1	1.3	1.9

[a] GDP is expressed in euro at market exchange rates.
[b] GNP at PPP is only expressed in relative terms and calculated from USD PPP values.

Sources: Data on GDP for CEE from EBRD (2000): selected economic indicators for each country. Data on GDP for EUR15 from EU Commission (1999): tables 1 and 5. PPP GNP data from the World Bank (2000): table 'Atlas method and PPP'. Author's calculation.

economic leaders of the region: with 60 per cent of the population of the region, they generate 77 per cent of its GDP.

Moving on to the PPP measures of GNP, the picture of the small East and the big West becomes somewhat more blurred. The PPP adjustments include non-tradables (like services) which are usually relatively cheap in poorer countries, and the internal purchasing power is therefore substantially larger than the market exchange rate conversion would indicate. In fact, at PPP rates, GNP of the ten applicants amounts to 10.7 per cent of GNP of the EUR15, whereas Danish GNP in PPP terms shrinks to 1.7 per cent. There is thus a substantial difference between expressing gross product at market rates or PPP rates, and the economic weight of the CEE countries in particular becomes more pronounced using the PPP measure.

Per capita income

Table 9.3 considers the issue of 'wealth', or standards of living, by listing per capita values of GDP at market exchange rates and per capita values of GNP at PPP exchange rates. The table shows per capita data for the ten applicant countries. Regardless of

Table 9.3 Per capita gross product at market and PPP rates, 1999

	per capita GDP, market rates [a]		per capita GNP, PPP [b] per cent of EUR15
	euro	per cent of EUR15	
Bulgaria (ii)	1,369	6.5	23.5
Czech Republic (i)	4,917	23.3	58.8
Hungary (i)	4,553	21.5	50.1
Poland (i)	3,740	17.7	37.8
Romania (ii)	1,423	6.7	27.0
Slovak Republic (ii)	3,273	15.5	46.9
Slovenia (i)	9,235	43.7	72.1
Estonia (i)	3,313	15.7	37.4
Latvia (ii)	2,421	11.5	28.4
Lithuania (ii)	2,705	12.8	29.2
Total CEE	3,262	15.4	38.2
EUR15	21,133	100.0	100.0
Denmark	30,641	145.0	116.2
Portugal	10,494	49.7	72.5

[a] GDP is expressed in euro at market exchange rates.
[b] GNP at PPP is only expressed in relative terms and calculated from USD PPP values.

Sources: Data on GDP for CEE from EBRD (2000): selected economic indicators for each country. Data on GDP for EUR15 from EU Commission (1999): tables 1 and 5. PPP GNP data from the World Bank (2000): table 'Atlas method and PPP'. Author's calculation.

the measure used, the CEE average is clearly below the EUR15, and also clearly below the value for Portugal, which is one of the poorest member countries. However, using the PPP measure, Slovenia comes extremely close to the Portuguese per capita GNP and actually surpasses Greece on this measure. Also the Czech Republic is in reach of the lowest values of per capita GNP at PPP for the existing EU member states.

In fact, the five first-wave countries are all among the six 'richest' CEE countries, the only outlier being the Slovak Republic which ranks fourth in the PPP measurement. It is noteworthy that the Slovak Republic received one of the most favourable reviews, in terms of economic performance, in the 1998 evaluation exercise. From these observations we can deduct that 'wealth', as measured by per capita income, is correlated with success in the accession procedure. Put differently, high per capita income is considered a basis for and/or indicator of a functioning market economy.

Overall, it can be concluded from the Tables 9.2 and 9.3 that the applicant countries are relatively poor, and were they to be admitted in 1999, they would have been net recipients from the EU budget. Their economic importance is also moderate, but given their population sizes and growth prospects, the economic potential of the applicants is substantial. Given resumed growth, a number of applicant countries might actually be able to overtake the poorest EUR15 countries in terms of per capita income by the time of accession.

Main sectoral structure: the role of agriculture

Turning to the composition of GDP by main sectors, it is relevant to ask if the distribution in sectors of the applicant countries is similar to that of the EU. Due to lack of data, the simple distinction between primary, secondary, and tertiary sectors, i.e. agriculture, industry, and services, will be maintained. As already mentioned, centrally planned economies put relatively large emphasis on industrial production at the expense of the service sector. This trend is reversed in the process of transition. Consider the case of Latvia: in 1991, approximately 22 per cent of GDP was generated in agriculture, 36 per cent in industry, and 42 per cent in services. By 1994, the composition of Latvian GDP had become 9 per cent in agriculture, 20 per cent in industry, and 70 per cent in services. These early developments need not necessarily indicate a huge growth in the service sector, but could simply result from a collapse of the industrial and agricultural sectors—combined with a slightly growing service sector.

Table 9.4 shows the composition of GDP in 1999 for all ten applicant countries and EUR15. The sectoral structure of the individual EU member states was the subject of Chapter 5. The table demonstrates that the decisive difference in sectoral structures between the EUR15 and the CEE countries is the size of the agricultural sector. In terms of country variation, the proportionally largest agricultural sectors are found in Bulgaria, Romania, and Lithuania, which were all in the second wave, and this might indicate that their economic structures are incompatible with the EUR15. Consulting Table 5.3, we find that the largest agricultural shares in EUR15 in 1997

Table 9.4 Distribution of GDP on main sectors in per cent, 1999			
	Agriculture	Industry	Services
Bulgaria[a] (ii)	21.1	28.7	50.2
Czech Republic (i)	5.0	36.0	59.0
Hungary[a] (i)	5.5	26.5	68.0
Poland (i)	5.2	28.2	66.6
Romania (ii)	13.9	27.8	58.3
Slovak Republic (ii)	4.4	25.3	70.3
Slovenia (i)	3.4	27.9	68.7
Estonia[a] (i)	4.6	15.4	80.0
Latvia (ii)	4.2	17.9	77.9
Lithuania (ii)	8.8	20.8	70.4
CEE	7.2	28.7	64.1
EUR15[b]	2.1	30.5	67.4

[a] 1998.
[b] 1997, showing gross value added, reproduced from Table 5.3.
Source: EBRD (2000): selected economic indicators for each country. Author's calculation.

were found in Greece, Ireland, and Portugal with 8.1, 4.5, and 4.1 per cent, respectively.

In the EUR15 countries, the size of the service sector varies between 54.6 per cent in Ireland and 70.1 per cent in France (with Luxembourg at an exceptional 78.1 per cent), whereas in the CEE countries, the size of the service sector ranges from 50.2 per cent in Bulgaria to 80.0 per cent in Estonia. In this respect, the applicant countries are a rather heterogenous group. Industry, on the other hand, which is normally the sector accounting for the largest fall in output, actually has a proportion similar to the levels of the EU member countries. Although the reorientation of the sectoral structure in transition economies away from industry and agriculture towards services has been impressive, not all countries have reached a structure fully compatible with the EU average. However, the structures of most applicant countries are well within the variations found among the existing EU members, and they have assimilated the main sectoral structure of a typical market economy.

Let us return once more to the role of the share of agriculture in GDP. It was established in Chapter 5 that there is an intriguing relation between a high agricultural share in total value added and a low per capita GDP. Is this relation valid also for the CEE countries? Correlating the GNP per capita data of Table 9.3 to the share of the agricultural sector, we find a value of − 0.5, i.e. a negative relation similar to the one found in the data of Figure 5.1. The more a country relies on agriculture, the poorer it is. So the observed relation between per capita GNP and first-wave membership, and the relation between the share of the agricultural sector and second-wave membership, are just two sides of the same coin.

Unemployment: following Western Europe

A final item for consideration in the description of the economies of Central and Eastern Europe is the labour market situation. Historically, the centrally planned economies had virtually no unemployment. This was the result of a compulsory labour allocation, where firms were commanded to take on labour, which they might not need. This, combined with the transitional recession, left the economies with three major factors with which to adjust the labour market: rectifying the potential mismatch between workers and jobs (i.e. hiring people to work in areas which match their skills the best); redirecting employment from collapsing sectors into growing sectors; and firing idle and excessive labour. All three elements will, at least in the medium term, result in lower employment. Whether or not this results in growing unemployment depends on the development in labour force participation. Because of the coexistence of these two forces—employment and participation—the unemployment picture is not clear-cut. Another problem in identifying the true level of unemployment is that unemployment figures can vary widely depending on the definitions and methods used. Additionally, unattractively low benefit levels, strict registration systems with limited duration, and widespread black economy activities contribute to a wide margin of error in Eastern European labour market statistics.

Table 9.5 presents the development over time in unemployment figures for the ten applicant countries. The data are taken from the EBRD and at times differ widely from the official figures quoted by national sources. Differences in accounting and definitions are the main source of such discrepancies. The table also shows EUR15 figures as well as the calculated CEE average.

Although the CEE countries have rather heterogeneous performances, it is striking that the average unemployment rate in Central and Eastern Europe is in line with the unemployment level of the EUR15 despite the presence of those three factors which reduce employment during transition: rectification of the worker–job mismatch, reduction in employment in collapsing sectors with 'slower' recovery in the growing sectors, and the elimination of idle and excessive labour. This evidence hints at a steep reduction in participation rates in the CEE countries. Consulting the *World Development Indicators* (World Bank, 1998: table 2.3) this interpretation is confirmed: while the world labour force has grown on average by 1.7 per cent per year from 1980 to 1996, labour force growth in e.g. Russia is only 0.1 per cent, 0.3 per cent in the Czech Republic, and 0.2 per cent in Slovenia. In fact, the six countries which have experienced a negative annual growth rate (– 0.1 to – 0.5) are, without exception, transition economies. How, then, does a reduction in the labour force come about? Two central causes can be identified. First, the female participation rate was very high in communist countries, and after 1990, many households may have reassessed their labour supply decision. Secondly, many older workers, who were made redundant from state-owned enterprises, may have been transferred onto a pension scheme and thus have exited the labour force.

Comparing Eastern European unemployment with the EUR15, based on the

Table 9.5 Unemployment as percentage of labour force

	1991	1995	1999
Bulgaria (ii)	11.1	11.1	16.0
Czech Republic (i)	4.1	2.9	9.4
Hungary (i)	7.4	10.4	9.1
Poland (i)	11.8	14.9	13.0
Romania (ii)	3.0	9.5	11.5
Slovak Republic (ii)	8.3 [a]	13.1	19.2
Slovenia (i)	8.2	7.4	7.5
Estonia (i)	n.a.	9.6	11.7
Latvia (ii)	2.3 [a]	18.1	19.4
Lithuania (ii)	0.3	17.5	13.3
CEE [b]	8.2	11.7	12.6
EUR15	8.2	10.7	9.2

[a] 1992.
[b] Calculated as the weighted average using population size as an approximation of labour force size.

Note: CEE data for 1999 are EBRD estimates.

Sources: EBRD (1998): selected economic indicators for each country. EBRD (2000): selected economic indicators for each country. EU Commission (1999): table 3. Author's calculation.

extensive analysis by Boeri *et al.* (1998), it can be argued that the Eastern European labour markets feature more of the EU-type structural unemployment problems (identified in Chapter 3) than the frictional type of unemployment found in the USA. Hence, in terms of labour market problems, whereas this is certainly not an advantage, the applicant countries appear to be rather similar to the EUR15.

Consulting Table 9.5 once more, it is also possible to establish a relation between unemployment levels and first- and second-wave countries. Calculating the unemployment rate for the first- and second-wave countries respectively (again using the population size as weights), we find that first-wave country unemployment increased from 9.7 per cent in 1991 to 11.8 per cent in 1995 and settled at 11.6 per cent in 1999. For the second wave, percentages were 5.7, 11.5, and 14.0 per cent respectively. It appears that the first-wave countries experience an earlier surge in unemployment than the second-wave. If temporary high unemployment is seen as a necessary feature of transition, then this data can be interpreted as an indication that the first-wave countries have embarked on the road to market economy earlier than the second-wave countries.

Let us summarize the main findings of this section on the economies of Central and Eastern Europe. Even though, in terms of population size, the applicant countries would account for more than 20 per cent of a union with twenty-five member states, at present they do not account for much more than 4–8 per cent of GDP of such a union. The conclusion is that the applicant countries are generally poor. The industrial structures of the CEE countries indicate that they have incurred a high degree of transformation away from the focus on industry of the centrally planned economy, but not all countries yet have main sectoral structures similar to those of the EUR15. It is important to bear in mind that low capacity utilization in transition economies may distort the picture. Regarding the unemployment levels of the applicant countries, the levels are as high as those of the EUR15. Finally, using the distinction between first- and second-wave countries, we found that, compared with the second-wave countries, the first-wave countries are relatively richer, closer to the EUR15 average in terms of main sectoral structures, and have experienced and begun the recovery from periods of high unemployment sooner. All three features indicate that they have proceeded further on their journey towards becoming fully fledged market economies.

9.5 Privatization and restructuring

ONE of the main features of the centrally planned economies was that almost all productive capacity was state owned, so a major challenge during transition is privatization—the first part of structural adjustment. Privatization in itself is meaningless if it does not result in the identification of new owners who behave as optimizing agents, i.e. run their firms according to the principles of profit maximization. This second element of structural adjustment is called restructuring and addresses the efficiency of firms.

This section will first describe the possible privatization outcomes, i.e. the new ownership patterns, and discuss advantages and problems with different outcomes. Then we look at the actual privatization routes chosen by the applicant countries. Finally, the restructuring performance of different countries will be examined.

Privatization in transition

Table 9.6 illustrates some of the main privatization methods and some of the important new owner groups. A combination of a method and a new owner results in a particular privatization outcome. Table 9.6 introduces a number of terms which need some prior explanation. Management-employee buyout (Mebo) describes a situation where the management and workers of a firm become its new owners. Corporate governance, or just governance, concerns the way in which a firm is managed and controlled, and is therefore closely related to the issues of restructuring. Ownership concentration is a typical example of corporate governance. Disperse versus concentrated ownership relates to the number of different owners who have to agree on a course for their firm. Disperse ownership (many small shareholders) might result in certain governance problems, for example, the gain which individual (small) share-holders will obtain from actively interfering with the firm's management may not be worth the effort, whereas concentrated ownership avoids this risk. Share resale describes a set-up where an investor with a business idea can obtain control over a firm by purchasing shares from its present owners. *Voucher privatization* is a method whereby the government allocates vouchers to the public which can then be used like money—but only to purchase state assets. Consequently—and in contrast to most of the other privatization methods—no privatization revenue is generated for the state budget in case of voucher privatization.

Table 9.6 introduces only a sample of the possible methods and owners. The main body of the table introduces a popular name and identifies the pros and cons of the resulting privatization outcome. Issues of interest are, for example, the speed and effectiveness of privatization, the resulting corporate governance structure, or the generated revenue of the privatization.

Looking at the different privatization methods, there are some points worth expanding upon. Auctioning state assets, even where they are offered to the general public, may result in a successful Mebo-bid, and hence be associated with some

Table 9.6 Overview of the pros and cons of privatization outcomes

		New owners		
		Insiders (workers, managers, other stakeholders, etc.)	Outsiders (general public, other firms, institutions, etc.)	Foreigners (firms, individuals, etc.)
Privatization method	Auction	*Mebo-bid* Pro: determines right price, swift. Con: requires wealth, governance problem.	*Treuhand-type* Pro: determines right price, swift, fosters concentrated ownership. Con: requires wealth.	*FDI* Pro: know-how owner. Con: public resentment, risk of discount prices.
	Sale of shares	*Mebo* Pro: easy to resell shares to outside bidder. Con: requires wealth, governance problem.	*Public offering* Pro: nation of shareholders. Con: requires wealth, disperse ownership risk.	*FDI* Pro: know-how owner, some shares remain domestic. Con: public resentment.
	Vouchers	*Mimicked Mebo* Pro: popular. Con: governance problem, no privatization revenue.	*Czech-type* Pro: fair, popular. Con: disperse ownership risk, no privatization revenue.	Unobserved.

Source: Adaptation from Schröder (1999).

corporate governance issues. The sale of shares needs not result in a sale at all, so the state will remain the owner, and the firm will not be privatized. A common feature for both methods is that the new owner requires some initial wealth. This condition is a major constraint in transition economies, because the public has not had the opportunity to accumulate wealth under central planning. Whatever savings people may have had were typically eroded during the first years of high inflation. This also explains the popularity of the voucher privatization programmes.

Another—and possibly decisive—result of any privatization programme concerns the new owner. An important question is, which type of owner will a priori be effective in restructuring, i.e. optimizing all processes within the firm. Here, insiders are usually assumed to suffer from the so-called 'stakeholder' conflict. This means that they hold a stake in the firm which may distort their willingness to maximize firm profits. For example, if the workers in a firm are also its owners, they may opt to maximize wages paid, or prevent employment reductions, rather than optimizing the firm. Outside ownership should circumvent such conflicts, but may create a disperse ownership problem. Foreign ownership has an advantage in terms of access to new technology and capital, and as such should result in the widest possible restructuring of firms.

What, then, have been the choices of actual privatization programmes? Table 9.7 outlines the present situation, showing the dominating privatization outcome for each country, indicating method and new owner, as well as progress in large-scale privatization.[1] Starting with column 4, we see that none of the applicants reaches a

Table 9.7 Main privatization methods (owners) and progress, status 1999

	Main programme	Secondary programme	Progress[a]
Bulgaria (ii)	Sale (outsiders)	Voucher (public)	3
Czech Republic (i)	Voucher (invest. funds)	Sale (outsiders)	4
Hungary (i)	Sale (outsiders)	Mebo (insiders)	4
Poland (i)	Mebo (insiders)	Voucher (public)	3 +
Romania (ii)	Mebo (insiders)	Sale (outsiders)	3 –
Slovak Republic (ii)	Mebo (insiders)	Voucher (public)	4
Slovenia (i)	Mebo (insiders)	Sale (outsiders)	3 +
Estonia (i)	Sale (outsiders)	Mebo (insiders)	4
Latvia (ii)	Voucher (public)	Sale (outsiders)	3
Lithuania (ii)	Voucher (public)	Mebo (insiders)	3

[a] Progress replicates an EBRD measure of progress in large-scale privatization (status 1999). 1: little private ownership, 2: some sales completed, 3: more than 25% of large-scale assets in private hands, 4: more than 50% of state-owned enterprises in private hands, 4+: more than 75% of enterprise assets in private hands.

Sources: EBRD (1997): 90. EBRD (1999): 32.

[1] Large-scale privatization concerns large SOEs. Progress in small-scale privatization has typically been much faster. Small-scale indicates small shops, restaurants, flats, etc.

4+, which is the measure indicating 'standards and performance typical of advanced industrial economies' (EBRD, 1998: 27). This can clearly be related to the Copenhagen Criteria. On this progress measure, the first-wave countries on average rank higher than the second wave. However, this measure also indicates that privatization has not yet been completed.

Turning to the method of privatization and the new owners, management-employee buyout programmes appear to be the dominating privatization method, followed closely by the extensive use of voucher privatization schemes. Overall, insider ownership appears to be the main resulting ownership form in a number of countries, but it should be remembered that insider ownership is associated with potential restructuring problems. However, many of the voucher programmes appear to have resulted in ownership being allocated to the general public, which might be associated with disperse ownership. Sales to outsiders, which is the typical Western privatization method, only ranks third.

Restructuring: addressing efficiency

The primary aim of privatization is to introduce owners, who will engage in active restructuring of the firm. An increase in efficiency and productivity boosts the competitiveness of a country and hence relates directly to the Copenhagen Criteria, but the restructuring record of the transition economies has been mixed. There is intriguing evidence of persistent overmanning, i.e. maintaining unproductive labour, well into the structural adjustment phase. This implies stagnating labour productivity and will finally reduce profitability. Table 9.8 provides an introduction to the restructuring record.

The table shows a link between increased labour productivity and profitability. It also shows how the qualitative measure of restructuring progress correlates with the two, more concrete, measures of restructuring. Examining the role of restructuring and first-wave membership, profitability appears to be a fair indicator, just as the first-wave countries generally rank highest on the progress measure. As indicated above, progress in restructuring should be seen as a clear precondition for the ability to withstand the competitive pressures of the Internal Market, and Table 9.8 shows that this relation has indeed found its way into the opinion of the European Commission. However, the table also indicates that none of the applicant countries has reached a restructuring and corporate governance structure identical to 'Western' economies, i.e. 4+.

As a final item in this section, we return again to the relation between ownership and restructuring. Does the evidence from Central and Eastern Europe indicate that some owners, and hence privatization programmes, are better than others in terms of stimulating effective restructuring? The evidence is mixed. Several case studies and samples of firms in transition economies repeatedly show the following features: Firms that remain state owned usually have the worst restructuring performance, leading us to conclude that privatization *per se* is a must. The difference between

Table 9.8 Restructuring measures and progress

	Profitability[a] (1995)	Annual percentage growth in labour productivity (1992–5)	Restructuring progress[b] (1998–9)
Bulgaria (ii)	1	−2	2+
Czech Republic (i)	14	7	3
Hungary (i)	8	3	3+
Poland (i)	7	5	3
Romania (ii)	1	−1	2
Slovak Republic (ii)	12	5	3
Slovenia (i)	10	3	3−
Estonia (i)	n.a.	n.a.	3
Latvia (ii)	n.a.	n.a.	3−
Lithuania (ii)	n.a.	n.a.	3−

[a] Average operating cashflow as percent of revenue.
[b] Restructuring progress replicates an EBRD measure of corporate governance and enterprise restructuring. 1: soft budget constraint, few reforms, 2: moderately tight credit and subsidy policy, 3: hard budget constraints, actions to promote corporate governance, 4: substantial improvements in corporate governance, e.g. significant new investments, 4+: Standards and performance typical of advanced industrial economies, market driven restructuring.

Sources: Djankov and Pohl (1998): table 1. EBRD (1999): table 2.1.

insider- and outsider-owned firms is by no means clear-cut, so the presupposition made in the beginning of this section is not supported, meaning that there is little evidence that insider-owned firms persistently perform worse in terms of efficiency. However, one repeated finding is that foreign-owned firms are clear leaders in terms of restructuring, and that newly established ('*de novo*') firms perform extremely well.

The main findings of this section on privatization and restructuring are as follows. Privatization is a core element of transition in Central and Eastern Europe. The privatization programmes have often relied on voucher schemes and frequently resulted in insider ownership, but as yet, the privatization process has not been concluded. For many countries, more than half of the large-scale state assets remain to be privatised. In terms of restructuring, which concerns the efficiency of firms, a clear link between restructuring progress and first-wave membership was identified. Still, none of the applicants has a structure (neither privatization nor restructuring) which reaches the level of advanced industrial countries.

9.6 The 'degree' of being a market economy

THERE is no clear-cut way of defining what being a market economy is all about. In fact, it covers a host of institutional arrangements, including such disparate items as the right to private ownership, some form of social safety net, and effective bankruptcy legislation. In this section, we will focus on two dimensions in which the CEE economies have had, and sometimes still have, a long way to go, namely the degree to which GDP is produced in the private sector, and, secondly, the extent to which the state has withdrawn from using subsidies. The level of subsidies is a measure of the extent of state interference with the decisions of economic agents and corresponds to a hardening of the budget constraints of enterprises.

On the face of it, the share of GDP derived from private sector production appears to be a measure remarkably similar to the degree of privatization, but in fact it is not. There are two forces at work differentiating the share of privatized state assets from private sector share of GDP. First, the foundation of *de novo* firms generates an entire branch of the economy which is private but was not state owned before. Secondly, and less obvious, a higher growth rate in the private (and privatized) sector than in the remaining state sector will skew the balance (over time), even if privatization were stopped. What, then, is the private sector share of GDP? Table 9.9 gives the answer.

Table 9.9 Private sector share of GDP, per cent		
	1994–5	1999
Bulgaria (ii)	n.a.	60
Czech Republic (i)	64	80
Hungary (i)	65	80
Poland (i)	55	65
Romania (ii)	35	60
Slovak Republic (ii)	n.a.	75
Slovenia (i)	40	55
Estonia (i)	55	75
Latvia (ii)	34	65
Lithuania (ii)	55	70
EUR15	85	n.a.
Sweden	75	n.a.
UK	87	n.a.

Notes: Data for CEE are EBRD estimates and differ from the official sources. Data for the EU are calculated from the share of 'services from general government and non-profit-making bodies'.

Sources: EBRD (1995): table 2.1. EBRD (1999): table 2.1. Eurostat (1997): ch. 3. Author's calculation.

The table provides private sector share of GDP at two points in time. The residual up to 100 indicates the level of state sector activity. It is common for all transition economies that the share of the private sector increased between 1994–5 and 1999, and it is also safe to assume that, at the outset of transition (1989–90), the share was much lower, in some cases only a few per cent, as private ownership of the means of production was rare. The table also provides data for the EUR15, Sweden, and the UK. Sweden is a member country with a very high level of state sector activity, while the UK is a member country with a very low level of state sector activity. Data are not available for EUR15 for 1999, but they will be very close to the ratios of 1994–5. Although none of the applicant countries has reached the EUR15 average of 85 per cent private sector share of GDP, four countries have reached, or even surpassed, the lower boundary constituted by Sweden, but as these are percentage measures, part of this observation is caused by a collapse of the state sector rather than by a boom in the private sector.

Among the first-wave countries, two perform notably poorly, i.e. Poland and Slovenia with 65 and 55 per cent, respectively. Given that private ownership, and consequently private economic activity, is at the heart of a market economy, and given that being a market economy is a central element of the Copenhagen Criteria, the above measure appears to be surprisingly uncorrelated with the grouping of first- and second-wave countries. However, it could be argued that a large private sector share is not a core theme of the European market economy model. Far more relevant for Europe is some version of '*Sozialmarktwirtschaft*', which, by definition, will have a significant level of state activity.

The extent of state subsidies

The second dimension in measuring the 'degree' of being a market economy is the abolition of state subsidies. This is a particularly important feature of transition, as it addresses the issue of state intervention and state ownership. In other words, if firms operate in the expectation that the state will intervene to support them, which gives them a so-called *soft budget constraint*, their actions will reflect such expectations. Only if firms survive without state aid can they be said to be able to withstand competitive pressure—another important Copenhagen criterion.

Table 9.10 provides data on subsidies for six of the ten applicant countries and also includes data on the EUR15, Ireland, and the UK (two boundary cases within the EUR15). First of all, data for the CEE countries demonstrate an impressive reduction in the use of subsidies over the examined period, the only exception being Romania, which has an initial surge in subsidies followed by a rapid reduction in the years 1993 and 1994 (note that the data presented are in per cent of GDP). Given the general fall in GDP over that period, the absolute reduction in subsidy levels is even more rigorous. By 1994, all the countries surveyed are within the margins of EU subsidy levels, which is a major accomplishment for the transition governments and certainly makes them qualify as market economies using this benchmark.

Table 9.10 Government expenditure on subsidies, per cent of GDP

	1989	1990	1991	1992	1993	1994
Bulgaria (ii)	15.5	14.9	4.1	1.8	2.2	1.3
Czech Republic (i)	25.0	16.2	7.7	5.0	3.9	3.4
Hungary (i)	12.1	9.5	7.4	5.5	4.3	4.5
Poland (i)	12.9	7.3	5.1	3.2	2.2	2.2
Romania (ii)	5.7	7.9	8.1	12.9	5.5	3.8
Estonia (i)	n.a.	n.a.	n.a.	0.8	0.9	0.8
EUR15	2.3	2.2	2.3	2.2	2.4	2.3
Ireland	4.6	5.8	5.7	4.8	5.1	4.5
UK	1.1	1.1	1.0	1.1	1.1	1.1

Notes: Data on the EU are defined as 'Current transfers to enterprises, general government'. EUR15 excluding Luxembourg.

Sources: IMF (1996): table 20. EU Commission (1998): table 64.

What may have compelled such austere policies? The first reason that springs to mind is the desire to withdraw the state from economic activity. In fact, the removal of subsidies is one of the most visible policies of the liberalization phase. An additional reason, and maybe the actual driving force, is the need to stabilize the economy. The stabilization packages of transition economies (in reaction to output collapse and high inflation) usually include tight fiscal policies, a sound fiscal policy being both a signal to the outside world and a means to avoid inflationary pressures stemming from the need to monetize the government deficit. Hence, cutting government expenditure is of major importance, and cuts in subsidies provide a central tool.

Despite the vagueness of measuring the 'degree' of being a market economy, this section has examined two dimensions: private sector share of GDP and the use of government subsidies. In both dimensions, the transition economies have performed well, and particularly the countries of the first wave are reaching levels compatible with the EU level.

9.7 Trade and FDI

THIS section will examine the trade and FDI relations between the EU and the applicant countries. Trade is important for the discussion of eastern enlargement in several respects. First, trade has always been the vehicle of European integration and will certainly also be so in the current enlargement round. Secondly, the Copenhagen Criteria explicitly state that the prospective new members must prove their ability to withstand the competitive pressures of the internal market. If a nation can successfully penetrate the EU market and tolerate import competition from the EU before full membership, without using protective measures such as tariffs and/or home producer subsidies, then that nation must certainly be able to withstand the competitive pressures once it becomes a full member. Asserting trade relations is thus one way of checking the fulfilment of the Copenhagen Criteria. Turning to the role of FDI, its importance in creating economic links across borders and its beneficial effect on the economic development of the host countries should be recognized. We have already established that CEE firms with foreign participation perform significantly better in restructuring, and it can thus be deduced that FDI strengthens structural adjustment.

Trade flows and deficits

Table 9.11 shows the share of extra-EUR15 trade with the CEE countries, which is a group of countries slightly larger than the ten applicants (see the note to the table). To put the data into perspective, recall that by 1996, intra-EU trade accounted for approximately 60 per cent of all foreign trade of the EU member countries, and it follows that the extra-EU trade was in the range of 40 per cent. The table presents trade with CEE countries as a percentage of this extra-EU trade.

The table lists the percentages of extra-EU imports from and exports to CEE countries for the EUR15 and Germany, and it is evident that the role of the CEE countries has increased since the beginning of transition. The data for Germany show that the region is relatively more important for German foreign trade than for the EU on average, and this is certainly one of the reasons that Germany is in support of eastern enlargement. At EU level, exports to the CEE countries countries are higher than imports, which is an indication of the trade surplus that the EU has with the region. Part of the explanation of this imbalance is the role of capital goods, as the build-up of

Table 9.11 Trade with CEEC[a] as a percentage of extra-EU trade		1991	1993	1995	1997	1999
EUR15	Imp. from CEEC	5.8	6.7	8.7	9.0	10.3
	Exp. to CEEC	7.2	8.3	10.2	12.1	13.3
Germany[b]	Imp. from CEEC	10.6	12.3	16.1	17.3	20.0
	Exp. to CEEC	10.9	12.5	14.8	17.6	19.5

[a] In the Eurostat definition, apart from the 10 applicant countries, CEEC also includes: Albania, Bosnia-Herzegovina, Croatia, Serbia, and Montenegro.
[b] The percentage relates to Germany's total extra-EU trade.

Sources: Eurostat (1996): tables 1801, 1802, 1915, and 1916. Eurostat (2000): tables 1801, 1802, 1915, and 1916. Author's calculation.

the Eastern European capital stock has caused a surge in the import of investment goods, mainly from the EU. In terms of enlargement, the region has become increasingly important over time, hence the postulate of trade as a vehicle for integration, but the causality is by no means clear. Do the association status and the implementation of trade agreements cause the swell in economic cooperation, or does the increase in trade activity encourage the political groundwork?

Considering the role of the EUR15 in the foreign trade of the different applicant countries, it is important, first of all, to note that the economies of Central and Eastern Europe experienced a bold reorientation of trade away from the members of the Council for Mutual Economic Assistance (CMEA, or better known as COMECON) towards the OECD countries. It was the COMECON that directed (and upheld) trade flows within the eastern block during the period of central planning. Kaminski *et al.* (1996) estimated an index of export reorientation, and for the years 1991 to 1994, they found that the applicant countries had increased their trade with OECD countries by 100 to 200 per cent. In their overall ranking of export reorientation among twenty transition economies, the applicant countries cover the top nine places (Slovenia is not included in the analysis), and in fact, Czech Republic, Poland, Estonia, and Hungary hold the top four places (in that order). This is a striking coincidence with first-wave membership found in an analysis conducted more than a year before the Commission issued its opinion in 1997.

Turning to the relative importance of trade with the EU compared to other regions, Table 9.12 provides data on the main trade flows of the ten applicants for the year 1997. In the table, trade shares are classified according to their regional grouping, i.e. belonging to either the EU, the rest of Europe, excluding the former Soviet Union (FSU) republics (i.e. predominantly the ten applicant countries), or FSU (including Eastern non-applicant countries, mainly Russia).

The table states the share of total imports and exports respectively, the residual for each country indicating the trade share with the rest of the world, ranging from a few per cent in the Baltic Republics to more than 20 per cent in the case of Romania. Overall we find that the EU is the single most important trading partner for all the applicant countries, and that, on average, the first-wave countries conduct a relatively larger share of their trade with the EU. Note that it appears from the table that the Baltic Republics conduct an unduly large share of their foreign trade with the Former Soviet Union. However, part of this observation stems from the fact that trade between the Baltic Republics is included in this category so that e.g. in the case of Latvia, 6.4 and 6.0 per cent of imports stem from Lithuania and Estonia, respectively, and are included in the 31.3 per cent. Similarly, the fact that the Czech Republic and Slovak Republic conduct substantial parts of their trade with the group 'Other Europe' is caused by the historically strong trade links between these two countries.

As a final point under trade matters, the current account situation arising from the above flows should be considered. Disproportionate growth in imports and sluggish export performances in particular have generated current account problems in most transition economies. Table 9.13 provides some recent data. For both 1998 and 1999, it shows substantial current account deficits for almost all applicant countries. The current account balance is composed of the balance of goods (merchandise trade

Table 9.12 Main trade flows, 1997, per cent of total trade

	EUR15		Other Europe[a]		FSU[b]	
	Imp.	Exp.	Imp.	Exp.	Imp.	Exp.
Bulgaria (ii)	38.3	44.7	8.7	10.4	33.2	14.3
Czech Republic (i)	61.5	59.9	16.0	25.2	7.6	5.4
Hungary (i)	62.4	69.9	9.5	12.7	10.0	7.0
Poland (i)[c]	64.0	66.6	8.8	9.2	9.0	13.6
Romania (ii)	52.5	56.6	8.4	9.0	14.5	5.7
Slovak Republic (ii)	39.5	45.0	30.7	41.9	18.3	7.6
Slovenia (i)	67.4	63.6	16.1	23.9	2.9	5.0
Estonia (i)	59.1	48.6	4.6	5.0	19.1	40.0
Latvia (ii)	53.2	48.9	8.9	3.9	31.3	39.9
Lithuania (ii)	47.7	36.7	12.6	5.4	32.9	49.4

[a] 'Other Europe' consists mainly of the applicant countries, excluding the Baltic Republics, and EFTA countries.
[b] FSU contains the European part of the former USSR and is mainly composed of non-applicant countries, but includes the Baltic Republics. Figures are mainly accounted for by Russia.
[c] 1996.

Source: United Nations (1999): individual country tables: table 3. Author's calculation.

Table 9.13 Current account balances of the applicants, per cent of GDP

	1998	1999	Percentage point change
Bulgaria (ii)	−0.5	−5.5	−5.0
Czech Republic (i)	−2.4	−2.0	0.4
Hungary (i)	−4.9	−4.2	0.6
Poland (i)	−4.4	−7.6	−3.2
Romania (ii)	−7.0	−3.4	3.6
Slovak Republic (ii)	−10.1	−5.7	4.4
Slovenia (i)	0.0	−3.0	−2.9
Estonia (i)	−9.2	−6.2	3.0
Latvia (ii)	−11.7	−10.2	1.5
Lithuania (ii)	−12.1	−11.2	0.9

Notes: Mismatches of differences in the third column are caused by rounding. Data for 1999 are EBRD estimates.

Source: EBRD (2000): table 1.5.

balance) and services traded. Background data show that all ten countries have a surplus on the service balance, so the underlying problem must stem from the import and export of goods. Part of the explanation is the above-mentioned surge in the import of capital goods, but much of the deficit also stems from ever-increasing imports and sluggish export performances. This underlying problem is exacerbated— if not caused—by continuous real appreciation, driven by fixed or semi-fixed exchange rate regimes and two-digit-level inflation. We will return to this issue in Section 9.8.

FDI inflows

Let us turn to the inflow of foreign direct investment into the CEE countries. Table 9.14 shows absolute and cumulative per capita FDI inflows into the CEE countries, as well as per capita inflow for 1999. The use of cumulative FDI data measures an increase in the stock of foreign capital. Adjusting data to per capita figures eliminates variances caused by differences in country sizes.

A number of observations can be deduced from the data on FDI. First, the cumulative inflow varies a lot. Secondly, adjusting the figures to per capita terms still leaves wide variation. As an example, for the nine years from 1989, per capita FDI inflows of Romania and Bulgaria amount to only around 15 per cent of the Hungarian level. Thirdly, first-wave countries hold three of the top five ranks in terms of cumulative per capita inflow, the exceptions being Poland and Slovenia with relatively low per capita FDI. Finally, whereas the 1999 figures disclose that the first-wave countries

Table 9.14 Foreign direct investment inflow into CEE, US dollars

	Cumulative 1989–99 (millions)	Cumulative 1989–99 per capita	Inflow 1999 per capita
Bulgaria (ii)	2,265	273	89
Czech Republic (i)	14,924	1,447	476
Hungary (i)	17,770	1,764	140
Poland (i)	20,047	518	172
Romania (ii)	5,264	235	36
Slovak Republic (ii)	2,111	391	130
Slovenia (i)	1,135	568	20
Estonia (i)	1,615	1,122	162
Latvia (ii)	2,135	880	151
Lithuania (ii)	2,012	545	129

Note: Data for 1999 are EBRD estimates.
Source: EBRD (2000): table 1.7.

remain in the top ranking, many second-wave countries have clearly caught up, illustrating yet again that, by the end of 1999, the rationality behind the grouping into waves was no longer as clear-cut. It should also be borne in mind that since a variable like FDI inflow is strongly dependent on a country's membership prospects, there is a causality issue.

The relative position of FDI is one thing, the absolute levels is another. In a paper by Sinn and Weichenrieder (1997), cumulative FDI inflow is compared to the level of FDI inflow into East Germany, using East Germany as a benchmark. The findings (data up to 1996) indicate a disappointing performance for all CEE countries. In per capita terms, FDI inflow into the CEE countries is only a few per cent of the East German level, the highest figures being found for Hungary and Slovenia at approximately 10 per cent. Possible causes of this disappointing performance are the larger risk, lack of expertise, and information deficiencies associated with the CEE countries. Further, the 'oversupply of investment objects' has depressed the FDI market, i.e. Western FDI is spread out thinly throughout the whole of Eastern Europe. Finally, low FDI levels could also be caused by a certain resentment towards foreign investors and/or owners, and some evidence to this effect has been presented by Sinn and Weichenrieder (1997: app. 1).

This section on trade and FDI has identified the following main conclusions: The European Union is the single most important foreign trade partner for the applicant countries. Trade reorientation has been massive for the transition economies, and the EU accounts for an ever-increasing trade share, just as the CEE countries account for an expanding share of extra-EU trade. Nevertheless, in relative terms, the EU is more important to the CEE countries than they are to the EU, but this will usually be the case when comparing a large economic area to a smaller one. Turning to the current account positions, all applicant countries suffer from substantial current account deficits.

9.8 Monetary aspects

THIS section will be dedicated to an examination of the final Copenhagen criterion, the 'adherence to the aims of [. . .] monetary union'. Even though participation in the monetary union is not a precondition for Union membership (nor is it presently achievable for any of the applicants), it is certainly a dimension according to which the countries are monitored, and policy makers in the CEE frequently use monetary union criteria as a benchmark for domestic economic policy. Before turning to the Maastricht criteria, it is appropriate to introduce the applicant countries' monetary and exchange rate arrangements.

Fighting inflation and introducing exchange rate policies

As demonstrated in Table 9.1, all CEE economies have had spells of high inflation, but all ten applicants have had impressive inflation stabilization records, even though the 1999 inflation levels were still clearly above the EU average. A core feature of almost all stabilization packages has been some form of fixed or semi-fixed exchange rate system. In addition to the initial high inflation experienced at the outset of transition, some countries have had to start their own monetary system from scratch, such as the Baltic Republics, which had to introduce their own new currencies after their membership of the rouble zone.

What were the causes of the initial high inflation? The two principal forces were the monetary overhang and price liberalization. Monetary overhang is the counterpart of the goods rationing in the economy, which forced agents to have savings, as many goods were not available. With the removal of price controls, and only slow quantity adjustment, prices were pushed upwards, sometimes reaching monthly inflation rates of more than 1,000 per cent. However, this was a one-off effect. The causes of persistent transition inflation are different.

A major driving force behind the continuous high inflation has been the substantial budget deficits of transition governments. State-owned firms were initially kept alive by state subsidies (soft budget constraints), and the transitional recession strained the public budget further. Given the infant financial markets of transition economies, the only source of financing budgets was monetization—with the usual inflationary consequences. Another feature of transition economies was a high industry concentration, where large firms with considerable market power in principle could act as monopolists and abuse their market power by raising prices. A further vehicle for continuous high inflation was the appearance of widespread currency substitution in the early years of transition. As agents substituted to safe currencies, such as US dollars or Deutschmark, the domestic monetary authority controlled only part of the monetary base. Parallel to currency substitution, growing de-monetization—the reliance on barter trade—can fuel inflation.

Today, most of the applicant countries have managed to bring inflation down to 10 per cent or less. In all cases, a main ingredient of this stabilization has been a close tightening of money growth, typically facilitated by some sort of exchange rate peg. The ultimate exchange rate-based stabilization took place first in Estonia and later in Lithuania and Bulgaria, where the monetary authority was substituted by a currency board. A currency board arrangement reduces the central bank to an issuing authority, covering the entire monetary base with foreign currency. Hence, in principle, the central bank—or rather the currency board—is able to exchange any amount of domestic currency into the peg currency at the fixed rate. In the case of Estonia, for instance, eight Estonian kroon are covered by one Deutschmark. Growth of the monetary base is thus limited to the inflow of foreign currency. In hindsight, the Estonian arrangement has been extremely effective as an inflation stabilization device;

however, the tight peg combined with the remaining inflation (which is still several percentage points higher than German inflation) has caused persistent real exchange rate appreciation. Thus, in principle, Estonian competitiveness deteriorates, and only a substantial initial undervaluation or persistent productivity gains can justify such appreciation. This problem relates to the severe current account deficits demonstrated in Table 9.13.

It is obviously not always feasible to operate with tight exchange rate pegs, such as the currency board, and larger economies find it particularly difficult to maintain such constructions. A different exchange rate regime, also aimed at stabilizing inflation, was chosen by Poland, which opted for a crawling peg arrangement. This means that the Polish zloty is allowed to adjust (devalue) at regular intervals by a certain pre-announced, but limited, fraction. The permitted monthly devaluation is approximately 1 per cent. This system creates stability in the sense that investors and markets need not fear sudden devaluations, and in addition, it prevents harmful real appreciations, thus protecting Poland's competitiveness. In 1997, the Polish system was modified to allow for a small fluctuation margin of the zloty rate against a basket of foreign currencies, similar to the EMS, but the central rate of that margin is still adjusted by the crawling peg mechanism.

To summarize the description of the monetary and exchange rate arrangements, the ten applicants can be grouped by the degree of exchange pegging. Estonia, Lithuania, and Bulgaria rely on currency board arrangements, whereas the Slovak Republic has pegged the koruna to a basket of foreign currencies with fluctuation margins. Latvia relies on a strong independent central bank, but shadows its exchange rate to the SDR in a virtual peg. Poland and Hungary use crawling peg mechanisms. The Czech Republic initially had a pegged exchange rate, which included fluctuation margins and occasional devaluations, but later moved to a managed float. After severe troubles, Romania has relied on a managed float since 1998, whereas Slovenia relies on a strong independent central bank and engages in a managed float.

Transition economies and the convergence criteria

We noted earlier that adherence to the aim of monetary union was part of the Copenhagen Criteria. The first Maastricht convergence criterion—on exchange rate stability—is of course driven by the exchange rate regimes introduced above. Data on the other two monetary criteria (inflation and interest rates) as well as the budget deficit criterion are shown in Table 9.15. Two of the ten applicant countries fulfil the inflation criteria, but none fulfils the interest rate criteria. As discussed in Chapter 8, the interest rate level traces the inflation performance, i.e. high inflation is associated with higher interest rates.

On the deficit criterion, the applicants perform better than expected. Two effects are at work. On the one hand, as transition strains the public budget, tax collection collapses, the transitional recession reduces revenues, and pressures on social spending increase, one would expect transition governments to run large deficits. On the

Table 9.15 Applicants and the convergence criteria, 1999, per cent

	Inflation	Interest rate	Deficit (per cent of GDP)
Bulgaria (ii)	6.2	14.1	−1.0
Czech Republic (i)	2.5	8.0	−3.8
Hungary (i)	11.2	15.4	−5.6
Poland (i)	9.8	14.4	−3.5
Romania (ii)	54.8	68.6	−3.1
Slovak Republic (ii)	14.0	13.5	−3.6
Slovenia (i)	8.0	15.2	−1.0
Estonia (i)	3.9	8.6	−4.7
Latvia (ii)	3.2	12.5	−3.8
Lithuania (ii)	0.3	13.0	−8.6
Criteria	2.7	7.8	−3.0

Notes: Data on inflation are reproduced from Table 9.1. Interest rate data are EBRD estimates and show the longest quoted lending rate, typically one year.

Source: EBRD (2000): country data and table 1.3.

other hand, as mentioned above, stabilization of the economy, in particular avoiding inflationary pressures, forces governments to pursue sound fiscal positions (which is also the typical recommendation by the IMF). The latter effect appears to dominate for many CEE countries.

Data on government debt (the final Maastricht criterion) are not consistently available. From the available data, there is evidence of relatively low debt positions among the applicants, but this is not so much caused by a balanced budget approach as by the short period of time during which the CEE countries have accumulated debt.

The main findings of this section, addressing monetary issues of the applicant countries, can be summarized as follows: Fighting inflation has been a major concern of the stabilization packages of all transition countries. The CEE countries have applied various versions of exchange rate pegging as inflation fighting devices. In terms of monetary union, whereas the applicant countries are far from fulfilling the Maastricht criteria, their direction and pace are right. On the budget condition, the applicants aim at strict discipline in the spirit of the Maastricht 3 per cent.

9.9 Concluding remarks

THIS chapter has dealt with the eastern enlargement of the European Union, a central element of which is the fulfilment of the so-called Copenhagen Criteria: stability and democracy, being a market economy able to cope with competitive pressures, the ability to adopt the *acquis*, and adherence to the aims of the EMU. These are the conditions, which the ten applicant countries have to fulfil before membership becomes feasible, and the chapter has examined the economies of the CEE countries with respect to these conditions. In several instances, the differences between the first-wave countries—i.e. those that started membership negotiations in 1998—and the second-wave countries—i.e. those that started negotiations in 2000—have been highlighted.

The main findings were that transition from a centrally planned system towards a market economic system is always accompanied by output collapse and high inflation. Transition was divided into three phases: liberalization, stabilization, and structural adjustment. Examining GDP data, we found that, although the applicant countries are all relatively poor in per capita terms, some first-wave countries may soon be able to overtake the poorest EU countries. Concerning main sectoral structure, it was established that, traditionally, the industrial and agricultural sectors have been dominating in the CEE, but a substantial reorientation has occurred among the leading applicant countries, and several applicant countries feature a main sectoral structure well within the margins of the present EUR15.

A central aspect of the shift from a centrally planned system towards a market economy is privatization of SOEs. Progress in both privatization and restructuring was examined, since they are the basis of a market economy. We found that privatization is far from concluded, and evidence on sluggish restructuring was presented. However, in terms of the private sector share of GDP, a number of first-wave countries reach levels of up to 80 per cent, which is comparable to the levels found among EUR15 countries.

On trade and FDI, a major reorientation among the CEE countries was identified. The EU is now by far the single most important trade partner for most of the applicant countries, and again the widest reaching progress was found for the first-wave countries. Eastern Europe has attracted FDI inflows throughout the 1990s, but the allocation between the different countries is very uneven, and, by some accounts, absolute FDI levels in the CEE are disappointing.

Overall, the presented material indicates that, judged by economic data alone, a number of the applicant countries appear very similar to the poorest of the existing EU members. However, having said that, we must realize that the present analysis does not take into account the economic costs and benefits, which will arise for both the applicants and the EUR15. It is the allocation of these costs and benefits which is at the heart of the ongoing negotiations. Eventually, the conclusion on enlargement will not be made on economic grounds alone, but will be determined rather by political restrictions and resilience.

Further reading

A recent book addressing the issues of economies in transition in a descriptive manner, and including ample information on the development of reforms up to the present date, is M. Lavigne (1999), *The Economics of Transition: From Socialist Economy to Market Economy*, 2nd edn., Macmillan, London. A more formal treatment of transition economics, but with no particular focus on eastern enlargement questions, is given in O. Blanchard (1998), *The Economics of Post-Communist Transition*, OUP, Oxford. The most influential economic article on the enlargement question to date, including a review of the impact of enlargement on the EU budget, is R. Baldwin, J. F. François, and R. Portes (1997), 'The Cost and Benefit of Eastern Enlargement: The Impact on the EU and Central Europe', *Economic Policy*, April. Finally, the annual *Transition Reports* of the EBRD provide a rich source of facts and data on all transition economies.

References

Boeri, T., M. Burda, and J. Köllö (1998), *Mediating the Transition: Labour Markets in Central and Eastern Europe*, CEPR, Economics Policy Initiative.

Bruno, M. (1993), 'Stabilisation and the Macroeconomics of Transition—How different is Eastern Europe?', *Economics of Transition*, 1 (1): 5–19.

Djankov, S., and G. Pohl (1998), 'The Restructuring of Large Firms in the Slovak Republic', *Economics of Transition*, 6 (1): 67–85.

EBRD (1995), *Transition Report 1995*, European Bank for Reconstruction and Development, London.

—— (1997), *Transition Report 1997: Enterprise Performance and Growth*, European Bank for Reconstruction and Development, London.

—— (1998), *Transition Report 1998: Financial Sector in Transition*, European Bank for Reconstruction and Development, London.

—— (1999), *Transition Report 1999: Ten Years of Transition*, European Bank for Reconstruction and Development, London.

—— (2000), *Transition Report: Update*, European Bank for Reconstruction and Development, London.

EU Commission (1998), *European Economy*, 65.

—— (1999), *European Economy*, 69.

Eurostat (1996), *Eurostatistics: Data for Short-Term Economic Analysis*, 7/1996.

—— (1997), *Yearbook 1997: A Statistical Eye on Europe 1986–1996*.

—— (2000), *Eurostatistics: Data for Short-Term Economic Analysis*, 7/2000.

IMF (1996), 'World Economic Outlook: A Survey by the Staff of the International Monetary Fund', *Occasional Papers*, May 1996.

Kaminski, B., Z. K. Wang, and L. A. Winters (1996), 'Export Performance in Transition Economies', *Economic Policy*, October.

Schröder, Philipp J. H. (1999), 'On Privatization and Restructuring', *European Studies Working Papers*, 33/1999, Dept. of Economics, University of Southern Denmark, Odense.

Sinn, H. W., and A. Weichenrieder (1997), 'Foreign Direct Investment, Political Resentment and the Privatization Process in Eastern Europe', *Economic Policy*, April.

United Nations (1999), *1997 International Trade Statistics Yearbook*, 1, United Nations, New York.

World Bank (1998), *World Development Indicators*, World Bank, Washington, DC.

—— (2000), *World Development Indicators*, World Bank, Washington, DC.

Chapter 10

From European Economies towards a European Economy?

Jørgen Drud Hansen and Finn Olesen

10.1 Introduction

INTEGRATION is an evolutionary process which involves economic, political, and historical elements. The previous chapters have mainly illustrated economic integration in Europe. It has been clearly demonstrated that the EU countries have forged much closer bonds, in particular through the establishment of the Internal Market, where the institutional barriers to free mobility of goods, services, persons, and capital by and large have been removed. The establishment of the Economic and Monetary Union (EMU) has created equal conditions in the monetary area for those countries participating in the common currency, the euro, and the mutual transactions between these countries are no longer burdened by currency exchange costs and exchange rate insecurity. At the economic policy level, the monetary policy for the euro countries has become a matter of common interest under the competence of the European Central Bank (ECB), and the fiscal policies of individual member states are now governed by the regulations of the Stability and Growth Pact. The conditions of the agricultural sector are regulated by the Common Agricultural Policy (CAP) based on an extensive market regulation of production and prices. Based on the structural funds, the regional policy programmes of the EU have attempted to equalize the differences in standards of living between the rich and poor areas of the EU. A common framework for manufacturing and services has been created by prohibiting trade-distorting state subsidies and anti-competition agreements between dominating firms in the European market. The free mobility of goods, services, and factors of production has created a pressure on the member states to harmonize taxation rules, in particular on interest earnings and corporate income.

It is the cooperation between the EU countries in all these areas which has been examined in the previous chapters. In this final chapter, the integration experiences gained so far will be summarized in Section 10.2 in order to answer the question whether the EU still consists of a club of economies, or if it has developed into one economy. We find that nominal convergence, i.e. convergence of inflation and interest rates, has been extensive, in contrast to the synchronization of the business cycle, which has been less successful. Section 10.3 takes a look into the future by examining recent initiatives of, and discussing the prospects for, further integration. It will be identified that the major challenge for the EU will follow from the enlargement by new member countries from Central and Eastern Europe (CEE). This will necessitate a reform of the EU institutions, and enlargement will also create a pressure for reforms of the CAP and regional policy of the EU. Section 10.4 concludes the chapter.

10.2 European integration so far

Is it fair to conclude that, in the last decades, the economies of the EU member states have become so integrated that they form one coherent European economy? There is no immediate answer to this question, as there is no clear consensus concerning the meaning of the word integration. Loosely speaking, integration refers to a process where formerly independent entities melt together to form a unity. Integration can take several forms.

First, the concept of integration can be related to the degree of convergence with respect to formal and institutional frameworks, i.e. whether the EU members face the same conditions, and it is obvious that the EU cooperation has created equal formal and institutional conditions for the economic environment in a number of central areas. As the Internal Market is based on 'the four freedoms', the state borders no longer constitute an institutional barrier to economic transactions, and as a result, the institutional conditions for producers and consumers in the Internal Market have become more uniform in several crucial respects. The Common Agricultural Policy (CAP) is another striking example that the EU cooperation has created similar institutional frameworks, as the production of all farmers in the EU takes place under the same set of market regulations. Finally, the EMU has created similar institutional conditions in the monetary area for the countries participating in the euro. So by the measure of similarity of formal and institutional frameworks, integration has proceeded a great deal, and the EU must be said to be highly integrated.

Secondly, the concept of integration can be related to the degree of similarity in measured outcome, for example uniform prices, interest rates, unemployment rates, and standards of living. These two aspects of integration—similarity in institutional and formal frameworks and similarity in outcome—do not necessarily lead to the same conclusions with respect to the development in the degree of integration. The new literature on 'economic geography' thus indicates that it is possible that there will be persistent differences in the development in standards of living between different areas, even though the barriers to mobility of goods, services, and resources are reduced. Such differences persist as a consequence of the existence of economies of scale and agglomeration economies (Krugman (1991)).

The complexity of the concept of integration is not the only hindrance to examining the effects of the actual integration process within the EU. The removal of barriers is a global trend, another example of which is the trade liberalization taking place under the aegis of the WTO, and it is difficult to distinguish the specific effects of the European integration process from the more general effects stemming from the global process. Keeping these caveats in mind, in the following, we will try to summarize and evaluate the process of integration in specific economic areas in the EU from the outcome point of view only.

Indications of integration

Table 10.1 evaluates the present stage of economic integration from a micro- and macro-economic perspective. In the following, we will expand on the findings of the table.

Markets for goods and services

As demonstrated in Chapter 6, intra-EU trade has increased significantly because of the formation of the customs union and the Single Market, and this has led to a substantial reduction in the price dispersion of individual products or services between member countries. However, the effect of trade liberalization on price differences varies a great deal from one product to another. More precisely, the decrease in price dispersion depends on the level of transport and other trade costs after the elimination of tariffs and quotas. If trade costs of tradables are low after liberalization, price dispersion is similarly low, i.e. trade liberalization leads to significant market integration. For non-tradables, on the other hand, trade costs after liberalization are significant and, as a consequence, the markets are segmented. In this case, the formation of the customs union and the Internal Market has only to a limited degree reduced price dispersion. The distinction between tradables and non-tradables applies to both goods and services, but most services are non-tradables, because the production and consumption activities take place at the same locality. Typical examples are healthcare, nursing homes, and tourist facilities.

The empirical assessment of the degree of market integration is related to the change in price dispersion. The EU Commission (1996) has carried out a survey of the effects of the Single Market measured by the development in price dispersion for

Table 10.1 Rating of the degree of integration

	Rating	Comments
Microeconomic convergence:		
a. Markets for goods and services		
Tradables	+++	Intense intra-EU trade, nearly full equalization of prices
Partly tradables	+	Increasing trade flows, some equalization of prices
Non-tradables	0	By definition no trade flows, no equalization of prices
b. Markets for factors of production		
Labour market	0	No mobility, and hence no equalization of wages
Market for real capital	++	Some mobility manifested through FDI flows, mergers and acquisitions — equalization of real profit rates
Macroeconomic convergence:		
c. Nominal convergence		
Price level	++	Labour intensive non-tradables cheaper in poor countries, hence not full equalization of price levels
Inflation rates	+++	Intense intra-EU trade and stable exchange rates (especially the introduction of the euro) have led to a convergence of inflation rates
Nominal interest rates	+++	Massive cross-border financial activities in the framework of stable exchange rates has led to a convergence of interest rates
d. Real convergence		
Business cycle synchronization	+	Member state specific business cycles because of different economic structures ·and lack of coordination of fiscal policy
Unemployment	0	No equalization of employment because of country-specific business cycles and different labour market structures
Living standards	+	Mixed trends of convergence of standards of living because of ambiguous effects of mobility of goods and resources on spatial distribution of economic activity

Notes: Rating of integration according to outcome, i.e. degree of equalization between member states. Ratings from o (no integration) to full integration ++++.

Table 10.2 Price variation among member states (EUR12), 1985 and 1993

	Coefficient of price variations (prices including taxes)	
	1985	1993
Consumer goods	22.5	19.6
Services	33.7	28.6
Energy	21.1	31.7
Equipment goods	14.0	14.5
Construction	22.1	27.4

Notes: The table shows the weighted average of the coefficient of price variations in each group for selected groups of goods and services. The coefficient of variance is defined by the spread divided by the mean in the statistical distributuion of prices for specific goods or services between countries.

Source: EU Commission (1996): 134.

groups of goods and services. Some of the main findings of the survey are reported in Table 10.2.

For the two groups consumer goods and services, which are by far the most important of the selected five groups, there was a clear tendency towards price convergence between the member states in the period 1985 to 1993. Note that the level of price dispersion for services is relatively high in both 1985 and 1993, which is due to the fact that a number of services are less tradable. In contrast to consumer goods and services, price dispersion has increased for energy and construction. This is no surprise, as the prices examined include indirect taxes (VAT and excise duties), and the development in taxation on energy has been particularly different between the countries. Note also that the areas of energy and construction had not been fully deregulated in 1993, which is why the markets were still segmented at the time.

To sum up, in the products and services which are the most traded, the national markets seem to some extent to have been replaced by a *pan-European market*. More competition on the pan-European market improves the efficiency, or welfare, of the economy, as price convergence limits the differences in the consumers' marginal utilities of the consumption of specific goods. Furthermore, as previously indicated in the analysis of industrial concentration (Chapter 5), welfare will increase as keener competition reduces the mark-up in the price determination.

Although, when measured by price dispersion, the two most important markets— for consumer goods and services—have become more integrated in recent years, there is undoubtedly a potential for further price level convergence in Europe. Surveys indicate that the geographic price differences are larger in the EU than in the USA, i.e. the markets for goods and services generally continue to be less integrated in the EU than in the USA. A survey by the EU Commission based on price data excluding taxes thus shows that, in 1996, the dispersion of aggregate price levels for goods and services was 14 per cent in the EU, but only 11 per cent in the USA (EU Commission (1999a): 217).

Markets for factors of production

Contrary to the markets for goods and services, there is very little integration of the labour market, especially for unskilled labour, across the member states. The mobility of labour has remained on a very low level leaving only marginal impacts on wage or employment dispersion (see Chapter 3 on labour market issues in the EU). The reasons for this low mobility are mainly language and other cultural barriers which, by and large, have remained unaffected by the endeavours to integrate the EU economies into one economy.

However, indirect integration effects have appeared on the labour market. The integration of the goods market and the introduction of the euro have emphasized the need for a flexible labour market, and as a consequence, the national trade unions have exercised more caution in their wage demands, as the demand for labour in the national market has become more sensitive to wage claims. It is therefore fair to say that, as a consequence of the integration process, trade union behaviour in the wage determination process has become interrelated across member states.

The level of foreign direct investment (FDI) and number of mergers and acquisitions has increased rapidly during the 1980s and 1990s. This development is analysed in Chapter 7 on foreign direct investment, which also demonstrates the increasing importance of intra-EU FDI flows. Where the mobility of goods is limited, the rationale for establishing subsidiaries has been to circumvent the distance barriers and use the owner-specific advantages of the firm to engage in production in more locations. In such cases, integration through FDI compensates for the lack of integration of the goods market. Chapter 7 furthermore demonstrated that there are comprehensive, two-way FDI flows taking place between member states, which also reflects the endeavours of firms to utilize their owner-specific advantages, e.g. superior knowledge of a specific production activity.

Significant restructuring and specialization have taken place in European business. The home market-oriented diversification strategies of individual firms have been replaced by strategies building on internationalization and development of core activities. As underlined in an article in the *Economist* (2000), this has created a more competitive and dynamic environment in the EU, where company behaviour has changed from destructive caution to creative destruction. The upsurge in capital flows — real as well as human — in the EU has therefore been a significant contributor to the economic integration of the member states and specifically, it has served to speed up the diffusion of technological know-how.

Nominal convergence

Integration has also left its significant mark at the *macroeconomic level*. As an example, monetary integration has led to clear convergence of price levels, inflation rates, and interest rate levels between the member states. Differences in price levels will be discussed below in connection with Figure 10.5.

The development in differences between member states with respect to inflation rates is illustrated in Figure 10.1. The middle curve (EUR15), indicated by a solid line, shows inflation in the EU as a whole in the period 1980–99. This period was characterized by a fixed exchange rate cooperation between most member states. The top (Max) and bottom (Min) curves give a year-by-year account of inflation in the countries with the highest and lowest inflation rates, respectively, and the distance between the two rates thus visualizes the maximum difference in inflation rates between the member states. The curves of maximum and minimum inflation are, however, sensitive to exceptional events in individual countries. The figure therefore also indicates the development in inflation in the countries with the third largest and third lowest inflation rates. These quartile curves offer a more informative picture of the actual inflation spread, as they exclude outlier countries. Statistically, the two curves approximately delimit the upper quartile and the lower quartile, respectively, in the

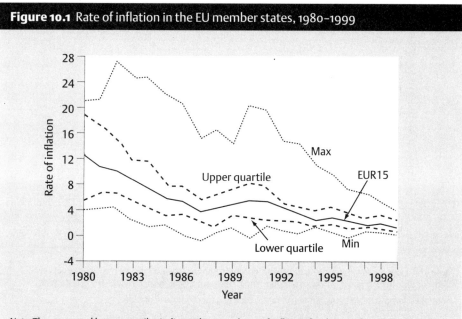

Figure 10.1 Rate of inflation in the EU member states, 1980–1999

Note: The upper and lower quartiles indicate the annual rate of inflation for the member countries with the third highest and third lowest rate of inflation, respectively, in the specific year.

Source: EU Commission (1999*a*), Annexe: table 24. Authors' calculation.

distribution of inflation rates between countries for the specific year. It appears from the figure that inflation in EUR15 as a whole has decreased, and this is an expression of the increased emphasis on the objective of price stability. Furthermore, the spread in inflation rates has visibly decreased throughout the entire period, and looking at this macroeconomic variable, integration has proceeded successfully.

The nominal convergence, measured by the convergence of interest rates, is even more explicit. Differences in long-term nominal interest rates essentially reflect differences between the expected inflation rates of the member countries. Figure 10.2 illustrates the development in the nominal long-term interest rate. Confidence in the feasibility of the EMU project significantly influenced the differences in interest rates throughout the 1990s. After the breakdown of the fixed exchange rate cooperation of the EMS following the two currency crises in 1992 and 1993, there was widespread scepticism concerning the realization of the EMU project, and as a consequence, there were significant differences in exchange rate levels. This scepticism gradually disappeared concurrently with the political determination to realize the project from 1 January 1999, and compared with previous years, differences in exchange rates were therefore reduced to a moderate level.

Figure 10.2 Nominal long-term interest rates in the EU member states, 1980–1999

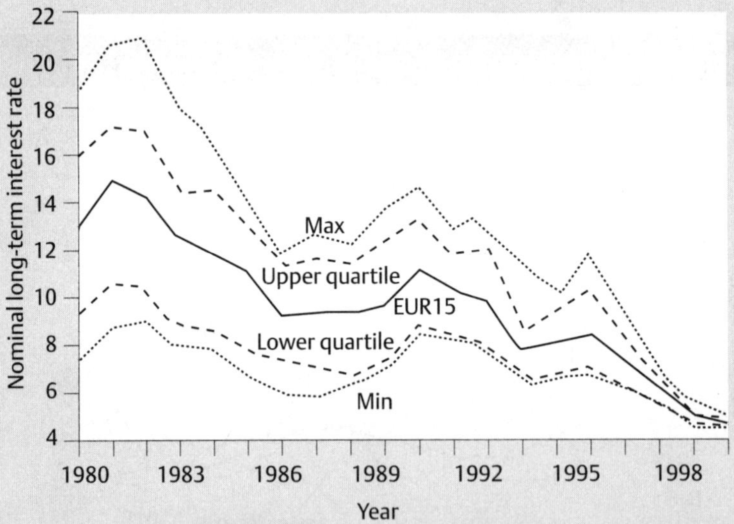

Note: The upper and lower quartiles indicate the long-term nominal interest rates for the member countries with the third highest and third lowest long-term nominal interest rates, respectively, in the specific year.

Source: EU Commission (1999a), Annexe: tables 24 and 52. Authors' calculation.

Business cycle synchronization

Whereas the monetary integration in the EU is obvious, the macroeconomic effects of the integration process on total output and employment are less clear. Economic developments, which are described in a more long-term perspective in Chapter 4, thus often differ between the individual member countries, especially in the short run. In other words, there is a lack of *synchronization* of the business cycles between the member countries, and this factor has not changed markedly since the early 1980s. Figure 10.3 shows the development in the annual real growth rate in GDP since 1980. It is immediately apparent from the figure that the differences in growth rates vary a lot when the country with the strongest growth in a specific year is compared to the country with the weakest growth. This significant variation is particularly due to the exceptional conditions which have characterized the economic development in the two countries, so one will get a more precise picture of the real differences in growth by looking at the differences in growth rates for the upper and lower quartiles of the countries. The figure shows that there are significant differences between the upper and lower quartiles, and the curve does not indicate a more synchronized development in business cycles in the 1990s compared with the 1980s.

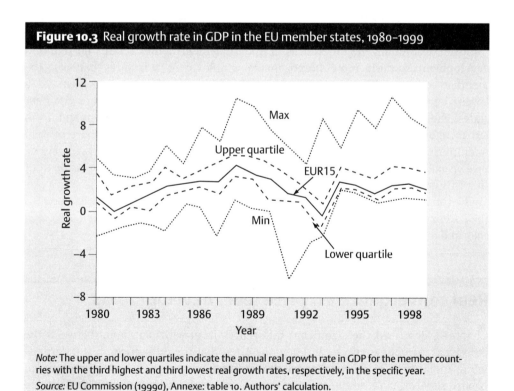

Figure 10.3 Real growth rate in GDP in the EU member states, 1980–1999

Note: The upper and lower quartiles indicate the annual real growth rate in GDP for the member countries with the third highest and third lowest real growth rates, respectively, in the specific year.

Source: EU Commission (1999a), Annexe: table 10. Authors' calculation.

At first sight, it may seem surprising that the development in business cycles has not been synchronized more in recent years. As demonstrated in Chapter 6, the Internal Market has contributed to a significant increase in trade between the member states. At the same time, exchange rates between most of the current member countries have been relatively stable as a result of their participation in the fixed exchange rate cooperation of the EMS, irrespective of whether this participation has been of a formal nature. In such macroeconomic conditions, there are strong links between the developments in aggregate demand in individual member countries, so that a change in aggregate demand in one member country, e.g. in the form of an increase in the demand for investment, will lead to an increase in activities in the other countries, which in turn will lead to an increase in imports (and thus to increased export possibilities and higher activities in the other member countries). Consequently, extensive intra-EU trade under fixed exchange rates should contribute significantly to increased synchronization of the business cycles.

There may be various reasons for the lack of synchronization of the business cycles of the member countries in the 1980s and 1990s. First, as pointed out in Chapter 5, there are significant differences in industrial structures between the member countries, and similarly, the functioning of the labour markets differs from member state to member state (see Chapter 3). It is obvious that such structural differences may mean that the economic development in the individual countries will not concur when external conditions change. Secondly, the economic policy of individual member states is determined by domestic considerations rather than by the concern over a coordinated development in business cycles in the EU.

Indeed, examining the differences in unemployment figures reveals no sign of a development towards more homogeneous employment structures between the member countries. Figure 10.4 illustrates the differences in unemployment via a Lorenz curve of unemployment in 1985 and 1998 for the current fifteen member states. The countries are ranked according to their rate of unemployment and, from left to right, the Lorenz curves display coordinates of the cumulated share of total unemployment and the cumulated share of total labour force in EUR15. The curvature visualizes the inequality in the distribution of unemployment, and it is apparent that this inequality has not changed substantially between 1985 and 1998. More precisely, the inequality is expressed by the Gini coefficient, which is the area between the Lorenz curve and the diagonal in the figure. The Gini coefficient made up 0.11 in 1985 and 0.10 in 1998, so in reality, the inequality remains unchanged.

Real convergence vs. price level developments

Chapter 4 described the significant differences in growth per capita between the individual member countries and demonstrated that the differences in standards of living are far from being equalized. It also pointed out that the increased mobility of goods, services, and resources can exacerbate such diverging developments in growth.

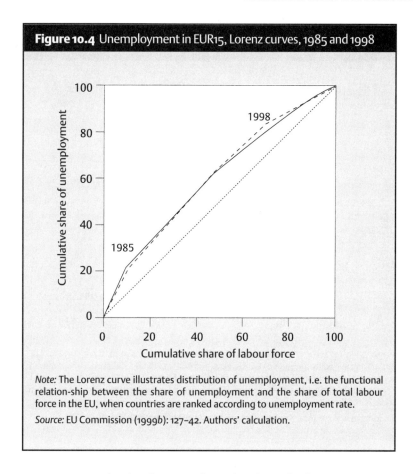

Figure 10.4 Unemployment in EUR15, Lorenz curves, 1985 and 1998

Note: The Lorenz curve illustrates distribution of unemployment, i.e. the functional relation-ship between the share of unemployment and the share of total labour force in the EU, when countries are ranked according to unemployment rate.

Source: EU Commission (1999*b*): 127–42. Authors' calculation.

Figure 10.5 contrasts the development in real and nominal convergence, measured in GDP per capita in PPS, to the price levels of individual member countries from the mid-1980s until the end of the 1990s. In case of perfect integration, both price levels and real GDP per capita will be equal in all member countries, i.e. all economies will converge at the point (100,1). If EU integration is effective, the expectation is that the countries will move closer to the point (100,1) over time. As it appears from the figure, the relative price level generally increases concurrent with the relative standards of living. This correlation between price level and standards of living is particularly due to the fact that the wage level in the poor member countries is relatively low, and as a result, non-tradables, and services in particular, are relatively cheap.

For six member states (Germany, Greece, Spain, France, Portugal, and Sweden) there is a clear convergence with the EU level of both standards of living and price levels. Belgium diverges both with respect to standards of living and price level, while the picture is more blurred for the remaining countries, which either converge in one dimension but diverge in the other, or over- or under-shoot in relation to the EUR15 average in terms of standards of living or price levels.

Above, we examined the question of whether or not economic conditions in the EU member countries have become more similar. It is evident that the countries have

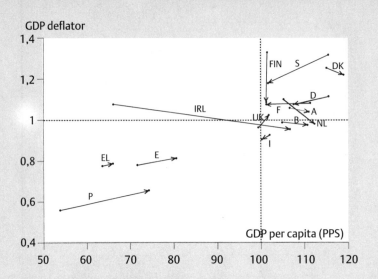

Figure 10.5 Convergence of standards of living and price levels, 1984–1986 and 1997–1999

Note: The arrows illustrate the change between the three-year averages 1984–6 and 1997–9. The GDP deflator is calculated as the ratio of GDP in euro and GDP in PPS. B = Belgium, DK = Denmark, D = Germany (1984–6 excluding East Germany), EL = Greece, E = Spain, F = France, IRL = Ireland, I = Italy, NL = The Netherlands, A = Austria, P = Portugal, FIN = Finland, S = Sweden, UK = United Kingdom (Luxembourg is not listed).

Source: EU Commission (1999a), Annexe: tables 5, 6, and 9. Authors' calculation.

forged closer ties in the past forty to fifty years and that the creation of the customs union and the Single Market has stimulated trade between the countries, thus contributing to more uniform prices of individual goods. Similarly, in the monetary area, the development has clearly been towards increased homogeneity with respect to inflation and interest rates, and the fixed exchange rate cooperation of the EMS, and later the euro project, have been determining factors towards this end. With respect to synchronization of the business cycles, unemployment levels, and standards of living, there are still differences between the countries, and it is questionable whether integration has progressed in these dimensions.

10.3 Prospects for the European Union in the years ahead

IN the following, we shall look at current development trends in the EU cooperation as well as at the long-term development perspectives. Integration often creates a need for further integration. This perception of integration as a politically dynamic process, which will automatically lead to increasing integration, is the fundamental idea of neofunctionalist political integration theory.

There are several examples in the history of EU integration which support such a perception of the development. The removal of visible trade barriers, such as tariffs and quotas, following from the creation of the EU customs union, led to an increase in various forms of invisible trade barriers, such as discriminatory public procurement, national technical standards, and abuse of the tax systems for national protectionism. This created a need for further integration, which in turn led to the creation of the Single Market (see Chapter 6). Unstable exchange rates are partly incompatible with the Common Agricultural Policy (CAP) and may partly be perceived as a trade barrier in the Internal Market, as exchange rate insecurity hampers trade. Thus, both the CAP and the Single Market have created a need for fixed exchange rates. In the 1980s and early 1990s, it was attempted to accommodate this need via the fixed exchange rate cooperation of the EMS, and when the EMS broke down in August 1993, the wish for full, monetary integration, through the formation of the EMU, was enhanced (see Chapter 8). Furthermore, the restrictions, which the establishment of the customs union and the Single Market put on the possibility of individual countries to give state subsidies, created a need for an active regional policy at the EU level (see Chapter 4). In order to accommodate this need, there has been a heavy expansion of the regional funds of the EU since the 1970s.

Given this procedural assumption, that integration often creates a need for further integration, it is possible to conjecture the future development. At the turn of the century, the following areas were, formally or informally, on the agenda of the political decision makers of the EU:

- Concerted efforts to improve employment in the member states
- Tax harmonization
- Enlargement of the European Union with several Central and Eastern European countries
- Reform of the regional policy related to the structural funds
- Reform of the Common Agricultural Policy (CAP)
- Institutional reforms of the decision-making process in the European Union.

On a longer horizon, discussions may possibly also include:

- Reform of the welfare state, since the above steps, once implemented, might affect the existing welfare system, as extensive legal and illegal migration must be expected.

These perspectives for the current and future development in the EU will be discussed in more detail in the following.

Decreasing the relatively high level of unemployment has increasingly become the focal point of EU cooperation. Concern about unemployment has been enhanced by the establishment of the monetary union, which has limited the member states' possibilities of pursuing an independent, national economic policy. At the same time, the European Central Bank is obliged to ensure price stability, which has put further emphasis on a joint EU effort to increase employment. In concrete terms, this has led to an incipient cooperation on labour market and employment policies. The obligation to cooperate in this field was originally spelt out in the Amsterdam Treaty's chapter on employment, and has subsequently been elaborated by a decision of the European Council in 1997 and by the Employment Pact (see EU Commission (1999*b*)). Cooperation has, however, been rather sketchy so far. The individual member states are obliged to prepare an annual national action plan for employment, and these plans are then coordinated by the Commission, which elaborates a common strategy for the employment and labour market policy. The proposal for this strategy is submitted to the European Council for approval and following this, the strategy is expected to be implemented on the basis of recommendations to the individual member countries. The cooperation so far has thus mainly consisted of exchanging information, making joint analyses, and issuing recommendations without limiting the competence of the individual countries to carry out their own labour market and employment policies.

In the first instance, the objective of the cooperation is to increase employment and create a flexible labour market, but in the long run, the problem may turn out to be labour scarcity as a consequence of the demographic developments (see Chapter 2), and the aim of the employment and labour market policy cooperation will therefore also be to contribute to larger 'employability', i.e. increasing the job supply by increasing labour market association of individual generations.

There are similar dynamic policy spill-over effects from previous to future integration in other areas. This applies to taxation policy, where the free mobility of capital following from the Internal Market has created a need for a harmonization of the rules on corporate taxation and on taxes on capital gains. The geographic location of firms, and especially of financial investments, is sensitive to differences in taxation, so unless the taxation rules are harmonized, competition between countries in these areas will either lead to a reduction in the tax rates or to distortions in the allocation of capital and tax revenue between countries. Differences in excise duties and value added tax on consumption may also induce consumers to make their purchases in the countries with the lowest taxation level. Although several member countries (e.g. the UK and Denmark) are reluctant to give up their national competence in the taxation area, there is nevertheless a strong market pressure to introduce common regulations in this area. This pressure is enhanced by the increasing use of the internet for trade in goods, and the specific problems in this area will also call for a solution at the EU level.

The most important, immediate challenge of EU cooperation will arise if the current accession negotiations between the EU and a number of CEE countries are completed successfully. In the first instance, the Czech Republic, Hungary, Poland, Slovenia, and Estonia are expected to obtain membership, but several other countries, such as the Slovak Republic, Latvia, and Lithuania are expected to rapidly follow. The desire for enlargement of the European Union is especially politically motivated, as the admission of these countries will be the best bulwark against a renewed European political and economic split into an Eastern and Western block.

The financial and administrative implications of the expected enlargement of the EU with the CEE countries are, however, significant. As described in Chapter 9, the applicant countries have substantially lower standards of living than the poorest of the current EU member countries, and this will create a need for massive support from EU structural funds. As several of the applicant countries are relatively large, measured by population size, the fulfilment of this need may increase the requirement for EU expenditures on structural funds. It is unlikely that there will be political support to increase the total EU budget significantly, and the enlargement will therefore presumably lead to reforms of the principles governing the structural funds. Several of those countries which have received substantial support from EU structural funds so far (Greece, Portugal, and Spain) are unlikely to be willing to accept that this support is redistributed to the new, poor member states. In future, this may therefore lead to a redistribution of the structural funds according to national quotas so that those countries which have received a certain extent of this kind of support so far will keep this advantage.

But the true hindrance of a swift enlargement might well be the need for reforms of the CAP and of the political decision-making process. Poland has a large potential for agricultural production, and accepting Poland into the EU will therefore significantly increase EU expenditures on the CAP. This may mean that new member countries will only be comprised by the CAP after a long transition period and concurrently with an enhancement of the efforts made so far of adapting the agricultural sector of the EU into the world market conditions.

It is also likely that the political decision-making process will be changed in the nearest future. Again, it is especially the impending enlargement of the EU with several new member states from Central and Eastern Europe which necessitates such institutional changes, the aim of which is to maintain a dynamic and effective decision-making process in a future EU with more than twenty member states. The considerations move in the direction of enhanced possibilities of majority voting in the European Council of Ministers, changed representation in the European Parliament, so that the number of members of Parliament from each country will reflect the population size of the countries to a higher degree, and changed rules for the rotation system regarding the chairmanship of the European Council of Ministers. In this connection, it is possible that in future, groups of countries rather than individual countries will fill this post. There are also considerations of changing the practice of appointing the Commission. Until the present, the Commission has consisted of two citizens from each of the large countries (Germany, France, Italy, Spain, and the UK), and one citizen from each of the remaining, small countries. The

Commissioners are appointed by the Council of Ministers after prior nomination by the governments of the individual member states. If this principle, which is laid down in the Amsterdam Treaty, is maintained, the Commission will become unmanageably large. Changing the rules is therefore being considered, so that the small member countries are not necessarily represented in the Commission.

Also the so-called democratic deficit will be enhanced by the expected enlargement. This problem relates to at least the following three aspects. First, it must be expected that in future, the Parliament will be accorded more powers and decision-making competence vis-à-vis the Council of Ministers and, perhaps in particular, the Commission, just as it must be expected, as already mentioned, that the number of seats in the Parliament will be reallocated in proportion to the given number of member states and may be extended to include more than the current 626 members. Secondly, the political decision-making process in the EU may be made more democratic by making it more open in line with what is applicable to the national parliaments of the member states. Thirdly, the Commission has been criticized for being subjected only to a limited form of parliamentary control. Admittedly, the entire Commission as a body may be dismissed by the Parliament, as happened in 1999, but none of the Commissioners are subjected to anything similar to ministerial responsibility.

Finally, it must be assumed that the enlargement of EU cooperation will actualize the need for a reform of the EU bureaucracy with a view to simplifying the functioning of the EU system (see the reflections on this in Chapter 1). Bearing the integration efforts made so far in mind, such an organizational and administrative simplification may, however, prove to be a highly difficult task to solve in practice.

In the long run, the enlargement may lead to an inclusion of the social welfare systems of the individual countries into the integration process. The free movement of persons may give rise to extensive migration from the new, poor Central and Eastern European member countries to the richer Western European member countries. With the current social benefit regulations, the contribution of the migrant towards the production in the host country will be smaller than the wage and social benefits received by the migrant after tax. This will result in a welfare loss (Sinn (2000)) of the current citizens in the host country. As the migrant's choice of destination country will depend on wages and social benefits after tax, individual countries will have an incentive to offer the lowest social standards to make the country less attractive as a host country compared to the other member countries. Such competition between the member states may lead to an erosion of the welfare state. In order to avoid such a development, and at the same time preserve the principle that a citizen of the EU enjoys the same rights everywhere in the EU, it stands to reason to harmonize the social standards of the member countries. Social policy may thus become a new object of integration.

The above discussion of the perspectives of the future development in EU cooperation illustrates the three dimensions of integration: functional scope, geographical domain, and institutional capacity (Laursen (1995)). These three dimensions are illustrated in Figure 10.6. Integration in *functional scope* consists of the transfer of policy areas from decision-making at the national level to decision-making at the EU level.

Integration in *geographical domain* captures the geographical dimension, i.e. the area where the integration rules apply. Finally, integration of *institutional capacity* represents the establishment of institutional bodies to monitor the development and decision-making at the EU level.

EU integration has progressed in all three dimensions in the past. Increasingly more areas have been submitted to decision-making at the EU level. The formation of the customs union and the EMU constituted significant steps towards increased integration in functional scope, as each country transferred its national sovereignty in trade policy and monetary policy to the EU level. Integration in space has taken place as the number of member states has increased from six in 1958 to fifteen in 1995. Also institutional capacity has been increased, especially with the adoption of the Maastricht and Amsterdam Treaties, which delegated more decision-making powers to the Council by limiting the cases requiring unanimous decisions. A new powerful institution has also appeared by the establishment of the European Central Bank.

The simultaneous integration in all three dimensions is hardly erratic, but reflects linkages in the integration process, which may also appear in future. Integration of functional scope may lead to integration in geographical domain. When the Internal Market was established, countries outside the EU got a stronger incentive to seek membership of the EU to get full access to the Internal Market, likewise if the euro project develops successfully, more countries will want to participate. A widening of the EU with more member countries creates a demand for efficient decision-making,

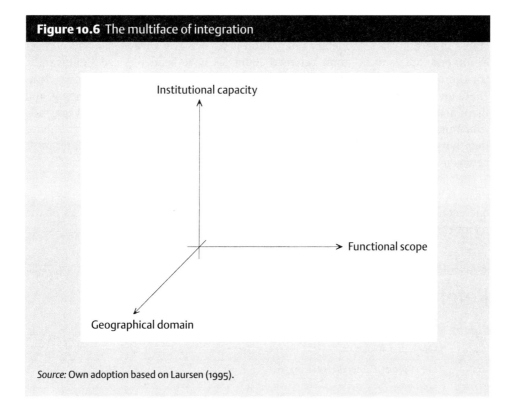

Figure 10.6 The multiface of integration

Source: Own adoption based on Laursen (1995).

which points to the need to establish more powerful, federal institutions instead of relying on intergovernmental cooperation. A future enlargement of the EU with several CEE countries will make the need for institutional capacity immediate. Enlargement without securing an efficient decision-making mechanism through a strengthening of the federal institutions may bring the integration process to a stalemate.

In a Union with many member states, there may be opposing views on the future course of the Union and, especially, disagreement on the degree of federalism. If the stalemate scenario is to be avoided, a possibility would be to open up for membership at different layers, where some member states are allowed to proceed into deeper stages of integration without committing all member states. However, allowing for such flexibility has its costs, as it will contribute to a weakening of the EU institutions and confuse the decision-making process.

10.4 Closing remarks

R ETURNING once more to the main question of this chapter and of this book, namely whether the European economies have evolved towards one European economy, the answer is yes, but there is still a long way to go before we can truly speak of one economy.

It is obvious that the economies of the EU member states have become more integrated in recent years. Monetary integration is particularly advanced, as differences in interest rates and inflation between countries have been reduced significantly. Looking upon the changes in total output and employment, results are less clear. There are still substantial differences in unemployment and standards of living, and there are no definite signs that the development in business cycles between individual member states will become more synchronized. National characteristics have thus not been blurred, even if, in a number of areas, the economic differences between member countries have decreased.

The clash between unity and diversity still characterizes the European Union at the turn of the century, also in the economic sphere. It makes sense to perceive the EU as one economy, where, if one takes a closer look, the individual economies of the member states are still discernible.

References

EU Commission (1996), 'Economic Evaluation of the Internal Market', *European Economy Reports and Studies*, 4.

—— (1999a), *European Economy*, 69.

—— (1999*b*), *Employment in Europe*.

Krugman, P. (1991), *Geography and Trade*, MIT Press.

Laursen, F. (1995), 'On Studying European Integration Theory and Political Economy', in F. Laursen (ed.), *The Political Economy of European Integration*, European Institute of Public Administration, Kluwer Law International, Maastricht.

Sinn, H.-W. (2000), 'EU Enlargement and the Future of the Welfare State', *Distinguished Address*, International Atlantic Economic Conference, 14–21 March 2000, Munich.

The Economist (2000), 'Lean, Mean, European', *European Business Supplement*, 29 April.

Index